ROME, POSTMODERN NARRATIVES OF A CITYSCAPE

Warwick Series in the Humanities

Series Editor: Tim Lockley

Titles in this Series

1 Classicism and Romanticism in Italian Literature:
Leopardi's *Discourse on Romantic Poetry*
Fabio A. Camilletti

Forthcoming Titles

Picturing Women's Health
Kate Scarth, Francesca Scott and Ji Won Chung (eds)

Gender and Space in Rural Britain, 1840–1920
Gemma Goodman and Charlotte Mathieson (eds)

www.pickeringchatto.com/warwick

ROME, POSTMODERN NARRATIVES OF A CITYSCAPE

EDITED BY

Dom Holdaway and Filippo Trentin

PICKERING & CHATTO
2013

Published by Pickering & Chatto (Publishers) Limited
21 Bloomsbury Way, London WC1A 2TH

2252 Ridge Road, Brookfield, Vermont 05036-9704, USA

www.pickeringchatto.com

BRITISH LIBRARY CATALOGUING IN PUBLICATION DATA

Rome, postmodern narratives of a cityscape. – (Warwick series in the humanities)
1. Rome (Italy) – In literature. 2. Rome (Italy) – In motion pictures. 3. Rome
(Italy) – Buildings, structures, etc. 4. Rome (Italy) – Civilization – 20th century.
5. Rome (Italy) – Civilization – 21st century.
I. Series II. Holdaway, Dom, editor of compilation. III. Trentin, Filippo, editor
of compilation.
945.6'3209-dc23

ISBN-13: 9781848933491
e: 9781781440001

This publication is printed on acid-free paper that conforms to the American
National Standard for the Permanence of Paper for Printed Library Materials.

Typeset by Pickering & Chatto (Publishers) Limited
Printed and bound in the United Kingdom by the MPG Printgroup

CONTENTS

Acknowledgements   vii

List of Contributors   ix

List of Figures   xiii

Introduction: Rome, Postmodern Narratives of a Cityscape
   – *Dom Holdaway and Filippo Trentin*   1

Part I: Knowing Rome

   1 Between Rome's Walls: Notes on the Role and Reception of the
     Aurelian Walls – *Marco Cavietti*   19

   2 The Explosion of Rome in the Fragments of a Postmodern Iconography:
     Federico Fellini and the *Forma Urbis* – *Fabio Benincasa*   39

   3 Centre, Hinterland and the Articulation of 'Romanness' in Recent
     Italian Film – *Lesley Caldwell*   57

Part II: Fragmented Topography

   4 Topophilia and Other Roman Perversions: On Bertolucci's *La luna*
     – *John David Rhodes*   79

   5 Marcus Aurelius and the Ara Pacis: Notes on the Notion of 'Origin'
     in Contemporary Rome – *Filippo Trentin*   101

   6 A Postmodern Gaze on the Gasometer – *Keala Jewell*   119

Part III: Situating Rome

   7 Ecclesiastical Icons: Defining Rome through Architectural Exchange
     – *James Robertson*   137

   8 'Roma Interrotta': Postmodern Rome as the Source of Fragmented
     Narratives – *Léa-Catherine Szacka*   155

   9 Las Vegas by Way of Rome: The Eternal City and American
     Postmodernism – *Richard W. Hayes*   171

Notes   189

Index   213

ACKNOWLEDGEMENTS

The editors would like to thank the Humanities Research Council, the Department of Italian and the Faculty of Arts at the University of Warwick for their support of the conference 'The Postmodern Palimpsest', which gave life to this book project. Extra thanks are (over)due to Jennifer Burns, Fabio Camilletti, Simon Gilson and Loredana Polezzi for their involvement from the very beginning of the project and their extremely useful comments and criticism on early drafts of the volume.

We would like to thank the contributors to the volume, whose comments and insight on postmodern Rome, as well as constant commitment and friendly collaboration was a pleasure and a privilege. Thanks are due to each anonymous reviewer of the articles for their invaluable insight which contributed much to each chapter. We are particularly grateful to Catherine O'Rawe, Robert Gordon, Knut Langewand, Mary Louise Lobsinger, Mario Moroni, Sergio Rigoletto and Jeanine Tuschling for their invaluable comments, assistance and support, and to Frances Lubbe, Mark Pollard, Stephina Clarke and Eleanor Hooker at Pickering & Chatto for their availability and advice.

Finally, this volume would not have taken shape without the assistance of the Department of Italian at Warwick, the Arts and Humanities Research Council and the British School at Rome, who, through financial and logistical support, have allowed us the time and space to develop this project fully.

LIST OF CONTRIBUTORS

Fabio Benincasa teaches at Duquesne University, Rome Campus. After graduating at the University of Rome 'La Sapienza', he worked for two years at Rai Educational, producing documentaries. In 2001 he moved to the USA where he completed his PhD at Indiana University. His doctoral thesis, under the supervision of Peter Bondanella, deals with the relationship between the Baroque and Italian auteur cinema. Back in Italy he writes a monthly column on the audiovisual for *Formiche* and is editor for the Festival of Architecture in Rome. He has published in specialized journal and websites such as *Italica*, *Paratesto* and *Italian Studies*.

Lesley Caldwell is Honorary Senior Research Associate in the Italian Department and Honorary Reader in the Psychoanalysis Unit at UCL, and a psychoanalyst in private practice. With Dorigen Caldwell she edited *Rome: Continuing Encounters between Past and Present* (Farnham: Ashgate, 2011) and has organized the Rome Lecture Series (UCL/Birkbeck). With Francesco Capello she edited the special issue of the *Journal of Romance Studies* on Italian Psychoanalysis and the Humanities (2011). With the psychoanalyst Helen Taylor Robinson, she is joint managing editor of the Collected Writings of Donald Winnicott.

Marco Cavietti is an art historian who collaborates with the Italian National Archive in Rome and with the Historical Archive of the Italian Ministry for Internal Affairs. He was educated at the University of Rome 'La Sapienza' and at the Warburg Institute in London. His research focuses on Renaissance Rome and museology. He published articles on fifteenth-century Rome, in particular on Pomponio Leto.

Richard W. Hayes is an architect and architectural historian, educated at Columbia and Yale universities. His previous publications include the award-winning book, *The Yale Building Project: The First 40 Years* (New Haven, CT: Yale University Press, 2007) and a chapter in *E.W. Godwin: Aesthetic Movement Architect and Designer* (New Haven, CT: Yale University Press, 1999). Another chapter is forthcoming in *Interior Lives: Biography, Identity and the Modern Interior* (Farnham: Ashgate, 2013). Hayes has received grants and awards from the Fulbright Foreign Scholarship Board, the Paul Mellon Centre for Studies in British Art, the Graham Foundation for Advanced Studies in the Fine Arts, the American Institute of Architects, the American Architectural Foundation, and the MacDowell Colony. He is currently a visiting fellow at Clare Hall, University of Cambridge.

Dom Holdaway is Fellow of the Institute for Advance Study at the University of Warwick, where he recently completed a PhD on Italian Cinema. His thesis interrogated the notion of *impegno* (political commitment) in Italian Mafia Film. He has published on meta-history and performance in Italian film, and co-edited a special issue of the journal *Italian Studies* on readings of crisis and rebirth in Italian cinema. His research interests include spectatorship, postmodern theory and queer studies.

Keala Jewell is Professor of Italian and Comparative Literature at Dartmouth College. She has published widely on Italian poetry, having co-edited an anthology of women poetry and authored a book on experimental poetry in post-war Italy. Her most recent book focuses on the intersections of literature and art history: *The Art of Enigma: The de Chirico Brothers' Politics of Modernism* (University Park, PA: Pennsylvania State University Press, 2004). Her current research delves into the 'magic realism' of Massimo Bontempelli and the neo-Gothic fiction of Tommaso Landolfi.

John David Rhodes is Reader in Literature and Visual Culture in the School of English at the University of Sussex. He is the author of *Stupendous, Miserable City: Pasolini's Rome* (Minneapolis, MN: University of Minnesota Press, 2007) and *Meshes of the Afternoon* (London and Basingstoke: BFI/Palgrave Macmillan, 2011) as well as the co-editor of *Antonioni: Centenary Essays* (London and Basingstoke: BFI/Palgrave Macmillan, 2011), *On Michael Haneke* (Detroit, MI: Wayne State University Press, 2010) and *Taking Place* (Minneapolis, MN: University of Minnesota Press, 2011). He is a founding co-editor of the journal *World Picture*.

James Robertson is Lecturer at the Manchester School of Architecture, and works on the architecture of sacred spaces. His current focus is the exceptional architecture of the twentieth-century Glaswegian practice of Gillespie, Kidd & Coia and the particular importance of their ecclesiastical work in an international context. He also has a keen interest in the twentieth-century ecclesiastical architecture of Rome, since his tenure as Rome Scholar at the British School at Rome in 2009.

Léa-Catherine Szacka is an architectural historian based in Paris and currently a post-doctoral fellow at the Laboratoire d'Excellence Création, Arts, Patrimoine. She studied architecture at the Université de Montréal and at the IUAV

University of Venice. She has recently completed a PhD on the history of the 1980 Venice Architecture Biennale at the Bartlett School of Architecture at UCL. She has done research and curatorial work at the Barbican Art Gallery in London and the Centre Pompidou in Paris and has taught architecture and history and theory of architecture at Nottingham Trent University as well as in various architecture schools in Paris.

Filippo Trentin is a doctoral candidate in the Department of Italian at the University of Warwick, where he is currently working on a dissertation on Rome's representations in literature and cinema from the 1940s to the 1970s. He was educated in Comparative Literature at the University of Rome 'La Sapienza' and at Dartmouth College. His research focuses on the representation of cities in written and visual cultures with a particular emphasis on the interactions between literature and cultural theory.

LIST OF FIGURES

Figure 1.1: Section of the Aurelian Wall under restoration at Porta
Maggiore   22

Figure 1.2: Section of the Aurelian Wall in the Parco Lineare Integrato project
at Porta Metronia   23

Figure 1.3: Map of Rome inside the Aurelian Wall designed by the American
artist Matthew Hural   35

Figure 2.1: The traffic jam in front of the Colosseum, in Fellini's *Roma*   54

Figure 3.1: The obelisk dedicated to Guglielmo Marconi in EUR   70

Figure 3.2: The last breaths of 'Il Terribile', between Libanese and Freddo
on the Spanish Steps in *Romanzo criminale*   73

Figure 3.3: Freddo and Libanese sitting in Garbatella in *Romanzo criminale*   75

Figure 4.1: Intertextual auto-citation in *La luna* (nodding in the direction
of *Il conformista*)   89

Figure 4.2: Bernini's elephant in *La luna* (nodding in the direction of
Strategia del ragno)   91

Figure 4.3: Santa Maria della Pace in *La luna*, next to Caterina's flat   93

Figure 4.4: The re-appearance of Accattone (Sergio Citti) in *La luna*   96

Figure 5.1: The original Marcus Aurelius equestrian statue inside the Capitoline Museums   105

Figure 5.2: The replica of the Marcus Aurelius equestrian statue at the
centre of Piazza del Campidoglio   106

Figure 5.3: The Museum for the Ara Pacis, designed by Richard Meier   112

Figure 6.1: The Gasometer at Ostiense   120

Figure 6.2: *Il gazometro a San Paolo* by Roberto Melli (1938)   123

Figure 6.3: *Periferia con gasometro* by Renzo Vespignani (1946)   125

Figure 7.1: Apse of the Church of Nostra Signora Ss Sacramento e Santi
Martiri Canadesi in Rome   125

Figure 7.2: Apse of the Church of Sacro Cuore di Gesù Agonizzante near
Rome   146

Figure 7.3: Apse of Church of St Columba in Glasgow   147

Figure 7.4: Apse of the Church of St Laurence in Greenock   148

Figure 9.1: Blueprint and photograph of the Maritime Theatre inside
    Hadrian's Villa in Tivoli   174
Figure 9.2: Design of Charles Moore's Piazza d'Italia in New Orleans   176
Figure 9.3: Photograph of Michelangelo's Porta Pia   180
Figure 9.4: Photograph of Constantine's colossal head   183
Figure 9.5: Collage of Giambattista Nolli's 1748 map of Rome with a photo-
    graph of Las Vegas's Strip   186

INTRODUCTION: ROME, POSTMODERN NARRATIVES OF A CITYSCAPE

Dom Holdaway and Filippo Trentin

It is history, above all, that one reads quite differently [in Rome] from anywhere else in the world.

J. W. Goethe[1]

Until the mid-twentieth century, a vast majority of cultural representations of Rome within the Western collective imagination relied, almost incessantly, on notions or echoes of the classical city: from 'Caput Mundi' or the 'Eternal City', to the 'Divine City' of Christendom or the 'City of Ruins' of the Grand Tour. Throughout the decades these temporalities have been preserved and have coexisted, moulding the image of the Italian capital as though a palimpsest of written and re-written layers, whose original traces never completely fade. The metaphor of the palimpsest, bound to the pre-modern topography of the city with its synchronic coexistence of different historical layers, was established throughout the centuries by the descriptions of fascinated travellers, amazed by the persistence of historical buildings and remnants of history within Rome's cityscape. For Goethe, visiting Rome meant visiting history itself,[2] while for Freud the urban fabric of 'The Eternal City' mirrored the inner structure of the human mind, in which layers of past memory-traces, conscious and unconscious, coexist.[3]

After the Second World War, when Italy was integrated into the Western bloc and consequently pressured to conform to a neo-liberal capitalist model, Rome was drastically redefined by the contemporary economic and social upheaval and the growth and expansion that accompanied this period. A general population increase, domestic migrations and a turn away from agriculture accompanied post-war regeneration and a relatively rapid re-building of infrastructure, forcing the city to spread far beyond its traditional limits. From the 1920s on, Rome's population multiplied approximately seven times and its surface became ten times larger, encompassing vast directional and commercial areas.[4] This triggered a rupture, a separation of the city into two distinct parts: the historical city centre, within the Aurelian Walls, and the modern periphery.

The separation of the city has reverberated through the various ways of thinking Rome in recent years, leading to two distinct and complementary approaches to the city. The first of these focuses on the fortune, or the decay, of the (historical) city's classical image, with the key paradigm of the city and unwavering point of reference thus being the 'Eternal City'. The second concentrates on Rome's urban and suburban *modern* growth, highlighting the sharp contrast between the beauty of Rome's ancient city centre and the ugliness or corruption of its modern peripheries. In many cases of the latter, the implicit dichotomy of the corrupt periphery with the beauty of the historical centre signals that the same patrimonial notion of 'Eternal Rome' pervades both of these approaches.

Examples of the first approach to the city include Peter Bondanella's *The Eternal City*, and Catharine Edwards's edited volume *Roman Presences*.[5] The former aims to identify the ongoing presence of the myth of Rome from the time of Livy and Tacitus to its use in Asimov's *Foundation* cycle and the *Star Wars* trilogy; the latter analyses the influential role that Rome's classical image had in the construction of a modern European identity. In spite of their different aims, both examples attempt ultimately to sustain the enduring legacy/legacies of Rome's classical past, stressing the existence of an archetypal Imperial imaginary. Another, more recent, example of this strand is Michael Herzfeld's *Evicted from Eternity: The Restructuring of Modern Rome*. Though Herzfeld's goal differs somewhat, since he describes the recent process of gentrification within specifically the Monti quarter, the framework that he uses is similar, as he nostalgically reads the disappearance of local life from this area of Rome in terms of the fading away of Rome's eternality: '[h]ere, eternally, eternity continues to fracture and to coalesce, repeatedly and without rest'.[6] For each of these studies, the signifier 'Rome' evokes images of its glorious, classical past.

The second approach to Rome, which focuses on its modern face, has been led by pioneering urbanists such as Italo Insolera and Antonio Cederna, and the important scholars that followed them.[7] While these studies are key to understanding the post-war restructuring of Rome, since they have unveiled the foundational role played by estate speculation and political corruption in the post-war reconstruction of the city, they have also established the basis for a conservative framework of rejection and complaint against every attempt to provide alternative readings of Rome's contemporary image. A clear legacy of this framework is the furious cries which followed the inauguration of the museum of the Ara Pacis, designed by American architect Richard Meier in 2006 (see Trentin's contribution to this volume on pp. 101–17).

The essays collected in *Rome, Postmodern Narratives of a Cityscape* emerge from a different position. Rather than lamenting the loss of the 'eternal' aspects of the city as a consequence of modernity and postmodernity, the essays collected here aim to problematize the universal idea of Rome by incorporating and absorbing the fragments, the detritus and the hidden zones of the city's contemporary image. In this sense, it participates in the ongoing formation of a *third* framework of studies on recent Rome, which follows some of the theoretical insights expressed by historian Vittorio Vidotto in his seminal *Roma Contemporanea*. As Vidotto writes, traditional approaches to Rome based on the complete rejection of its modernity produced 'una sostanziale incomprensione storica della città, incapace di cogliere e di volgere in positivo la complessità dei fattori della trasformazione urbana' (a substantial historical misunderstanding of the city, which was incapable of understanding and reading at all positively the complexity of the various factors that contribute to urban transformation).[8] Sharing in Vidotto's sentiment from a theoretical point of view, *Rome, Postmodern Narratives of a Cityscape* challenges both the grand narratives of Rome as 'Eternal City', and Rome as a modern hell, models which have limited the possibility to read, interpret and analyse the complexities of Rome's contemporary cityscape. While it is very important to recognize the singular importance of the first two fields of Rome studies, in founding itself on the third this book seeks to enact something of a shift from the critical framework in which the previous models participate.[9]

This third approach to the city, which has produced a number of important contributions to contemporary Rome studies in recent years, thus examines the contemporary city in open, plural and inclusive rather than binary terms.[10] Rejecting the dichotomy between the supposedly glorious ancient city and the allegedly squalid modern one in favour of a dialectical understanding nevertheless raises a very tricky question: how to go beyond the weighty presence of Rome's classical past, without rejecting it outright.

The special issue of *Annali d'Italianistica* entitled 'Capital City: Rome 1870–2010' represents a relevant instance of the third approach to Rome; the essays quite specifically focus on Rome's post-unitary modernity in a universal study of the city's specific trajectory (taking into account centre and periphery). In the introduction to the volume editor Cristina Mazzoni writes:

> the capital has served as a mirror in which to contemplate the problem of modernity. More than any other city, Rome typifies the insistent presence of the past in Italy, and the seemingly insurmountable challenge of freeing Italians from the constraints of tradition.[11]

While Mazzoni's understanding of Rome as an incubator for important insight on modernity is undoubtedly fruitful, it is in relation to this historical anxiety that we seek to offer, if not some resolution, then certainly some new insight. We do so in fact by turning to Rome's *postmodern* narratives, taking the city as a mirror in which to contemplate the problem of *postmodernity*, and its own, striking re-appropriations of history, as we illustrate below.

This collection of essays is the first attempt to frame Rome's cityscape in light of postmodern theories. As Mazzoni's edited issue illustrates, even the most valuable studies on contemporary Rome have been notably resistant to notions of postmodernity and have rather preferred to articulate their analyses singularly within the framework of *modernity*. In Mazzoni's introduction, notwithstanding the fact that the volume covers a temporal arch which stretches to 2010, and that some of the included contributions explicitly address postmodern concerns,[12] the discussion turns singularly around the notion of Rome's modernity, never its postmodernity.

In many senses this evident hesitation to confront Rome's postmodernity is understandable, not only because of a critical tendency to emphasize Rome's comparatively late modernity, but also due to the glaring incompatibilities of the city with the majority of theoretical, urban conceptions of the postmodern. Rome cannot easily be likened to Los Angeles, or to New York, London or Paris, within the frameworks of canonical postmodern concepts: it is not an emblematic city in terms of flexible accumulation, nor is it a world city of multinational capital or of post-industrialization. The Italian capital has never been an important global–industrial centre, rarely an important *domestic* centre: instead it is typically Milan which assumes this status (indeed the Italian headquarters of numerous multinational companies are in Milan). According to recent research conducted by the Globalization and World Cities Network – an organization which every few years publishes a list ranking the most important global cities based on the impact of their advanced tertiary services – Rome does not belong to the so-called 'Alpha Cities', the first group of global cities which comprises, among others, Milan, New York, London, Tokyo, Paris, Los Angeles, Shanghai and Beijing. Rome is instead a 'Beta City', grouped together with other capitals like Manila, Tel Aviv and Cairo.[13]

Yet in spite of its apparent financial peripherality, Rome is at the heart of Italian media production, and throughout the past eighty years it has remained an important international hub of cinematic production. Rome furthermore is undoubtedly at the forefront of global tourism. There is little doubt that Rome's historical city centre – with its ancient stones and temples, its Renaissance buildings and Baroque churches – is one of the most attractive entertainment industries in the world. Every year it attracts millions of people from all over the world; people who circulate around the city, take in the city and capture the spectacle of the city with their cameras. It is precisely the relationship between its relative industrial and financial peripherality and its centrality in media and tourist production which, in our interpretation, makes Rome one of the most interesting cases for capturing the reticular complexity of the postmodern shift.

The following essays do not seek to impose a view of what the postmodern is by attempting, deductively, a general definition of it through which we frame the object 'postmodern Rome'. Nor do they do this inductively, by combining the individual definitions in order to give a general idea of what 'postmodern Rome' might be. The volume approaches the postmodern by skipping the idea of universality that is intrinsic to both these ways, and instead attempts to construct an idea of postmodern Rome which is open, inclusive and osmotic. In sum, the aim is not to define once and for all the idea of postmodern Rome, but rather to open up the possibility to think of Rome in pluralistic (including postmodern) ways, in other words an idea of the city that is detached from any claim to universalism or eternality. To re-semanticize Rome it will be necessary to turn to a series of alternative narratives.

Postmodern Rome

The question remains: why has such difficulty arisen in the study, analysis and description of Rome as postmodern? This has a threefold answer. First, it is a consequence of the infamous history that this term had within the Italian academic context, since the latter has typically informed international studies of modern Rome. As Pierpaolo Antonello and Florian Mussgnug put it, in their explanation of the resistance against the postmodern in studies of political engagement, 'the category of the postmodern has experienced critical resistance, if not outright opposition, within the Italian intellectual field'.[14] Monica Jansen too has noted how publicly during the 1980s 'la stampa italiana ha reso impossibile ogni seria riflessione sul postmoderno rifiutandolo già dal principio come civetteria, come cedimento alla moda' (the Italian press made any serious reflection on the postmodern impossible, dismissing it from the beginning as coquetry, as submission to the latest fad). Though she then goes on to illustrate lucidly the importance of postmodern Italian thought, the fact that thanks to continued disputes and a lack of public acknowledgment this ultimately reaches little more than 'un postmoderno ambiguo' (an ambiguous postmodernity) demonstrates a first important motive for the lack of studies of Rome and postmodernity.[15]

This aspect intersects with the second reason, the strong legacy that the romantic idea of Rome as 'Eternal City' still has today. This image, which was reproduced inside and outside Europe during the Grand Tour, has found a strong ally in the contemporary tourist industry. One of the most well-known tourist publications, the Michelin guide to Rome, (though we could have chosen descriptions from the Rough Guide, Lonely Planet, Time Out or any other mainstream guidebook), describes Rome as follows:

> Far more than a city, [it] is a series of eras stacked atop one another. Ruins, churches and *palazzi* provide spectacular detail to this modern metropolis that is, despite its fast pace, quite pleasant. Wide pedestrian boulevards, splendid parks and grand piazze – the spaces where residents and tourist converge – give Rome the feeling of an open-air museum. No other city in the world can compare.[16]

What this paradigmatic and traditional image evidently does not take into account, however, is the vast expanded urban space that followed Rome's expansion during the twentieth century. Nowadays Rome is an impressive labyrinth of highways and junctions, suburban malls and gated communities which go far *beyond* the ancient Aurelian Walls that demarcate the historical centre. It has a metropolitan area of some four million inhabitants and an enormous communal area, the second biggest in Europe after that of Greater London.[17] However, in spite of this rapid expansion, and unlike any of Europe's other global cities, what 'Rome' signifies in the vast majority of cases is still the space contained in the city centre.

The third motive of resistance to the idea of a postmodern Rome involves the apparent incompatibility of its contemporary urbanscape with that of, for example, Los Angeles – by many considered the quintessential postmodern city. In the introduction to his *The Postmodern Urban Condition*, urban geographer Michael Dear identifies in the cityscape of contemporary Los Angeles the 'prototype of contemporary urbanization'.[18] This privileged status is for Dear a consequence of the city's contemporary processes of deindustrialization and reindustrialization: the dismantling of the traditional space of the factory, and the constitution of new spaces of hi-tech production. In urban terms, what this produces is a highly dispersed, polymorphous and decentred cityscape characterized by the cohabitation of First and so-called Third-world forms of urbanism: gated communities as well as edge cities. Similarly, in *Thirdspace* Edward Soja, in a perhaps too predictable way defines Los Angeles as a 'postmetropolis'. According to Soja, the six characteristics which define a postmetropolis are 'a productively post-fordist industrial metropolis', 'a globalized and localized world city', a 'hyperreal scamscape of simulations and simulacra' as well as a dispersed and expanding cityscape, the increase of inequalities and polarities between social classes and control over the territory.[19]

While Rome's contemporary cityscape is indeed a dispersed, non-homogeneous and highly polarized territory which goes from Ostia and the Tyrrhenian Sea to the Apennine Mountains, it is certainly not the completely decentred suburban landscape that Los Angeles is. Though one of the aims of the last *piano regolatore* (urban master plan), approved in 2003, was to rebalance the unequal relationship between centre and periphery, in Rome the centre is still the dominant urban feature. The needs of the suburbs are very often subordinated to those of the centre, which absorbs most of the city's financial resources.[20] Moreover, crucially, Rome was never a major industrial centre and thus the postindustrial turn has affected very little of the Roman urbanscape (excluding the Ostiense area, as Keala Jewell observes in her contribution to this volume on pp. 119–36), which further removes any straightforward or obvious links between Rome and the typically postmodern.

Despite the motives that have historically stood against postmodern readings of Rome, the following essays testify to our belief not only that Rome can indeed be studied and approached in this context, but that it represents one of the most interesting examples of postmodern cityscapes within the global metropolitan map. 'Postmodernizing' the idea of Rome as the 'Eternal City' – that Eurocentric notion which for centuries mirrored the root of Western identity – is a necessary move that can help us to marginalize our Eurocentric gaze. In this respect, our idea of postmodern Rome finds its root in the deconstruction of the classical palimpsest, that image of a Rome as a stack of different eras which the contemporary tour guide still proposes, and finds instead its theoretical backbone in an anti-universal, anti-eternal, fluid and decentred idea of its cityscape.

Rome, or the Postmodern Palimpsest

As has been done elsewhere, in order to situate any particular stance on the postmodern, it is necessary, as Remo Ceserani writes,

> distinguere fra la postmodernità come etichetta storica inevitabilmente interpretativa – e quindi da discutere – e il postmoderno come adesione ideologica a movimenti culturali o letterari sorti nella stessa condizione – e quindi ancor più da discutere[21]

> (to distinguish between postmodernity as an inevitably interpretable historical label – and thus open to debate – and the postmodern as an ideological adherence to cultural or literary movements of a connected condition – and thus even more debatable).

In addition to his sentiment that both cases are fertile grounds for discussion, the same dual categorical definitions from Ceserani are usefully brought forward here.

The advent of the postmodern condition has been widely disputed according to different temporal patterns. We could roughly divide the various positions in this field into two views, one of which might be labelled the metahistorical, and the other the historico-materialist. According to the metahistorical interpretation, postmodernism would be nothing but the cyclical re-emergence of a mood, or a state of mind, which stresses paradoxes and parodies in periods of crisis and the redefinition of ideas; thus it is one which has no particular historical root. On the other hand, the historico-materialist interpretation reads the coordinates of postmodernity as the late stage of capitalism, and aims to capture the logic of the informational, hyper-technological and global society which progressively took shape after the end of the reconstruction period during the 1950s. Postmodernism would then be the architectural, artistic, literary, cinematic, etc. response to this historical shift.[22]

While we situate ourselves within a historico-materialist approach to postmodernity and postmodernism, we are also very conscious of the complexities inherent in such periodizations. In this respect, we share Fredric Jameson's preoccupation that 'periodizing hypotheses ... tend to obliterate difference and to project an idea of the historical period as massive homogeneity' and make use of his definition of postmodernism as a 'cultural dominant'.[23] For this reason, we prefer to see postmodernism as a force field coexisting within a more complex and intricate set of tensions which characterize late capitalist societies. As Jameson puts it, using Raymond Williams's categories, postmodernism is the 'emergent' cultural category which reacts to other 'residual' cultural categories that nonetheless do not cease to exist. The emergence of a postmodern condition would thus not obliterate features of modern or even pre-modern temporalities, which continue to coexist even in postmodernity. The consequence of this, as will be further argued below, is as much the search for entirely new modes of being or of representation as it is the re-appropriation, re-articulation and re-semanticization of models or focal points that belong to residual historical paradigms. The manner in which the relationship between the centre and the periphery is played out in Rome is a key example here.

The exposition of such a complex temporal model is necessary in order to undertake the attempt to frame postmodern Rome. If the cohabitation of emergent and residual forms of cultural production is a feature of any object of analysis, this is even more evident and true for Rome, given the multi-layered strata that the course of history has impressed on its cityscape (the church of San Clemente to which Caldwell makes reference is a useful physical embodiment of this; see pp. 57–77). In spite of stereotypical, over-simplistic and homogenizing categories which are usually attached to its idea (from the 'Eternal City' to 'Cloaca Maxima', from 'Caput Mundi' to 'Modernist Hell'), Rome's cityscape *is* a contradictory, ambivalent and dialectical territory where different temporalities, styles and forces interweave and clash against each other. In this respect, this investigation finds its point of origin in the attempt to move from the idea of Rome as a classical palimpsest to that of a 'postmodern palimpsest'. This theoretical notion incorporates styles, shapes and features which go far beyond those that characterize its traditional imagery, and shifts its emphasis from the historical traces in the background to the unified recombination of fragments from the perspective of the present.

In its application to the city of Rome in the following essays, the concept of the 'postmodern' is dialectical. As much as the term 'modern', it is a neutral term which refers to what Althusser defines a 'structure in dominance', and thus acquires characteristics which can be considered positive or negative according to the specific circumstances in which they appear.[24] The 'incomplete' project of postmodernity has included features which we can decide to support strategically, or to refute. Surely, many would welcome the end of logocentrism, sexual and identitarian normativity and a positivistic and linear notion of history. At the same time, though, there is a risk of accepting blindly the cultural logic of contemporary times, and ending up simply supporting the neo-liberal logic – a logic of exclusion, social hierarchy and class privilege – which is at work in every capitalist society.

This volume understands Rome as a complex territory where alternative forces cohabit and coexist rather than proposing a singular and total narrative of the city. Across the contributions, Rome presents itself as a city where classical monuments and temples lie alongside modern gas houses; where ancient churches such as San Clemente coexist with contemporary ones such as the Dives in Misericordia in Tor Tre Teste, designed by Richard Meier and inaugurated in 2000; where the city of cinema – Cinecittà – exists side by side with the Vatican; and where museums of classical art share space with museums of twenty-first century art, such as the Maxxi, designed by Zaha Hadid and inaugurated in 2010. Yet this coexistence is not singularly the topographical cohabitation of diachronic elements conceptualized and designed in different epochs, but also and above all the mutation and evolution of meaning that these elements underwent and continue to undergo throughout time. As Marco Cavietti and Filippo Trentin argue in their contributions to this volume, the Aurelian Walls or the Marcus Aurelius equestrian statue are not simply remnants of the classical past to be discovered and understood 'as it was'; they are significant keys to a diagnosis of the way in which different eras have dealt with that past. Rather than points on a linear timeline, past and present become axes of intersection in a historical constellation.

Together the following essays present Rome not only as a city that is legible within the framework of the postmodern, but moreover as an incubator of postmodernism, and in particular one which extends beyond the national borders of Italy. A key example is the architectural project 'Roma Interrotta', the focus of Léa-Catherine Szacka's essay, in which several architects undertook a double process of de-composition and re-composition of the pre-modern and unitary map of Rome, forcing it into an assemblage of fragments. Richard W. Hayes, in his contribution, argues that the Italian capital's complex, hyper-stratified and fragmented cityscape provided the architect Robert Venturi with a prototype for envisioning the postmodern cityscape. In his reading, a strong thread links the scattered and falsified urban landscape of Las Vegas with that of Rome. For Venturi, Rome's cityscape represented the antithesis of modernist utopias of urban order such as Paris or New York, and could thus provide anti-totalitarian alternatives to the rigidities of modernist urban planning.

The fragmentary and anti-unitary aspect of Rome brings us back to Vidotto's argument about its 'precocious postmodernity'. For him:

> La Roma del dopoguerra, rimane del tutto estranea all'adozione di un canone, e in questo senso è già paradossalmente e precocemente e, anche se inconsapevolmente, postmoderna. Se una città come Milano può identificarsi in una cultura imprenditoriale di efficenza e di operosità fino a riprodurre per oltre un secolo un proprio primato e rivendicare gli attributi di capitale morale, a Roma convivono tante culture e tanti modelli diversi.[25]

(Post-war Rome came nowhere near the adoption of a canon; in this sense it was already paradoxically and precociously, and even if unknowingly, postmodern. While a city like Milan can be identified by its entrepreneurial culture of efficiency and industriousness, such that it could maintain a position of leadership for over a century and lay claim to the attributes of moral capital, Rome on the other hand is made of plural coexistent cultures and many different models.)

In Vidotto's view, the plurality of Rome that lies at the root of its postmodernity has emerged in part due to the limited success of its modern regeneration. In this discourse, what is quite remarkable is Vidotto's distinction between Milan – the most 'modern' Italian city – and Rome, whose absence of a strong modern project marked the emergence of anti-systematic structures and features. As John David Rhodes also recognizes in his essay in this volume, 'perhaps Rome, never having been sufficiently modern, was already postmodern'. The lack of secondary activities and the limited presence of industrial landmarks, together with the predominance of tertiary activities such as cinema, radio and television productions are the economic structures which put Rome in a privileged position in order to witness and specifically record the postmodern shift.

In this regard, it is no surprise that Fabio Benincasa's essay reads Fellini's cinematic representation of Rome as the paradigmatic vision of a 'multilayered, fragmented and substantially abstract' cityscape. Read in Fellini's terms, Rome appears at the forefront of the representation of a fluid, polymorphous and deconstructed urbanscape, all features which will come to be addressed as intrinsic characteristics of the postmodern city. In Fellini's films, the image of Rome as an organon disintegrates into a fragmented map which finds its unity only in the director's gaze and montage. As Benincasa writes, 'Fellini is the author who, departing from the fundamental and unitary iconography of Baroque Rome, first elaborated the pluralistic city image of our time'. Thus, the uniformity of the modernist city that had found in Fritz Lang's *Metropolis* (1927) its most convincing depiction, finds in Fellini's multifarious and anti-unitary idea of Rome its symmetrical opposite.

Fellini's snapshot of Rome's fragmentary and osmotic imagery, and its reliance on the medium of cinema itself is something that should be better considered in order to grasp the contours of Rome's postmodern narratives. In this respect, we might return to *Window Shopping: The Cinema and the Postmodern*, in which Anne Friedberg analyses the strict relationship between cinema and postmodernity. Her argument is that cinema and television are key factors that have marked the passage from a modern to a postmodern condition, thanks to their capacity 'to transform our access to history and memory' and to produce an 'increasingly derealized sense of "presence" and identity'. For Friedberg, cinema plays a key role in the process of construction of a 'decentered' subjectivity which marks the shift from the modern to the postmodern. As she writes, 'descriptions of a decentered, derealized, and detemporalized postmodern subject form a striking parallel to the subjective consequences of cinema and television specta-torship'.[26] It is precisely in this dematerialized and de-realized area of the subject rather than in the emergence of a corporate and fiscal economic structure – a process that could be also read as a reaction to fascist dreams of totality based on a unitary and fixed idea of Rome as root of Western civilization – that Rome's postmodern narratives unravel.

The importance of cinematic production for Rome's economy and the almost obsessive affair between Rome and the cinematic camera – it is not by chance that Rhodes defines postmodern Rome as 'too imaged, over-represented' and 'saturated by representation' – are the features which appear to mark Rome's centrality for any discussion on postmodernity and that place the city at the cen-tre of the intersection between high modernism and postmodernism.

Osmotic Dislocations, Rome's Postmodern Narratives

The shadow of tradition that, as mentioned, has long been cast over Rome stud-ies, is, unsurprisingly, by no means absent from this volume. In the question of approaches to Italy's capital, *Rome, Postmodern Narratives of a Cityscape* seeks to transcend the ingrained or dichotomic readings of the city that take Eternal Rome as its central and universal foundation. Yet to transcend this specific tradition is nev-ertheless to include it, as is repeatedly demonstrated in the essays in this collection: from the *not*-unfamiliar city centre in Rhodes's reading of Bernardo Bertolucci's film *La luna* to the 'modernist' postmodernity of the ecclesiastical architecture after the second Vatican council, described by James Robertson; from the function of the Aurelian Walls as *mediator* between past and present in Marco Cavietti's reading, to the constant centre–periphery dialogue in the films described by Lesley Caldwell and Fabio Benincasa; from the semantic metamorphosis of monuments and maps in the discussions of Jewell and Trentin and in the 'Roma Interrotta' project that is commented on by Szacka, to the surprising mutation of the 'Eternal City' into an incubator of postmodern architecture as outlined in Hayes's essay.

For this reason, not only have the contributors each adopted the same osmotic approach to history, modernity and postmodernity outlined above, but moreover the essays have been slotted together in order to have recourse, in a playful way, to the traditions of the city. In the first section of the volume, 'Knowing Rome', the juxtaposed essays offer a number of specific perspectives on a historical grounding of the city, that together offer an approximation of its history. The essay by Marco Cavietti, entitled 'Between Rome's Walls: Notes on the Role and Reception of the Aurelian Walls', takes as its focus the city's perim-eter walls, constructed between AD 270–3 under the rule of Emperor Aurelian. Cavietti treads the history of the walls, illustrating the reflection of important social, historical and urban change upon the minor and major mutations of the city perimeter, as well as its symbolic and practical uses. What is perhaps most interesting, though, is how the function of the walls has faded as Rome has sprawled outwards since becoming capital of the Kingdom of Italy: no longer do the walls today denote the limits of the city as they had done for 1,500 years. By focusing on some of the most interesting re-appropriative artistic engagements with the walls in recent years, however, Cavietti argues that they should by no means be left to slip into the realm of a historical shadow, but rather that they are best re-articulated as a *threshold*, one which could bridge that gap between the tradition of history (the city centre) and the modern or postmodern (the ignored urban expansion). In Cavietti's piece, the monument thus stands for a fragment of the 'Eternal City' that both invokes a very important history within the urban fabric, and yet which has been dislocated from it in such a way that ultimately allows its re-semanticization in a specific, (but not universal) postmodern position.

One of the historical snapshots that Cavietti draws upon is the *Mirabilia Urbis Romae*, those prototypical guidebooks that were essentially lists of monuments employed by the pilgrim to orient herself in Rome in the Middle Ages. In a striking point that is then re-articulated in the following essay, Cavietti illustrates how these fragmentary lists not only foregrounded the walls as the primary point of orientation, but in fact they (both walls and texts) acted as the concrete punctuation of an *imagined* map of the city. Fabio Benincasa, in 'The Explosion of Rome in the Fragments of a Postmodern Iconography: Federico Fellini and the *Forma Urbis*', extends this point, suggesting that the skeletal form of the *Mirabilia* indicated a specific *absence* in terms of representation of the city. Likening the guides to further contemporary representations of the city – such as in Francesco Petrarch's letters – Benincasa posits the dialectical interaction between the concrete and the imagined (such as the monument and the cognitive tour) as the paradigm for the representation of Rome's urban form. Beginning with a broad outline of the city's artistic representation in art and literature from this period, Benincasa then traces this interplay of the Italian capital's presence through to the films of Federico Fellini. The author finds the presence–absence dialogue that is characteristic of historical Roman representations throughout Fellini's career, from the early *Lo sceicco bianco* through to *La dolce vita*, *Satyricon* and *Roma*. In each case, the weight of tradition is both present and absent, and the overpowering grotesque of *Satyricon* that literally dissolves from the walls in *Roma* is highly significant here. Nevertheless, Fellini's representation not only adopts this model of Roman representation, but ultimately comes to mutate it. And Rome does indeed shift, moving from the mappable and knowable (albeit sporadically visited) city to the shadowy, unmappable sprawl of 'Toby Dammit' and *Roma*, offering us ultimately a further paradigmatic image of a cityscape that anticipates some of the most emblematic depictions of the postmodern cityscape, from Francis Ford Coppola's *Rumble Fish* (1983) to Ridley Scott's *Blade Runner* (1982), from John Carpenter's *Escape from New York* (1981) to David Lynch's *Blue Velvet* (1986).

The theoretical notion of the fragment, so commonly applied to studies of postmodernity, and which Benincasa employs and problematizes historically in his essay, offers a continued pertinence throughout the volume. In Lesley Caldwell's 'Centre, Hinterland and the Articulation of "Roman-ness" in Recent Italian Film', the fragment appears as an interesting allegory of the geographical and social development of Rome's peripheries. Continuing pluralistically the historical trajectory of the city begun by Cavietti and brought forward with a greater emphasis on the eighteenth to twentieth centuries by Benincasa, Caldwell provides a socio-historical introduction to the suburbs of Rome from their vast (and often illegal) expansion from the 1950s to the present. Many of Rome's *borgate* (suburbs) appeared as isolated 'nuclei' of communities that had been ousted by the *sventramenti* (demolition) of central Rome during the fascist period, and remained (barely) connected through linear lines to the city centre. Caldwell observes how through time these fragments within the Ager Romanus (the Roman countryside) have continued to be defined, relatedly, according to direct centre–periphery lines. However, as she demonstrates with reference to a series of films from the 1990s and 2000s, the connections to the historic centre for the people of Rome have become considerably weakened. In many cases, such as Daniele Vicari's film *Velocità massima* (Maximum Speed, 2002), the people of Rome exist comfortably, and with little compromise of their 'Romanness', outside of Rome's historical core. Caldwell's essay thus points to a complex and interesting model in which the very notion of 'Romanness' offers a means to come to terms with the contradictory creation, rupture and re-connection of the city's fragmented 'centres'.

The second section of the volume, entitled 'Fragmented Topography', foregrounds less the historical transition into postmodernity than the specific manifestations of the period on individual instances of the urban fabric, once again providing a useful juxtaposition of the city and its representations. The specific cases that are drawn upon – the historical centre, the Ara Pacis museum, the statue of Marcus Aurelius and the Gasometro – nevertheless do signal interesting lines of history and shifting relationships with it. What appears common to each of the essays in this section is the acknowledgment of the bypassing of a paradigm of 'modern' Rome, as designated by the work of Pier Paolo Pasolini. As, in fact, Jewell and Rhodes have argued elsewhere, Pasolini's poetry, novels and films from the post-war period can be read as a foundational model of Rome that opposes, if not *erases* the 'Eternal City' of Rome, replacing it with the bleak imagery of the fragments of the *borgate*.[27] In the following essays, then, the authors (consciously) transcend once again this Pasolinian model in order to refocus our attention back within the Aurelian Walls, nevertheless paying heed to the re-articulated city centre in light of what lies outside of it.

In Bernardo Bertolucci's *La luna* (1979), which is the focus of John David Rhodes in the chapter 'Topophilia and Other Roman Perversions: On Bertolucci's *La luna*', one of the symbols of Pasolini's Rome remains quite explicit. The film's male protagonist, Joe, stumbles into the Testaccio quarter where a local man attempts to pick him up. As Rhodes observes, this is the area in which Pasolini's archetypal Roman protagonist, Accattone, dies in the eponymous film after turning to a life of crime; the actor who plays the local in *La luna* is Sergio Citi, who not coincidentally also played Accattone twenty years earlier. This peripheral encounter thus accounts for much more than a casual nod to Bertolucci's mentor (the director of *La luna* assisted Pasolini in the filming of *Accattone*). Instead, once Joe has returned to the city centre and his home for the duration of the film, the differentiation from the periphery and the return of focus onto the centre becomes a political and a postmodern shift.

The nod to Pasolini in fact fits into a broader model of what Rhodes calls Bertolucci's 'auto-erotic cinephilia', in which he layers into the film thinly veiled cinematic references to his own work. While this very action has often led critics to dismiss Bertolucci's film as de-politicized, simplistic and self-obsessed, Rhodes demonstrates how a reading of the easily recognized – when combined into a topographic analysis of the 'over-familiar' monuments of Rome's city centre – returns the political to the film and its location. The overemphasis and fetishization of images of the monuments brings with it a further sense of historical confusion: though they belong to entirely different historical contexts, and are 'already lived' and 'after images', they not only remain present today but do so precisely within that context of postmodern Rome. Where postmodernity in the urban centres of Los Angeles or other typical instances is defined by a sense of the unmappable, Rhodes produces a striking new notion of the postmodern that exists precisely in its own overt 'know-ability' and 'mappability'.

The shift back onto the centre, and more specifically the re-semanticization of certain key monuments in the light of their historical significance is also the focus of Filippo Trentin's article, 'Marcus Aurelius and the Ara Pacis: Notes on the Notion of "Origin" in Contemporary Rome'. His case studies are the equestrian statue of Marcus Aurelius that sits on the Capitoline Hill, and the new shell and museum of the ancient Ara Pacis Augustae – the altar made in honour of the peacetime brought about by Emperor Augustus – redesigned by Richard Meier and opened in 2006. The historical import of both monuments is painfully apparent, and indeed has caused much controversy in relation to the protective removal of the horse and its replacement with a 'false' replica, and to the uncomplementary, 'international' style of the museum. Trentin argues, against the grain, that the criticisms aimed at both in terms of the 'undermining' of history and tradition is problematic, not to mention violent in their denial of the continued interaction and healthy re-interpretation of Rome's millennia of history. Using fruitful theoretical models such as Michel Foucault's readings of 'the origin', Trentin illustrates how such a denial ultimately offsets the historical development of the monument's fluid identities.

Like Rhodes, Trentin brings his argument back to the question of defining the postmodern in relation to a *return* to the city centre, thus implicitly accounting for the transcendence of Pasolini's paradigm. He moreover similarly relates the search for the postmodern between these specific topographical cases to the dominant urban models, such as Los Angeles and Las Vegas. Although the Italian capital remains problematic in its centre-led notion of urban space, the simulacrization of history in the statue, which appear highly compatible with the urban performances of Las Vegas, and the deconstructive approach to history of Meier not only offer profound evidence of Rome's postmodern turn, but offer a productive (albeit still problematic) way of grappling with postmodern history.

The third essay in this section of the book takes a further fascinating 'monument' as its focus: Rome's gasometro (gas house, or gasometer). Unlike the city centre or various statues, buildings and museums, the gasometer sits slightly awkwardly, 'suspended' between its creation not as a classical monument but as a modernist and industrially functioning tool, and its continued presence despite its discontinued use. In 'A Postmodern Gaze on the Gasometer', Keala Jewell attempts to interrogate the possibility of attaching postmodernity to the gasometer in relation to its recent iconic status, as triggered by its many artistic representations and alterations. Her mapping of the gasometer from the inter-war and post-war paintings that capture its industrial functions, through its presence within the industrial hub of Ostiense in mid twentieth-century painting and writing (Melli, Vespignani, Moravia and Pasolini) to the re-appropriated cultural symbol in more recent poetry and film (such as work by Sara Ventroni and Ferzan Ozpetek), traces a fascinating historical trajectory. Perhaps what is most striking about this alternative monument is how the gasometer, without moving, shifts from being peripheral to the city centre to being relatively close, as the city evolves and sprawls beyond it, and at the same time assumes some of the most categorical signs of post-industrial postmodernity. And yet, since this trajectory is now lurching towards its musealization, it remains to be seen quite how the artistic re-engagements with *modern* Roman history will continue to pan out.

From 'knowing Rome' in its layered histories according to broad representational outlines and individual monuments discussed in the first two sections of the book, the final section, 'Situating Rome', begins to re-contextualize the Roman postmodernity according to the global position of the city. Further tensions underlie this section: as mentioned, Rome is by no means a global postmodern city as per the rankings of the Globalization and World Cities Network. Nevertheless, as this introduction and each of the following essays attests, the models of postmodernity that intersect the various strata of Rome both draw from, and influence, pointedly international people, bodies, theories and urban plans. Given, as Fabio Benincasa observes, that the Roman urban model has been so powerfully influential in the creation of the imperial status in countless other cities, further tensions and clashes with Rome's postmodernity on a global level should be of little surprise.

The final three essays in the volume vary in their approach to 'Situating Rome': the authors at times focus their analysis on Rome, adopting international perspectives; at other times they focus on the postmodern legacy of the city across the seas. In combination, these three chapters avoid the pitfalls of any linear or simplistic notions of influence in favour of the pluralism and complexity which we have referred to constantly here.

The first essay, 'Ecclesiastical Icons: Defining Rome through Architectural Exchange', by James Robertson, continues the negotiation of the specific with the broader urban fabric by focusing on the development of churches in the Italian capital following the Second World War. Robertson's focus is on the churches outside the Aurelian Walls, thus foregrounding a narrative of postmodern Rome that stands in opposition to the dominant city-centre model. Robertson compares important churches such as the Chiesa di Nostra Signora del Santissimo Sacramento e dei Santi Martiri Canadesi, the Basilica di San Giovanni Bosco and the Basilica dei Santi Pietro e Paolo with those constructed by the Glaswegian company Gillespie, Kidd & Coia. By tracing the 'architectural exchange' between architects working in the two cities as they burgeon after 1945, Robertson illustrates the complexity of influences that are at play even in those aspects of Rome's architectonics that might be assumed to be fundamentally more traditional.

The 'exchange' that is at play in Robertson's chapter is ultimately revealed to go beyond the geographical, including also the temporal and artistic: an exchange between the modern and the postmodern. Not only, as we might have imagined, do certain modernist modes of building work continue to persist beyond Rome's postmodernity, but in fact, as he illustrates with reference to the Second Vatican Council and its effects on the (concrete) church, the process of postmodern architecture in fact pre-dates the typical chronological coordinates of the shift. Once again, then, Robertson's article signals the importance of history and of its reinterpretation in the context of Rome. The case of the church of Tor Tre Teste, designed – like the Ara Pacis museum – by Richard Meier, draws together an interesting combination of contemporary aesthetics with Roman traditions, including the ruins of the Ager Romanus and the use of local stone and concrete. As in other contributions to the volume, such as the essays of Jewell and Caldwell, then, the periphery remains an equally important site for the development of Rome's postmodern aesthetic.

The final two essays in the volume illustrate the importance of Rome in the development of an international, postmodern architecture. Léa-Catherine Szacka's essay, entitled '"Roma Interrotta": Postmodern Rome as the Source of Fragmented

Narratives', contextualizes and comments on the artistic project 'Roma Interrotta' (Rome Interrupted), in which twelve international architects dissected, redesigned and re-attached twelve pieces of Giambattista Nolli's 'New Map of Rome' (1748). Richard Hayes's 'Las Vegas by Way of Rome: The Eternal City and American Postmodernism' focuses on two of the most important and popular American postmodern architects, Charles W. Moore and Robert Venturi (the latter of whom was directly involved in the 'Roma Interrotta' project).

In Szacka's and Hayes's essays, the presence of Rome is surprising: in the latter essay, as the author puts it, due to the ongoing clash between Rome's universality and the postmodern disruption of master narratives; in the former as an apparently unlikely and forced challenge of this historical universality, represented by the Nolli map. Szacka first employs the 'Roma Interrotta' project as an illustration of the re-appropriation of history in the contemporary period that occurs in the twelve frames designed by the architects. The individual segments draw this re-appropriation into twelve fragmented narratives of Rome that not only unite deliberately international perspectives, but do so in a manner that comes to interact directly with the city space (first Rome, then internationally) in the interactive exhibition of the work. Using the cases of Antoine Grumbach, Léon Krier and James Stirling, Szacka observes the various influences that are drawn together in the re-envisioning of historical narratives, as well as the ultimate effects that the exhibition on Rome potentially had on the future careers and output of the architects.

In the final essay Hayes re-reads the work of these canonical postmodern architects – both theoretical, such as Venturi's *Complexity and Contradiction in Architecture* (1966), and practical, such as Moore's Piazza d'Italia fountain in New Orleans – through the lens of the Italian capital. In the case of the latter, the architectural influences of Rome and the historical weight of the empire, in particular through Hadrian's villa in Tivoli, become translated into a monument on the other side of the globe that is both interactive and symbolic, and a dedication to the Italian immigrant populace in New Orleans. Hayes's reading of these architects powerfully interrupts the typical dismissal of Rome from contemporary thought on postmodernism, not only by tracing the city's influence and heritage, but moreover by illustrating how the two architects destabilize the hegemony of 'Roma Eterna'.

In the citation of Robert Venturi from which Hayes draws the title of his essay, the architect describes the movement between Rome and Las Vegas as one which alters his vision of the city: '[it] is the Rome of evolving juxtapositions – of eternal incompleteness. It is a Rome acknowledging evolutions of many kinds and juxtaposing contexts of many kinds, a Rome that is never complete'.[28] Though this is the romanticized and fond account which pays testament to the influence of the city on just one architect, his repeated stress on the incompleteness of the city, as well as the contrasts and combinations of its various, mutating juxtapositions is something to which this chapter, as well as each of the contributions to this volume, attest. Happily, they draw together a vast range of approaches to the specific and the general in the case of Rome, producing insight on a series of crucial questions about the centre and periphery, the local and the international, the plurality of representations of the city, and the unavoidable weight of history; questions which are only part resolved, yet which we hope will trigger further thought and discussion in the application of postmodernity to this incomplete Rome.

We recognize that this volume is by no means exhaustive and that its absences point to the work which is still to be done in this fertile field of postmodern Rome studies. The chapters here merely signal certain major questions which remain unanswered, such as the relationship between race, gender and sexuality and the politics of space. It is our hope that the volume helps to clear away some of the detritus of the pompous and magniloquent imagery of Rome, in order to open it up to other potential meanings. The signifier 'Rome' should, in the future, include in its semantic field typically ignored features and characters: Ostiense, with its slaughterhouse converted into a museum for contemporary art (the Macro Ostiense), its power plant transformed into a gallery for ancient art (Centrale Montemartini), its train hub re-thought as a food mall (Eataly). Rome should mean that commercial and residential citadel which is Parco Leonardo and the scattered urbanscape located outside the physical limits of the actual city; the multicultural Piazza Vittorio, with its markets, its small shops and its ethnic restaurants; Via di San Giovanni in Laterano, the seat of the first Roman gay street, where everyday lesbian, gay and transsexual people gather.[29] The existence of these Roman presences should create together a breach in the image of the 'Eternal City', they should deconstruct its tradition, absorb a different temporality, propose a more osmotic notion of history in which a certain reading of the past no longer governs the present. Rome's postmodern narratives must replace a fixed and established notion of the city in order to re-think the cityscape of the future.

1 BETWEEN ROME'S WALLS: NOTES ON THE ROLE AND RECEPTION OF THE AURELIAN WALLS

Marco Cavietti

Le maree delle epoche sono passate e si sono ritirate lasciando sulla rena i relitti di lontani naufragi: come tutti i relitti, hanno attorno uno spazio prossimo e sconfinato, il mare e la spiaggia. È una città [Roma] vissuta di spoglie, poi di rovine, oggi di rifiuti.

(The tides of the ages rose and then fell, leaving behind on the sand the relics of distant shipwrecks: like all relics, they surrounded by close and unconfined space, the sea and the beach. [Rome] is a city lived of spoils, then of ruins, now of rubbish.)

G. C. Argan (1978)[1]

Introduction

At present Rome's urban space appears open and unconfined. The major housing expansion, which began during the post-war period and stretched through to the present, brought about a loss of coherency in the urban fabric. Over time, the city centre – while nominally preserved thanks to its historic value – has lost the specific, connecting function of 'the centre', becoming instead a discordant space. In its place, individual and disconnected fragments within the city have assumed its various 'central functions': be they administrative, economic, cultural, etc. Roberto Cassetti has commented on this situation, making particular reference to the 2003 *piano regolatore*, the urban master plan of the city. In Cassetti's view, the various 'centres' of Rome, which have materialized around the various focal points of urban activity, should be placed into dialogue with one another within a system of reciprocal relationships, so as to manage organically the dispersed urban context.[2] As a city develops, he writes,

Si formano nuovi intrecci di attività, variabili secondo i luoghi e quindi anche la nozione di periferia tende a svuotarsi di significato ... La città viene così a scomporsi in un insieme di frammenti legati tra loro da reti reciprocamente interagenti, e le 'centralità' più che in ruolo di riferimento del contesto, che pure si mantiene e che mette in moto una dinamica di ricostruzione sociale dei luoghi, diventano un attributo delle reti che le connettono fra loro in insiemi: sono queste che garantiscono il ruolo e il peso. In altri termini ciascuna centralità, più che al servizio di un ambito territoriale definito, si pone come parte di un insieme, al servizio dell'intera città o area metropolitana e, potenzialmente, dello spazio economico regionale e nazionale.[3]

(New bonds between different activities take shape, bonds which vary according to place, and consequently the notion of periphery tends to be emptied of significance ... The city thus breaks apart, forming a series of fragments that are linked between each other by reciprocally interactive networks. 'Centralities', then, rather than being a contextualizing reference point which nevertheless remains present and which kick-starts a dynamic of social regeneration of space, become an attribute of the networks which connect the fragments into a collective: these are what guarantee role and importance. In other words, each centrality, rather than being at the service of a given territorial context, posits itself as part of a whole, at the service of the entire city or metropolitan area and, potentially, the regional and national economic space.)

At present Rome continues to expand its presence and its influence in marginal areas. Yet this expansion raises a key question: what effect does this expansion have on its concrete relationship with the central, historical city? In order to begin to approach an answer, I will pose another question: in what ways can a monument such as the Aurelian Walls, one which was created in order to *confine* urban space and yet which certainly no longer does that today, continue to characterize the imagery of the city? Beginning with these questions, in what follows I intend to offer some reflections on the urban environment of Rome today.

The historical city centre of Rome is generally defined as those parts of the city which lie within the Aurelian Walls. Though traditionally this perimeter has always marked the confines of the city's urban development, today they survive only as a mute fragment of the ancient city that has been absorbed into the new one. In recent years, however, a renewed interest in the imposing monument has emerged in both urbanist and academic fields.

In 2003 the Aurelian Walls became the object of an ongoing regeneration project with the name Parco Lineare Integrato (Integrated Linear Park), under the scientific and organizational guidance of architects Paola Falini and Antonio Terranova.[4] The project aims not only to conserve the walls, but above all to reconsider their role as the point of interface between the historical centre and the extension of the modern city, in order to therefore imbue them with a new identity. Where this enormous, 18 km-long monument has traditionally been considered merely as the barrier which held in the ancient walled city, this project seeks to re-articulate the walls as a means of reconnecting the historical centre with the polycentric reality outside it, in the hope of forging an osmotic continuity between the two urban identities.[5] The completion of the park alongside the walls would thus renovate the presence of the walls within the urban fabric of the city and avoid organically entombing the ancient monument through the concrete expansion of Rome. It is not by chance, then, that the 2003 master plan placed emphasis on the position of the Aurelian Walls in order to allow their re-envisioning as an integral part of the city, and forge vibrant dialogues between the polycentric city and its historic identity, conserved inside the walls. The project leaders for the park believe that:

> intervenire su questa struttura significa intervenire sulla città, così come il centro storico si è espanso ed è diventato città storica, così gli interventi che riguardano le mura, anziché essere localizzati solo sulla cinta che circonda una parte di città, ed essere rivolti esclusivamente al restauro, devono, partendo proprio dal restauro, che è la 'grande valorizzazione' e la riconquistata dignità e salvaguardia, innescare un processo di coinvolgimento e sinergia rispetto allo 'spazio abitabile e vivibile' e trasmettere valorizzazione e valori ai luoghi circostanti.[6]

> (to modify this structure means to modify the city. Just as the historic centre has expanded and it has become a historic city, so any modifications of the walls must engage in a process of participation and synergy in relation to the 'open and liveable space' and produce value and appreciation in the surrounding areas, instead of being localized only to the belt that surrounds one part of the city, or indeed of being focused exclusively on their direct restoration. These modifications must begin with restoration, as this is the major source of value, of a returned dignity and of the monument's future safeguarding.)

The regeneration plan for the walls is to take place in six sections that relate to different sections of their perimeter: (1) from Piazzale Flaminio to Castro Pretorio, (2) from Castro Pretorio to Castro Laurenziano, (3) from Castro Laurenziano to Porta Metronia, (4) from Porta Metronia to Largo Chiarini, (5) from Largo Chiarini to the Tiber and, finally, (6) from Porta Portese to Castel Sant'Angelo. The modification project is to concentrate above all on the decayed sections of wall that are in a critical condition for a number of reasons: because of proximity to urban traffic, as has happened in the Muro Torto section, alongside Piazzale Flaminio, or at the Porta Maggiore (see Figure 1.1 on p. 22); because a section has become a common parking spot; or even simply due to decades of neglect and urban 'wear-and-tear'. At the time of writing, one area has already been successfully renovated, namely that situated adjacent to the Porta Metronia (see Figure 1.2 on p. 23).[7] There the project has created a new piazza and with it an open urban space that allows people to walk alongside the walls, at the same time diverting the flow of traffic and quickly producing an organic meeting place for locals. If completed, this project would undoubtedly bring about a semantic shift in the function of the walls, thus becoming a trail around the ancient city that crucially looks to its expansion, dialoguing with the contemporary city's growth.

In conjunction with this architectural project, in 2001 Rossana Mancini undertook historical research on the Aurelian Walls. Mancini has two aims: she

Figure 1.1: Section of the Aurelian Wall under restoration at Porta Maggiore. Photograph: Ireneo Alessi. Reproduced with the kind permission of the photographer.

Figure 1.2: Section of the Aurelian Wall in the Parco Lineare Integrato project at the Porta Metronia. Photograph: Ireneo Alessi. Reproduced with the kind permission of the photographer.

sought first to investigate their unifying function, and second to reconstruct the palimpsest of building work that has been created by the overlaying of various reinforcement and restoration efforts across the centuries, assuming in particular the identification and dating of this work as her particular focus. Mancini's study provides an extraordinarily comprehensive atlas of the walls, including for instance the events which led to Rome's transformation in the nineteenth century: from the pontifical city to the capital of the Kingdom of Italy after its annexation in 1870. For this reason, the study is no doubt a fundamental part of the Parco delle Mura (Park around the Walls) project.

A further instance of this renewed interest in the Aurelian Walls is well demonstrated by recent work from scholar Hendrik Dey, which reflects on their symbolic value from the ancient period through to the ninth century.[8] In his introduction, the author suggests that there are many different approaches to the study of the Walls, and he calls specifically for a possible new way of knowing and understanding them:

> As I believe that the Aurelian Wall both shaped and reflected the priorities, perceptions, and activities of those living within it, and those located (often far) without, I think there remain multiple histories of the Wall to be written, which jointly have much to reveal about the city of Rome during the tumultuous centuries spanning the end of antiquity and the beginning of the Middle Ages. In addition to more traditional architectural studies, there is the history of responses to the Wall, the story of how people more or less actively engaged with both its contemporary reality and its ever-growing legacy in ways that informed thoughts and actions alike. There is also the history of the Wall as agent: as an imposing presence that came to mould its surroundings in increasingly pronounced ways, and as an instrument used to further the political, military and ideological agendas of the city's ruling elite. The amalgam of these several histories should point the way to a new appreciation of the crucial role the Wall came to play in the evolution of the city around and within it.[9]

Taking inspiration from Dey's work, in particular his attempt to study the reception of the Walls diachronically, in this chapter I aim to interrogate the contemporary reception of the Aurelian Walls. While the ancient history of this imposing monument has been reconstructed on several occasions – as Dey's work helpfully confirms – the same can certainly not be said of its modern and contemporary history. For this reason, while in the first section I will offer a historical outline of the Walls from their construction through to the Second World War, in the second section I will linger on an analysis of their reception from the second half of the 1970s. Rome during this period experienced a moment of profound urban transformation led by the various public administrative bodies that, on the one hand, focused on the restoration of the historical centre inside the walls, and the vibrant reaffirmation of the city's cultural function outside of them, and on the other, concentrated on cleaning up the widespread illegal constructions in the periphery, outside the walls.

Rome Within and Without the Aurelian Walls: A Dichotomy across the Centuries

The Aurelian Walls have had, for centuries an important symbolic value and a strong identity: they protected the capital of the Empire and they marked out its authority. The Walls were first constructed between AD 270 and AD 273 under the order of the Emperor Aurelian, with the twofold aim of defending the city from the attacks of barbarian groups and of celebrating the power of their patron. In the centuries that followed, the walls were then continually conserved and restored in order to maintain these symbolic and practical functions. If the birth of Rome was the fruit of an effort to outline the confines of a space and a precise identity, not to mention consequently to distance those who did not belong to either, the same gesture of creating walls around that space not only spelled out the city's boundaries to anyone approaching it externally, and quelled any revolts internally, but more than anything else it gave the city a circumscribing form. With its walls in place, Rome thus became a model of urban form for each of the Empire's other cities. As Dey writes,

> Much would change before the Aurelian Wall developed into the embodiment of Rome's strength, permanence, and civic stature that it later became. This meta-morphosis could come about only after a cognitive revolution that encompassed a pervasive reshaping of traditional urban paradigms across the empire, via a lengthy and complex process that the Wall helped to inform and define.[10]

Not by chance, each of the cities in the Empire had to come to terms with the structural model of Rome, and often assumed the title of 'the new Rome': indeed across the following centuries such a title was applied to Milan and Florence, and even to Paris. The comparison with Rome became a mode to approximate and qualify the city according to the central model of the State capital.

In the following decades and centuries the Aurelian Walls saw continual adjustment alongside the evolution of the city. They represent a palimpsest that is on the one hand simply structural, but on the other *historical*, one that is able to restitute to us the traces of many of the changes undertaken by the city.

The first major restoration project to the Aurelian Walls (AD 401–2) took place under the Emperor Honorius, who, fearing barbarian attack, ordered that both walls and towers be raised by one level. Once the city had become the capital of Christendom, the papacy began to make use of the Aurelian Walls as a system of defence, and for this reason they continued the work on their maintenance. The most important restoration work was carried out under the pontificates of

Adrian I (772–95), while the first enlargement of the city walls took place under the order of Leo IV (847–55), who sought to construct new walls that included the living spaces around the Old Basilica of St Peter. At that point the city became a definitively Christian city, and its nerve centre moved from the Capitoline Hill (the centre of secular power) to St Peter's (the symbol of Christianity), and as such the latter needed to be included within the urban fabric. What was then called 'Leo's city' thus included a new area, one which until that point had been peripheral and distinct from the historical centre, yet once Rome sought to demonstrate its primary role as Christian capital the area was absorbed into the centre. This can be considered the first key moment of the city's expansion, tactically directed around the Basilica of St Peter, which of course needed protection but moreover would guarantee a certain economic development that was engendered by the influx of pilgrims. The urban development is thus directly connected to ideological motives, as much as economic and social ones.

During the Middle Ages, the Aurelian Walls had become little adept to the defence of the city, which in the mean time, having had a decrease in population numbers, had drastically diminished. Yet even in the years of the Commune of Rome, some restoration of the walls was carried out by the new-born judiciary, the *Magistri aedificiorum Urbis* (Magistrates of City Building), as is attested by an inscription on the Potra Metronia. With the return of the papacy to Rome after its detention in Avignon, urban regeneration and renewal became a fundamental prerequisite in order to sanction once again the supremacy of the Roman Catholic Church. In fact, from the fifteenth through to the seventeenth centuries, the popes continued to preserve the Aurelian Walls, and to make use of its gates for symbolic entrances into the city, as in the case of the Holy Roman Emperor Charles V of Spain, conqueror of the Turks, through Porta San Sebastiano (1536), or that of Cristina Queen of Sweden through Porta del Popolo (1655).

From this moment on the walls around Rome developed into a fundamental part of the imaginary of the city, becoming a constant image in the iconographic representations that defined the space occupied by Rome. The whole city within the walls became an imaginable and governable place, a town that could be represented geographically and which thus was 'knowable'. Taking into account, therefore, the fundamental value of the Aurelian Walls, it is possible to trace the evolution of the urban space of Rome through its historical phases. Literary sources and iconographic representations, such as maps, *vedute*, etc. from as early as the Middle Ages help us to reconstruct the development of Rome. To discuss its urban growth is also to confront the mythical image that the city still bears today; the space that Rome occupies has at the same time a concrete value and a symbolic essence, that comes from both political and religious roots. In parallel to the real city, an 'ideal' city exists only in thought, an idea that became the model for many European capitals that have continuously compared themselves with Rome and its central, imperial role.[11] Among the earliest descriptions of the city of Rome, worthy of note are the *Mirabilia Urbis Romae* (The Wonders of the City of Rome) that, from when they first appeared, around 1140–3, went on to have countless reprints and editions, and eventually began to appear quite commonly in the press, too. These prototypical guides offered lists of the city's monuments, beginning with the Aurelian Walls and turning then to the gates that punctuated the trajectory of the walls. As Lucia Nuti recalls in *Cartografie senza carte* (Cartography without Maps), these guides, when read in relation to the coeval regeneration of Rome, can very usefully show us how contemporary pilgrims understood the urban space of the city and how they orientated themselves.[12] Evidently the walls and their gates, together with the churches and ancient remains that are dotted across the urban fabric, can structure if not dominate the orientation of the pilgrim, allowing her to construct a mental map of her visit.

From the fifteenth century, following the return of the papacy to Rome, the city experienced not only a cultural renewal, but also urban and economic booms – in particular between the times of Martin V and Julius II – that sought to enhance its road layout and aimed to re-structure Rome as a religious and political capital. In 1425, Martin V founded the *Magistri Viarum et Aedificiorum* (Magistrates of Roads and Buildings), whose purpose was to control directly restoration and maintenance work on roads and buildings. The city then experienced the first major *sventramenti* (major demolitions) of the urban fabric that sought to renew (again) the image of the city in order to re-sanction the political presence of the popes. Rome remained, however, substantially within the confines of the Aurelian Walls, and the centre of the city remained that of classical Rome, leading Sixtus IV to symbolically and politically seize and appropriate the Capitoline. Giorgio Simoncini emphasizes how,

> Durante il Pontificato di Niccolò V la città storica continuò a evolversi in base al tradizionale modello urbanistico costituito da un nucleo centrale compatto rappresentato dalla città vecchia e da un insediamento circostante di densità abitativa irregolarmente decrescente verso l'esterno. Contemporaneamente si rafforzò anche il nucleo urbano situato nella parte inferiore dell'ansa del Tevere, concentrato intorno al canale di ponte, funzionale alla città leonina. I due nuclei, nonostante le continuità edilizia esistente nell'ansa del Tevere, si può ritenere che siano rimasti funzionalmente separati. La loro crescita era alimentata da fonti diverse: i traffici mercantili di Pira Grande e i consumi della città storica nel primo caso, e le funzioni religiose e di governo del Vaticano nel secondo. Questa diversità rientrava nel quadro della concezione urbana bipolare sviluppatasi in questo periodo.[13]

(During the pontificate of Nicholas V, the historic city continued to evolve according to the traditional urban model, consisting of a central, compact nucleus that represented the old town and of a surrounding settlement that has an irregularly descending population density towards the outer edges. At the same time, the urban nucleus situated below the curve of the Tiber and concentrated at the Canale di Ponte, operational since Leo IV, became more prominent. The two nuclei, we can argue, despite the consistency of building work within the curve of the Tiber, became essentially separate in their functions. Their growth was increased from different sources: the mercantile traffic from Pira Grande and the consumption of the historical centre in the first case, and the religious and governmental functions of the Vatican in the second. This difference had a great effect on the bipolar urban geography that developed in this period.)

Substantially, during the Renaissance and for much longer afterwards, there was a distinct urban separation between the classical settlement and the new areas that became populated in the following centuries. At that time, the division coincided culturally with the separation between sacred and profane spaces, while the Aurelian Walls continue to be simply a distant marker of confinement that encircled Rome.

In the the sixteenth and seventeenth centuries, Rome needed to maintain its image as the capital of Christendom while the papacy asserted its supremacy over the Protestant Reformation. The urban development ordered by Sixtus V is quite significant in this regard. The embellishment of the city was conceived as a sign of temporal and spiritual power that was destined to glorify not only the prestige of the papacy and the power of its reign, but also that of the church and of the Catholic faith. Sixtus V understood that urban development went hand in hand with the economic growth of the city, and, like his predecessors before him – in particular Sixtus IV – he established his legacy as the great restorer of Rome. Simoncini, in *Roma restaurata* (Rome Restored),[14] recalls and recapitulates the various historical interpretations that have alternatively posited the pontiff as the creator of a central urban plan of Rome or as the champion of a polycentric image of Rome. Others have argued for the complete absence of any default plan on behalf of the pope. Sixtus V had attempted various urban transformations that aimed at renewing the city for both architectural and liturgical reasons: on the one hand the improvements of road connections, on the other the facilitation of the many religious ceremonies that take place in the city. Simoncini recalls that,

il sistema viario centrale e radiale ammette motivazioni sia religiose che secolari. In questa logica la sua configurazione si può giustificare non solo con l'esigenza di collegare il centro religioso della zona collinare con le chiese situate ai margini della sua giurisdizione ecclesiastica, ma anche con la necessità di mettere in comunicazione il centro funzionale della zona, rappresentato dal luogo di smistamento di tutti i percorsi, con le porte urbane situate accanto o in direzione delle chiese: cioè Porta del Popolo (vicino a santa Maria del Popolo), Porta San Lorenzo (lungo la strada per San Lorenzo fuori le Mura), Porta Maggiore (adiacente a santa Croce in Gerusalemme), Porta Asinara e poi Porta San Giovanni (in prossimità di San Giovannni in Laterano).[15]

(the central road and radial system was governed by both religious and secular motivations. In this logic, its configuration can be justified not only according to the need to connect the religious centre in the hills with the churches situated at the margins of its ecclesiastical jurisdiction, but furthermore to the necessity to forge communication routes between the functional centre of the area, represented by the sorting location in all directions, with the urban gateways situated near to or in the direction of the churches. This included Porta del Popolo (near Santa Maria del Popolo), Porta San Lorenzo (along the road towards San Lorenzo Fuori le Mura), Porta Maggiore (adjacent to Santa Croce in Gerusalemme), Porta Asinara and Porta San Giovanni (in the proximity of St John Lateran).

With this in mind, it is clear that the relationship with the Aurelian Walls, in this period more than in the previous one, related directly to the connection of the internal roads with the external ones, to which corresponded a related gate in the perimeter of the walls. For instance, the new road ordered by Sixtus V, the Via Felice, connected Porta del Popolo and Porta Maggiore, facilitating internal to external movements and vice versa.

During the eighteenth century, the cityscape remained substantially the same, and the city took further advantage of its direct relationship with the Roman countryside. In this period the Grand Tour boomed, and the city became the main destination for the journey of young, wealthy Europeans. It was during this period that, alongside the ruins and the glories of the Eternal City, the Ager Romanus (Roman Countryside) system began to establish itself just outside the Aurelian Walls. From beyond the perimeter the Roman countryside expanded outwards, punctuated by archaeological ruins; the walls thus marked the beginning of a relationship between the closed city and the vibrant nature outside. That untouched nature conserved the poetic of the sublime. During this period, the papacy limited itself to a fairly conservative maintenance of the walls.

Interest in the walls then re-emerged during the nineteenth century, under Pope Pius IX, in parallel with the modernization of the city undertaken by this papacy. At the beginning of the nineteenth century, architect Giuseppe Valadier suggested a complete restoration project for the Aurelian Walls, proposing a regeneration through a planned walkway running all the way around its perimeter. Valadier then went on to work directly on the Muro Torto section, towards Villa Borghese (1822–6 and again in 1830),[16] while another architect, Virginio Vespignani, worked on the reconstruction of Porta S. Pancrazio (1857) and the exterior of Porta Pia (1868).

The fate of the Aurelian Walls was to then alter quite drastically after 1871 and the symbolic breach of Porta Pia, when the Italian army managed to enter into the city by breaking a 30 m gap in the walls alongside Porta Pia. The disappearance of the countryside surrounding Rome was initiated at that very moment. What had been quasi-mythical and sacred areas, inasmuch as they were untouched and organically preserved, began to disappear following the growth of new quarters, and the modern services that were needed by the capital of a state. The subsequent annexing of Rome to the Kingdom of Italy and its promotion to the status of capital city brought to fruition a transformation of the city and a hasty acceleration of the modernizing process that had begun with the previous pope. The expansion of the city in an effort to adhere to its new requirements triggered a frenetic growth in construction; in this context the Aurelian Walls quickly became a major obstruction to urban development. In order to facilitate circulation and take pressure off the road system, a series of openings were created in the city walls: in 1877, the limits of Porta del Popolo were widened, and again in 1896 the wall was opened up along Via degli Abruzzi by 70 m. Despite the necessity of growth, the master plan of 1873 envisages a walkway 40 m wide around the entire perimeter of the city walls, a distance which slowly diminished because of the need to expand. The Comune di Roma (Roman local authority) obtained official ownership of the walls only in 1895 after a lengthy dispute with the Demanio dello Stato (State Land Administrative Body). Unlike other European capitals, such as Vienna, in Rome there was never any plan to dismantle entirely the city walls in order to facilitate plans for urban expansion. Nevertheless, thanks to the unstoppable growth of the city, continual breaches and demolitions of the wall came in succession into the twentieth century.

At this moment the Aurelian Walls fell silent, and the city developed further and further beyond them, losing any sense of the organic; these traces of the ancient world became slowly suffocated by urbanization, in part forgotten where they no longer articulated the limits of the concrete city. New clearance and demolition began in the historic centre, which aimed to modernize the city in a way that stood against the previous modernization plans introduced by the papacy, instead instating the secularity of the new capital. At the beginning of the twentieth century, further openings were made along the entire stretch of the walls, in accordance with the Sanjust master plan. The walls began to be seen as a cumbersome presence, and during the fascist years – despite the rhetoric placed upon the ancient and its urban preservation – the civic functions of the walls were completely forgotten. Quite interestingly, in 1940, Porta San Sebastiano was assigned as housing to the Fascist Colonel-Lieutenant and pilot Ettore Muti, who (privately) entrusted the architect Luigi Moretti with its restoration and interior design.[17] The walls themselves, as well as their immediate surroundings, had been shelter for the homeless since the late nineteenth century, and this particular use of the structure intensified between 1920–30 following the enormous waves of immigration of agricultural workers, most of whom were soon employed in the city's booming building industry.

The process of the transformation of the capital that was brought about by fascist leadership constituted a point of rupture in the urban fabric, which had otherwise remained fairly steady since 1848. At this point, with the vast influx of people, the city expanded unstoppably, leaving the Aurelian Walls behind entirely. Even the powerful fascist policy that worked tirelessly and infamously to recuperate 'romanità' overlooked the monument completely: perhaps simply because it constituted a limit or a barrier, more than anything else.[18]

During the post-war period, the decision was made to preserve the historic centre, as a point of resistance and reaction to the fascist demolitions (*sventramenti*). While this facilitated the preservation of the historical centre and its memory, at the same time it sacrificed, again, the heritage of the Roman countryside, whose ancient ruins were being quickly erased by new housing blocks and residential quarters. It was not only the disappearance of the countryside which was problematic, however, but also the building work of the new city outside the walls which took place in an uncontrolled and random way. The walls signalled a rupture between the 'present', the new city which was dislocated and pushed outside, and the 'past', or the illusion of it, which was preserved inside, in the historical city. This philosophy of preservation refused and debased the problem of modernity: preserving and protecting the past does not necessarily mean remembering it.

The Persistence of the Aurelian Walls Today

The Aurelian Walls continued to be occupied throughout the post-war period by displaced migrants and the homeless. This situation changed little until around 1974, when the newly formed Ministero della pubblica istruzione (Ministry for Public Information) began to commit to the protection and preservation of cultural amenities. This included, in particular, a set of policy relating to the areas around the walls that aimed to prevent property speculation. In the same years, the local government became, for the first time historically, led by the left wing and by Mayor Giulio Carlo Argan, who immediately established the Assessorato per gli interventi nel centro storico (Department of Modifications to the Historical Centre).[19] The same Argan, in the dual roles of mayor and scholar of art history, understood the urban phenomenon ultimately as both a historical and an architectural one. For this reason he devoted much thought to the historical centre of Rome and to its periphery, the latter of which by that time had penetrated deep into the surrounding countryside.[20] Argan himself comments that:

La natura non è più al di là delle mura della città, le città non hanno più mura, si estendono in disperanti labirinti di cemento, si sfilacciano nelle luride frange delle baracche e al di là della città è ancora la città, la città delle autostrade e dei distributori, delle campagne coltivate industrialmente: e se anche qualche pezzo di natura sfuggito alla

speculazione immobiliare o all'industria turistica sopravvivesse, non lo vedremmo perché lo attraverseremmo a 200 km all'ora in automobile o sorvoleremmo in jet.[21]

(Nature is no longer outside the walls of the city; the city no longer has walls. They
extend out in desperate cement labyrinths, they unwind in the grimy fringes of shanty
towns, and all that lies beyond the city is more city: a city of motorways and of distribution companies, of industrially farmed countryside. And if some piece of nature
managed to survive, out of reach of housing speculation or the tourism industry, we
would never actually glimpse it because we would only speed across it in a car at 200
km/h, or far above it in a jumbo jet.)

Rome, as such, lost sight of the infamous countryside that once surrounded it,
and at the same time the walls suddenly no longer represented the limits of the
city: both the countryside and the city walls today constitute mere fragments
that are immersed in the highly dense contemporary city, almost entirely forgotten if not the subject of one or two distracted glances. During that period,
another art historian, Corrado Maltese, devoted the twenty-fourth congress
of the Comité International d'Histoire de l'Art (International Committee for
Art History), chaired by Maltese himself, to the theme of historical city centres.
Emphasizing the historical role of the centre in a contrasting juxtaposition with
the emerging periphery, the scholar argued that

> Le centre ancien constitue une source continuelle de messages sur le passé de la ville,
> ils constituent souvent une grandiose stratification de trace du véçu. Le centre ancien
> en tant que tel posséde la créativité et l'aspect organique des oevres d'art bien qu'il
> se présente souvent sans le nom des auteurs et comme une oevre collective. Par con-
> séquent le centre ancien nous apparaissent en conflit avec la ville dans son visage
> actuel. En réalité ils ont l'air d'émerger comme deux villes différentes: une ville-oeuvre
> d'art contre une ville non art, qui nie la primiére; une ville qui est bien définie avec
> son identité historique contre une ville anonyme, lieu et image d'une société affluente
> et consommatrice, partout structurellement épaule et semblablement aliénante.[22]

(The historical centre constitutes a continual source of messages that tell us about the
city's past; it often signifies a large-scale stratification of the traces of the lived. The historical centre possesses intrinsically the creativity and the organic face of its works of
art, despite the fact that they are often presented without the names of its original artists, but rather as a collective work. Consequently the historical centre appears to us in
conflict with the city of its current physiognomy. In reality they seem to emerge as two
different cities: one, the city-as-work of art against another, the city-as-not art, which
negates the former; one city which is well defined in terms of its historical identity
against the other which is anonymous, the space and image of an affluent and consumerist society, despite being structurally sound and superficially alienating.)

Maltese's focus here is on one of the consequences of urban expansion, which
is the distinct separation between the memory of the city, included within the

'defined' city as a repository of history and art, and its opposite, deprived of any characterizing quality, and the product of this new society.

Argan, like Maltese, returned on many occasions to the problem of the historical city centre, and of how the city must be considered in a unitary manner, with little distinction between centre and periphery. As such the scholar avoided any value-based hierarchies which automatically afforded the historical centre a greater prestige, and sought instead to support an organic design that nevertheless did make space to appreciate the historical status of a capital city such as Rome. In the same argument, he writes,

> Nel periodo in cui sono stato sindaco di Roma – una città-capitale in cui è molto forte la concentrazione di organismi direzionali – mi sono reso conto che la protezione locale circoscritta a una zona privilegiata della città, ancorché rigorosa, non è in nessun caso sufficiente e che i centri storici si possono salvare, e non soltanto prorogare per qualche tempo, solo nel quadro di una politica urbanistica che consideri globalmente tutti i problemi della città e del territorio.[23]

> (In the period in which I was mayor of Rome – a capital city in which the concentration of directional organisms is particularly high – I realized that local preservation, that was limited to one privileged part of the city, and despite being quite rigorous, was in no way sufficient; I realized that that historical city centres can be truly protected, and not simply prolonged a little further, only when placed within the comprehensive model of urban policy that considers, globally, *all* of the problems of the city and its territory.)

In spite of Argan's warnings and his important position within Rome's cultural and political circles, his ideas never found fertile ground for development. Indeed, as Luigi Ficacci observes, not only was Argan's work as mayor and his programme for Rome completely ignored by subsequent administrations, but moreover he not once received any of the just recognition that he deserved for his contributions to scholarship on art history.[24]

This clash between the historical reality that was closed inside the walls and the contemporaneous, dilated and limitless one outside seems never to have been resolved within the broad, complex reality of the city of Rome. The city's expansion beyond the walls not only continued to lack entirely the historical identity of the city centre, but, moreover, it actually *reinforced* this absence through constant juxtaposition. In fact, precisely within this dialectic we can reinvigorate and re-semanticize the Aurelian Walls as the symbol of the interaction *between* these two realities, and not as a fracture with the external. The walls should become the dual image of the city, which on the one hand looks to its millenary past, and on the other presents itself as communicative with the expanding future. Precisely because of their stratification in time, the walls appear to be the perfect polyvalent symbol of Rome, of a ramified city that is no longer constricted to its centre.

In any case, in 1980 the Comune di Roma announced their intention to make it possible for the public to visit the complex of the Aurelian Walls, having only a few years earlier managed to free the walls of 'improper' occupation (which by this stage included artist studios that had been set up on the *camminamento*, the chemin de ronde or ancient patrol path atop the walls).[25] Despite this renewed interest in the monument, in the same year a portion of the walls collapsed in the Janiculum stretch, another in 1997 near Porta Maggiore, again in 2001 in the stretch alongside Porta Ardeatina,[26] and recently, in 2010, some parts fell down near the Church of St Croce in Gerusalemme.[27] Today much work is still taking place to reinforce the entire city wall structure. On the one hand, then, it seems that the local authority remains interested in the restoration and the safe management of one of Rome's most important monuments, though on the other, it continues to appear almost completely indifferent to the walls.

The problem thus shifts from one of conservation of the monument, which has been underway already for several years, to one of its effectual valorization; what is missing is a cultural initiative on behalf of the city's public administration, which could seek to re-articulate the walls as a living symbol of the city that could attract the attention of the capital's tourists.

One example of a living approach, free from nostalgic melancholia and open to the role that the Aurelian Walls might play in the city's future, is the street art of American Matthew Hural (see Figure 1.3 on p. 35). The artist, who was awarded the Arnold W. Brunner Rome Prize in Architecture in 2008–9, reflected on how the image of Rome inside the walls constitutes an urban space that can be imagined, represented and walked through, despite the uncontrolled growth of the city. This conceptualization awakens the attention of the inhabitants to the important, forgotten monument. The idea of the walking tour of the city recalls the medieval visits of Rome, when in order to orientate themselves, pilgrims would employ those skeletal guides that used the Aurelian Walls and their gates as access points to the city. Today, like then, the visitor needs points of orientation, and not only do the walls offer precisely that, but they moreover actually categorize and frame this known city. As Hural writes,

> When looked at as part of a modern urban fabric that is necessarily layered and historically contingent, the function of these walls, gates, canals, or bridges I have been looking at transcend any one narrative, allowing multiple temporal and cultural interpretation of their surfaces to exist contemporaneously.[28]

The city thus becomes known through the rediscovery of this monumental fragment of history. The Aurelian Walls relocate their space within the urban environment, and their function shifts, from protective barrier and limit, to one of a guiding line in the discovery of the city. Consequently, Hural focuses on the coexistence of these fragments of history today, and he pushes for their recogni-

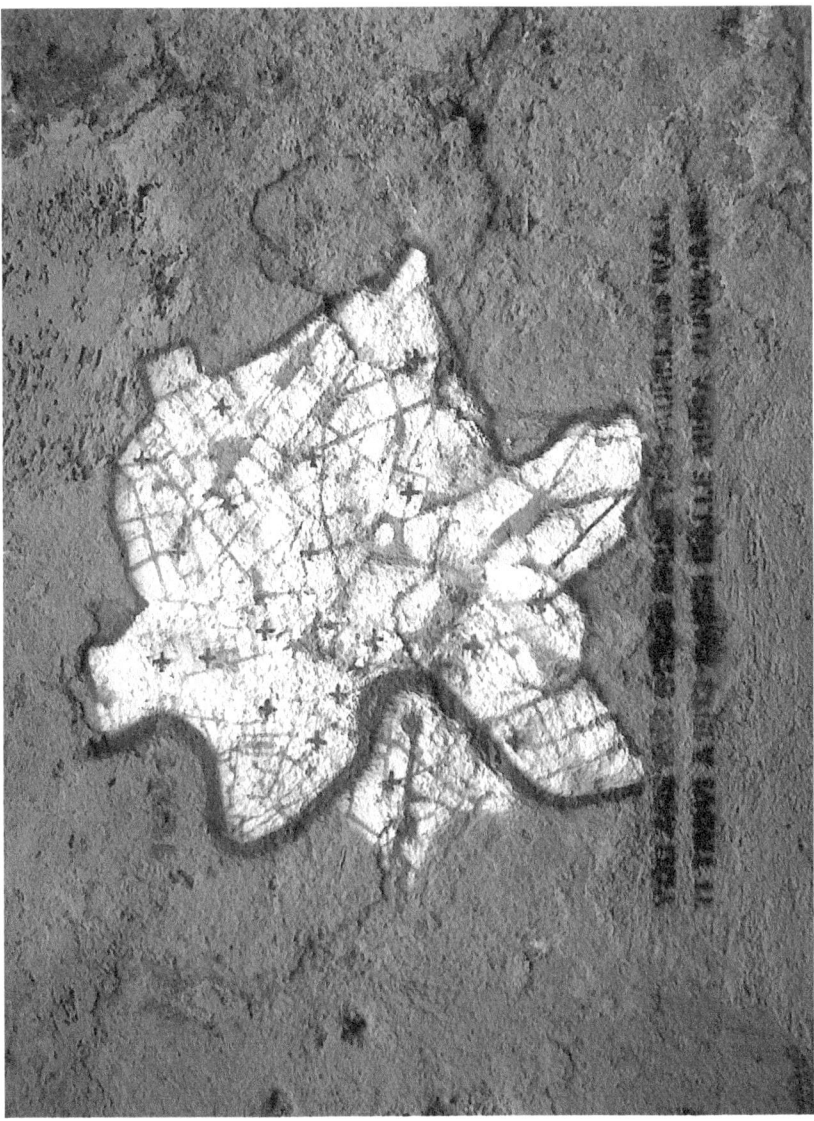

Figure 1.3: Map of Rome inside the Aurelian Wall designed by the American artist Matthew Hural. Photograph: Ireneo Alessi. Reproduced with the kind permission of the photographer.

tion through the action of the stroll. Walking thus becomes intended as a process of 'knowing' that is capable of putting together various temporal and spatial planes, at the same time forging one's own *personal* map. The artist's discovery of the city was concretized in a series of maps of the Aurelian Walls, made using stencils on various other walls across Rome, which signalled the viewer's position within this urban circuit. Hural's invitation to a process of re-discovery of the monument recalls that of Christo, another artist who in 1974 transformed the walls by drawing attention to their existence. A few years later, between April and July 1982, Achille Bonito Oliva exhibited his work 'Avanguardia Transavan-guardia' (Avantgarde Transavantgarde) along the stretch of wall between Porta Metronia and Porta Latina. The walls were thus transformed into an exhibition space, leading the architect Costantino Dardi to coin the term 'architettura della stratificazione' (stratification architecture).[29] Then Cultural Assessor Renato Nicolini defined the Aurelian Walls as:

> luogo simbolo per il rapporto con la storia che ripropone un interrogativo inqui-etante a cui l'arte moderna non ha dato risposte convincenti, e rispetto al quale il post-moderno costituisce, a ben vedere, forse l'ennesima evasione, l'illusione di un eterno presente.[30]

> (a place, symbolic of the connection with history, that re-articulates a worrying ques-tion – to which modern art has never responded convincingly – in relation to which the postmodern constitutes, on closer inspection, perhaps the umpteenth evasion, the illusion of an eternal present.)

If in these last examples the walls were made into a space that demands reinven-tion and reinterpretation, Hural, on the other hand, took the Aurelian Walls as a topographic element that is fundamental to visiting the city. To him it is an object that characterizes the historical and urban context, and for this reason he uses the city maps inside the walls and signals to the visitor her position in rela-tion to the confines of the walls. The stencilled maps, realized by Hural, are thus a figurative language that is capable of transmitting a spatial perception, as well as – contextually – a historical knowledge of the space covered by the visitor. The artist transfers onto the map of the centre inside the walls a description of Rome in relation to its own historical limits, created by the walls themselves. He thus creates a non-verbal description of the city that can nevertheless transfer the essence of urban space and push the visitor to discover more. Naomi Miller, in her volume *Mapping the City*, writes:

> Today maps are the fundamental metaphor. In the past decade, 'map', both as noun and as verb, has become the word of choice to describe states of mind, types of itin-eraries, codes of modern science, and secrets of the universe, as well as principles of paradigms and abstract concepts for organization, planning, and knowing.[31]

Miller then recalls how the metaphoric extension of the term 'map' and its use has brought to its approximation with the definition of 'representation', in other words the reproduction of reality. Relevantly, Hural's work not only communicates information relating to Rome's urban space, but he moreover offers a contemporary representation of it that is connected to its perception. It is interesting how the experience of discovery of the city on behalf of the artist is not distant from that of the many visitors in the past that orientated themselves in the network of Roman roads, and sought to grasp the nature of the city.

To reflect on the Aurelian Walls and on their history means to reflect on the entire city and on the conflict which continues to exist between the historical and modern cities. As it expands, Rome (first within the walls and later outside them), has always had to encompass the new, creating a relationship with its most recent developments. In this discussion I have broadly outlined how this happened historically with the inclusion of 'Leo's city', of the so-called 'new city' of Sixtus V, of the new quarters of the emergent Capital city and of the Fascist period: from the EUR to the most recent suburbs and peripheries. In all of these evolutions the Aurelian Walls remained in evidence as a mutating symbol of the entire city. For this reason they should be recognized not as a barrier, but as a threshold which forges, if not *forces* dialogue between the historical centre and the whole city, in order to begin to resolve the conflict between Rome and its own history.

2 THE EXPLOSION OF ROME IN THE FRAGMENTS OF A POSTMODERN ICONOGRAPHY: FEDERICO FELLINI AND THE *FORMA URBIS*

Fabio Benincasa

Much scholarship has been devoted to the unique development of Rome during centuries of European intellectual history as the symbolic *forma urbis*: it has repeatedly been perceived as the city that summarized all cities. Rome was at once a geographical location and an ideal, the cradle of antiquity and the holy site of Christianity.[1] The universal city of classicism since the Middle Ages, it represented an ancestral model on which the great Western metropolises were later to be founded or reshaped. In the cases of Paris, London, Berlin, and more 'recent' cities like New York City, Washington, DC and Buenos Aires, marmoreal colonnades, memorials, triumphal arches, domes and obelisks were the landmarks that characterized the shape of the urban landscape, marking the presence of a sacred aura of power and its culture that are direct descendents of the Roman Empire and its historical memory.

In the modern period, the relationship of the Italian intellectual with Rome has been pointedly visceral and contradictory. It was impossible to separate the symbolic importance of the city – in relation to national unification – and its reality: a chaotic and often provincial town, humiliated by the rigidity of the Papal bureaucracy and later by the presence of an asphyxiating and myopic Piedmontese government. From Giacomo Leopardi to Giuseppe Antonio Borgese and Carlo Levi, the disappointment of intellectuals over the contrast between ideal value of Rome and its real condition become almost a literary *topos*.[2] Since the birth of contemporary Italian literature, often conventionally marked by the publication of Luigi Pirandello's *Il fu Mattia Pascal* (The Late Mattia Pascal) in 1904, the capital of the newborn, unified Italian state has provided the perfect psychological background, the host to the wanderings and ruminations of the new nation's subjects. A large number of factors favoured this image of the city, including its multilayered and complex structure, its paradoxical status of Holy

City and former Imperial capital, its hectic urbanism and its contradictory modernization. The representation of Rome as a decomposed structure, pervaded by centrifugal dynamics in which relics of linguistic or even urban rationality are lost in an endless maze, was the long-sought achievement of Italian literature, culminating perhaps with Carlo Emilio Gadda's masterpiece *Quer pasticciaccio brutto de via Merulana* (That Awful Mess on Via Merulana, 1957).

This representation of the city soon translated to film, becoming a common starting point for several directors. The bond between the national cinema and the capital is deep, both thanks to the prominence of Rome in our collective imaginary, and simply enough, to the increasing centralization of the national film industry to the city during the wake of the First World War. Thus among the patrimony of countless identities that have emerged historically within the city, one most worthy of note is its metamorphosis into the 'city of cinema'. This concept is best expounded by Federico Fellini's *Intervista* (Interview, 1987),[3] in which moreover the *città* and Cinecittà (Rome's film studio complex that was built during the 1930s) perfectly overlap. Indeed, as I will discuss here, it was for Fellini, one of Italy's most acclaimed and famed directors, more than for anyone else, that the city functioned most frequently as a psychological landscape in his repeated depictions of Rome's mental and memorial fragments.[4]

Though ultimately Rome was to appear in many different guises throughout his career, the 'Eternal City' formed a part of Fellini's poetics from his first film, *Lo sceicco bianco* (The White Sheik, 1952), through to the late sixties and early seventies with 'Toby Dammit' (1968) and *Roma* (1972), and beyond, for instance in *Ginger and Fred* (1986) and *Intervista*.[5] Fellini's cinematic corpus founded a new paradigmatic vision of the city: multilayered, fragmented and substantially abstract. In the last twenty years, 'after Fellini',[6] Italian films such as Nanni Moretti's *Caro diario* (Dear Diary, 1993), Marco Bellocchio's *L'ora di religione* (My Mother's Smile, 2002) and Mario Martone's *L'odore del sangue* (The Scent of Blood, 2004)[7] have capitalized on Fellini's intuitions, demonstrating to their audience that the city is no more a humanistic *organon*, but now a disaggregated collection of iconographies. Fellini is the author who, departing from the fundamental and unitary imagery of Baroque Rome, first elaborated the pluralistic urban image for our time.

In these films it is apparent that the only possible means to interact with Rome that is left to the characters of the contemporary Italian cinema is a melancholic flâneurism into the *disiecta membra* of the iconic urban palimpsest. After Fellini the image of the city is never uniform: the wandering gaze of painter Ernesto Picciafuoco in Bellocchio's *L'ora di religione* chances upon sudden apparitions of monuments, such as the Vittoriano or Santa Maria Maggiore, while the dome of St Peter is proudly displayed during the duel against Count Bulla. The protagonist's car journeys around Rome never concretize the idea of a homogeneous urban complex, but rather they loosely trace out a collection of unrelated frames. The first episode of Moretti's *Caro diario* displays the same principle, in Moretti's musings over a film 'fatto solo di case' (made only of houses). In the images that accompany this, Moretti does not build the thread of an imaginary city, but rather provides us with a series of flashes of non-monumental spaces, refusing to offer a totalizing picture of the city. Residential neighbourhoods such as Garbatella, Spinaceto or Ostia are characterized by their heterogeneity; there appears to be little kinship among these places beyond that supplied by the director's visual montage.[8]

The young Federico Fellini moved to Rome from his native Rimini in 1938, one year after Mussolini inaugurated the monumental film studio complex, Cinecittà. The urban system of the capital at that time was substantially similar in its proportions and structures to the great Baroque space developed and articulated by Fontana and Bernini during the seventeenth century, but soon exposed to deep and lasting changes introduced by the fascist regime. The architectural characteristics of the earlier Roman Baroque were an ornamental extroversion that explicitly conveyed a multi-linguistic inspiration, which in turn sought to encourage the collective and social fruition of space. As architect Paolo Portoghesi has noted, thanks to the strong influence of counter-reformed Catholicism, Roman architecture has always been more eloquent in its articulation of class relationships and tensions than in its embodiment of the aesthetic self-representation of a dominant elite:

> Il linguaggio barocco romano postula un'architettura eminentemente cittadina che sfrutti ogni risorsa per trovare una risonanza profonda non solo negli intenditori e nei raffinati, ma anche nell'uomo della strada. Il programma politico della classe dominante di distrarre il popolo con le belle immagini della vita cittadina diventa nello sforzo linguistico degli artisti volontà di comunicazione universale, discorso articolato a più livelli di accessibilità in modo da conservare significato e pregnanza sia per l'uomo di cultura che per il più umile osservatore e spesso, nel suo campo di autonomia, diventa finzione o profezia di una diversa, più umana società.[9]

> (The Roman Baroque language postulates an eminently urban architecture which makes use of every available resource in order to find profound resonance, not only for the refined man and the connoisseur but also for the everyday man. The political agenda of the dominant class – to distract the people with persuasive images of urban life – becomes, through its artistic representation, a desire to communicate universally. It becomes a discourse that is articulated on multiple levels, so as to preserve meaning and weight both for the man of culture and for the humble observer; and often, through its autonomy, it becomes fiction or prophecy of a different, more humane society.)

The collateral additions imposed on the urban fabric during the reign of Umberto I and the fascist *ventennio* were often inspired by a similar conception of plurilingualism. It is worth noting that, once Rome had become the capital of a national state, there was a pointed effort to pinpoint a city centre in the disarticulated urban structure. The idea of opening a large, central square that was dominated by a monument, such as Piazza Venezia, or of building a crown of new neighbourhoods around the old city could be interpreted in the same way: as giving a centre to something that had been long fluctuating.[10]

An Experimental City

To understand how much the form of Rome could influence the aesthetics of artists and intellectuals we need to return to the early Renaissance when Rome, after its medieval decay, became mostly an imagined and imaginary city. As is visibly demonstrated by Petrarch's comments in his epistles on the past grandiosity of the city, the early modern image of Rome was based more on a reflection on absence than on the fragments of the city that are present. The ruins are material traces that evoke imaginary presences, but the intellectual evocation is nonetheless substantial and sensible.[11] An interesting counterpoint to these Petrarchan, 'absent' images is the series of early descriptions of Rome, written for pilgrims and visitors and known as *Mirabilia Urbis Romae* (The Wonders of the City of Rome). These prototypical tourist guides typically offered little more than lists of monuments and relics of the past city, without trying to supply a general or unifying description. In this case individual and fragmentary ruins and monuments characterize the city, without any need for context.

The constant juxtaposition in this period of the historical city and its ideal, transparent and metaphysical form thus made Rome into a ghost, impossible to express as an immutable space, yet continually reconverted through time. The humanist architecture that we can observe in the 'Città ideale',[12] comes across as the illustrations of a fantastic story, the fruit of a spectacular imagination. The architectural severity of classic orders germinates in a potentially infinite sequence of imaginative flashes, practically announcing the Baroque. The aim of these artists was to create a fluid, metaphorical structure of images that is otherwise theoretically infinite. The idea of the Classics therefore cannot be fixed into a mere Classicism: a standardized repertoire always remains lacking in its description of the unity of the city, identified not with a historical moment in the past, but with the vastness of space and time itself. The trace of ruins does not reflect anything more than itself and its unceasing variability.

In fact, this notion of the city is one which re-appears more recently in Armando Gnisci's essay 'Roma come sistema delle rovine' (Rome as a system of ruins). In it, Gnisci reads one of Rome's most unusual monuments as the ideal embodiment of the fluid state of ancient ruins: the Circus Maximus. Unlike the Colosseum, whose complex masonry still exhibits an imposing presence, the Circus Maximus no longer exhibits an architectural dimension. It remains only as a void, an imprint. The paradoxical absence of material allows an infinite structural reworking of the so-called *forma loci*.[13] It is the very place that maintains, in its floating morphology, a constant state of evolution: each visitor, observing the space, can forge a different constellation of signs and concepts. The semiosis is effectively unlimited and infinite.

The contradictory relationship between the fixity of a space with invariable coordinates and the fluidity of its representation in the case of Rome multiplies the possible interpretations of the classical, rather than philologically limiting them. Architecture becomes at times a theatrical background, such as in Giulio Romano's and Polidoro da Caravaggio's early sixteenth-century paintings, or an environment completely free from any system of visual cues, as in Annibale Carracci's and Pietro da Cortona's Baroque works. Even architects and urban planners such as Domenico Fontana and Gianlorenzo Bernini, when dealing with the monuments of Rome and their visual reference systems such as obelisks and fountains, sought to refocus the city into a new spatial coherence, yet often they used a personal–functional perspective. They did not try to recreate a lost unity: the classical rationality is instantly evoked in a *hic et nunc* that is projected on the future of the city itself. As Paolo Portoghesi states:

> In questo modo si ponevano le premesse perché Roma divenisse una città sperimentale, capace di produrre nuclei urbanistici di eccezionale qualità formale, senza peraltro riuscire ad acquistare la fisionomia di un vero organismo urbano in cui le ragioni del potere e gli interessi della comunità in qualche modo si equilibrassero.[14]

> (In this way, the foundations were set for Rome to become an experimental city, one capable of producing urban nuclei that were of an exceptional formal quality, without, nevertheless, managing to assume the physiognomy of a real urban organism in which the logic of power and communal interests balanced each other out.)

The system of ruins is thus multiplied in its potential for recombination thanks to the specific use of the Baroque metaphor. This approach openly applies to the city of Rome through the codification of an ad hoc pictorial genre: the urban view, the *veduta*, the purpose of which is situated at a crossroads of different needs. The push for a functional rationality replaced the metaphysical notion of a unified vision, suggesting an absolute point of view, and it is no coincidence that the first painter to precisely codify this genre in Italy, Caspar Van Wittel, was an accomplished engineer. This requirement of rationality – not from a universal point of view but more from an individual one – overlaps with a Baroque taste for fluctuation and suspended images, typically interpreted by artists such as Giovanni Paolo Pannini and the great designer and engraver Giovan Battista Piranesi.

A Collection of Fragments

At this point, in order to describe how Rome changed into 'the experience of Rome' in the eyes of its artists, there is little need to evoke the sublime, the picturesque or the speculations of theorists such as Edmund Burke and Johann Winckelmann. The Baroque sensibility opens our perception to ecstatic or romantic suggestions in their most trivial and unconscious articulations and meanings.[15] The concept of 'fragment' was not invented by postmodern thought; nor indeed were postmodern schools of thought the first to exploit the notion of the fragment. Instead, philosophers connected with idealist and historicist theory have repeatedly observed phenomena of disintegration, fragmentation and reorganization as continuously triggered by the historical process.[16] Important postmodern theorists, such as Jean-François Lyotard, did, however, discover the unique nature of the fragment as an autonomous element, existing without having to necessarily relate to the concept of totality.[17] It is as if the inductive process put in action by a philosopher or by an author in relation to the totality stopped in front of the extraordinarily composite nature which the fragment itself contains. The historical object, insulated from totality, maintains in itself a number of infinite reflections, as in Jorge Luis Borges's *Aleph*.[18]

In the history of Rome and of its image, it is precisely this quality that is difficult to identify: the relationship between particular and universal moves more and more towards singularity. Pannini, for example, established a series of fragmentary 'postcards' of the city, yet what does this ideal representation really mean in terms of a cognitive map of Rome? The artist was a step beyond the image of Rome developed during the Renaissance. The concept of *varietas* was central in the humanistic aesthetical speculation, but their artists tended to express an ordered and defined structure of reality through the strict use of perspective.

The relationship between metaphysical structures and their articulation in the visible reality becomes particularly close with respect to the uniqueness of the case of Rome: artists such as Brunelleschi and Donatello had a different attitude to pre-humanists such as Petrarch. The latter was still dealing with the shock of a total loss of antiquity that left but a few traces open to his interpretation; the two Renaissance artists believed it was possible to recover the relationship with the essence of the ancient itself through the study and analysis of the fragments. Through their artistic operations it was possible to fully restore the unitary conception of classical antiquity.

The Reframed Gaze

The approach of Fellini and other Italian intellectuals of the twentieth century is a derivation of an intellectual and figurative tradition: that of being immersed in a historical condition that prioritizes spatial articulation (with respect to the temporal and historical singularity) over 'historicist' buildings. These postmodern intellectuals developed an idealistic, nomadic gaze on the city that, in its deconstruction, becomes a metaphorical reference to the continuously unstable condition of modern man.

As I have briefly illustrated, for the Renaissance artist fragments of Rome and its ruins can still exist as a possible reference to a structure unified by imaginative thought. During the sixteenth century, one could conceive of monumental spaces such as the spectacular architecture of Raphael's *School of Athens* (1510–11) or the *vedute* of the *Città ideale*. For the twentieth-century artists, on the other hand, and Fellini is one of the most important examples here, in facing the tumultuous modernization of the urban space the tradition of the fragment opens up a continuous and fruitful development of singularity as opposed to any unity. Artists like Fellini offered a second, more important insight: by going beyond a single focal point on the city, he could describe the metropolis of the sixties as just as chaotic and imaginary as the ancient imperial city.

From the early modern period to the aesthetics of modernism – the latter emerging around the second half of the nineteenth century – intellectuals perceived antiquity as a fragmented field, whose conceptual unification could be accomplished only inside a dialectics of urban space and history. The modernist cities of Paris and London were already described as deconstructed and dystopian spaces, yet they found their possible conceptual unification in terms of historical development and progress. A century later, Fellini simply precludes these illusions.

In these cases, the artistic imagination is the instrument that juxtaposes the complexity of reality with historical fragments. The process of analysis and the tension towards synthesis are irreducible to one another. That dive into the audiovisual chaos of reality that Deleuze identifies as being central to Fellini's universe is nothing but the reflection of this attitude, always hovering between ecstatic abandonment and critical detachment. The rationality of his gaze consists not so much in a huge, logic composition but in a suspended state of consciousness within reality itself.[19]

Certainly Rome, as it appeared to the nineteenth-century visitor, was neither (singularly) the Renaissance dream nor the Baroque palimpsest, nor even the system of romantic and picturesque ruins known by the travellers of the Grand Tour. It was simultaneously an archaeological and mental space in which all the previous influences coexisted, animating a scene of ever-changing suggestions that were very different in comparison with the great European capitals, already on the verge of becoming metropolises. Nineteenth-century Rome was not a metropolis and would not be so until well into the following century. Nevertheless, a relationship existed between this city, the collective imagination of its landmarks and the disjointed space of the modern and postmodern metropolises. Baudelaire's or Benjamin's notions of Paris offered to its inhabitants an experience that was in some way comparable to that of the visitor to Rome, at least under the sign of vagrancy. As Georg Simmel states in his 'Die Großstadt und das Geistesleben' (The Metropolis and Mental Life), flâneurs, building their personal urban geography on the basis of their own sensibility, assign greater importance to the act of seeing than to the chaotic experience of their feelings. Flâneurs therefore are not so different from tourists, assembling through their memory the fragments of a metropolis that exist across time and space.[20]

First the early unified governments, and then the fascist regime tried with little success to rationalize the urban structure of a city that appeared incompatible with industrial modernity. The work undertaken by the Kingdom of Italy at the end of the nineteenth century magnified Rome in its urban structure, transforming it from a medium-sized town to a densely populated city; nevertheless, the chaotic map of the *urbe* retained its foundational characteristics. Demolitions and the attempted linearization of the street map could only emphasize the chaos of an urban fabric that increasingly exhibited its heterogeneity.[21] Even the call for the classic style ultimately created an awkward mix of various designs. The scenic architecture of unified Italy finds a strangely small paradoxical echo in the first historical epics of Italian cinema, such as the operatic *Quo vadis* (Enrico Guazzoni, 1913) or the lavish *Cabiria* (Giovanni Pastrone, 1914). These films blended together that classicism which originated from the traditional Roman monumentality and the new spatial sensitivity of the metropolitan vastness. The Rome of *Quo Vadis* is a space projected in an imaginary past, but also a concealed interpretation of the present metropolitan life. Therefore it lives in a kind of suspension in time, synthesized only thanks to the imagination of the viewer and her/his emotional life. The temporal ambiguity that has continually been embodied by Rome, a city of the past and of the future, becomes more complicated in its cinematic representation.

Lo sceicco bianco: An Unrealistic Flâneur

Federico Fellini is simultaneously a point of arrival and a departure of this complex iconographic layering that ranges (beyond the examples mentioned here) from Pirandello to Gadda, from the Futurists to the *Scuola Romana*, from Guazzoni to Camerini. The filmmaker's idea of Rome is connected directly to the imaginary of the metropolis, and his idea of urban experience is founded on the *absence* of a map that could host the actions of his characters. Rome is a mental place, dense with the changing suggestions that make impossible even the Proustian epiphany of lost time. *Lo sceicco bianco*, Fellini's debut film, is a comedy set in Rome, in the popular world of the *fotoromanzo*, or 'fotonovela', a sort of romantic soap opera made with photographs of real actors that was very popular in Italy during that period. In the film, two young newlyweds from the Italian countryside, Wanda and Ivan Cavalli, arrive in Rome for their honeymoon. Wanda is obsessed with the 'White Sheik', her favourite character in a *fotoromanzo* and escapes from her husband in an effort to locate him. Her husband wanders hysterically around the city, trying to hide the scandal of his missing wife from his local relatives. Finally, after many adventures, the couple is reunited and, in an atmosphere of hypocritical forgiveness, they attend a papal audience with their family.

In the film's original screenplay, written by Fellini along with his usual collaborators Ennio Flaiano and Tullio Pinelli, the Roman geography is fairly consistent.[22] The characters live in a hotel in Via XXIV Maggio, near the Quirinale, and after their separation, they move in a very coherent way. While Ivan walks towards Piazza Venezia and Piazza Campitelli, remaining within the city centre, the bride is projected outwards, reaching the pinewood of Ostia: the natural boundary of a formless city that can be given a perimeter only by the sea. Returning towards the city centre, after an awkward suicide attempt, she is admitted to the Santa Maria della Pietà asylum, on the Via Trionfale, once again at the (other) extreme geographical and moreover social limit of the city. Eventually Wanda, reunited with her husband, will return inwards and meet her new relatives, and the Pope, in a crowded Piazza di San Pietro. Anyone acquainted with the street map of Rome easily understands the consequentiality of these locations and their logical, well-defined relationship in the weaving of narrative construction.

Nevertheless, the film that Fellini ultimately created contradicts repeatedly the geographical continuity made by his scriptwriters. For a first example, a series of sequences that would otherwise explain the presence of the 'White Sheik' in the pinewood of Ostia are excluded, making his sudden apparition, swinging from a tree, strangely dreamlike. Fellini also chose not to shoot the scene of Ivan's unsuccessful attempt to cheat on his wife with one of the two good-hearted prostitutes he meets in Piazza Campitelli, making more enigmatic his night spent wandering *without* rational direction around the city's streets. Fellini's Rome in *Lo sceicco bianco* is thus a city where it is impossible to move in a planned and rational way. While Wanda follows her fictional hero, the space of Rome itself enters into a mutual relationship with the woman's desire, slipping rapidly into oneirism. The topographical relations are altered, as are the consequential links between the film sequences, almost in analogy with the couple's relationship. Ivan and Wanda's entrance into the city, and the loss of their familiar universe, makes Rome an uncomfortable and haunting space, marked by sudden apparitions and disturbing sounds.

The experience of Rome that began to take shape in *Lo sceicco biano* shows us a people driven from their unconscious impulses through a city defying any structure. *La dolce vita* (Fellini, 1960)[23] is the movie where this whole system of spatial poetics becomes central to Fellini's production.

The Theatre of *La dolce vita*

The tourist walking today along Via Veneto in Rome, looking for traces of past glory, will find an interesting memorial inscription, on a plaque installed by the Comune di Roma in 1995: 'A Federico Fellini che fece di Via Veneto il teatro della dolce vita', (to Federico Fellini who made Via Veneto the theatre of the 'dolce vita'). This inscription is interesting for many reasons: first and foremost because, ironically, the famous sequences set in Via Veneto were in fact not shot here, but on a fabricated set in the Cinecittà studios. The plaque thus commemorates an event, the film, that did not take place there, but that nevertheless indirectly helped to create a mythic bond between the people, the place and its history.[24] A second interest here is the use of the world 'theatre', which leads us to visualize Via Veneto less as a concrete place than as a stage, an urban artefact that manifests itself in the imagination and is dislodged from the mere reality. It becomes a Baroque theatre in the style of Calderón de la Barca, involving the whole human experience in dreamlike connotations and finding its fundamental manifestation in the international capital of Baroque. In *La dolce vita*, Fellini in fact extends this notion from Via Veneto to encapsulate the whole city. Rome is not even a palimpsest of places: fragmented but recognizable, it becomes a kaleidoscope. Fellini superimposes the elements of modernity over the already multifaceted image of Rome, not in order to underline their alienating function, but rather to further disarticulate the film narrative and iconic framework. The opening of the film is emblematic of this process: a statue of Christ suspended from a helicopter hovers over the ruined Roman aqueducts at the periphery, before moving inward over the *borgate* and some of Rome's tower blocks.

The semantic shift of Rome has always been underlined by Fellini, who emphasized the unique urban experience of Romans wandering through their own city as though it were a huge house. Leaving out its social and cultural implications, this statement illustrates quite usefully how Rome's experiential space becomes very different from a normal urban centre, being less a communal area that is subjected to different human experiences than one *created* by these experiences. Via Veneto, for example, which had already established itself as a mythical place for the social high life after the war, became a Fellinian theatre because it was connected with this imaginary. For an intellectual raised within the jet set, such as Marcello Rubini, this uncanny theatre is a familiar space where he can easily find his own way, a dream space where anything can happen and a set space where he performs himself as part of the society to which he wants to belong. Reality and theatricality in the everyday experience of the city are no longer separable. The *forma urbis* in *La dolce vita* is permanently distorted because it corresponds almost entirely to a mental landscape that the protagonist continuously builds and changes.[25]

We can identify a kind of double for Marcello in Steiner, a sophisticated intellectual who becomes his mentor and lives with his family in a beautiful, modernist house in the EUR. This neighbourhood was a favourite of Fellini, who used it again as a backdrop to the short film *Le tentazioni del dottor Antonio* (The temptations of Doctor Antonio, 1962).[26] The rationalist and classicist architecture of the forties and fifties represents a stronghold of modernity, and their functionality aspired to impose a definitive order for the confused map of the city centre. Mussolini's idea in founding the EUR was to build a second centre for the city, upholding and amplifying the rational characteristics of the classical and rejecting what was considered superfluous and chaotic.[27]

Fellini's camera overturns EUR's original conception. The geometries of arches and marble buildings, and the neighbourhood's sharp lighting look like quotations from a metaphysical painting. And indeed, at Steiner's home in *La dolce vita* a painting by Giorgio Morandi, one of the most metaphysical of the Italian painters of the twentieth century, hangs on the wall. Morandi's detachment from objects and his geometric precision anticipates Steiner's severity, which ultimately leads him later to despair and self-destructive madness. Fellini considered this quarter a space that dismantled the idea of the classical through the evidence of its unconscious references, giving such an extreme version of rational classicity that ultimately it changes into an essentially ironic toy. EUR, like Via Veneto, transfers the living experience of the classic to a mental level, a theatrical set where the marmoreal buildings appear as though made of papier mâché. Mussolini's recreation of Rome thus misses its target of being a *tabula rasa* that cuts the Gordian knot of the city centre. It ends up mirroring it the rest of the city through the minds and the gazes of those who are lost in this stunning, classicist carnival.

The most famous scene of *La dolce vita* could of course only take place in one of the most famous Baroque sites of Rome: the Trevi Fountain. The monument is a summary of two centuries of artistic speculation on the simulation of space and matter. This debate over time involved the greatest exponents of Baroque art theory such as Gianlorenzo Bernini, Pietro da Cortona, Giovan Pietro Bellori, Francesco Borromini and Cardinal Giovan Battista Agucchi. Everything in the fountain is simulation and theatre, so much so that Fellini did not try to rebuild it in Cinecittà and used, for once, the true location, a scenic palimpsest of perceptual experiences in itself. The relationship between reality and fiction in the fountain is multifaceted: sculptures blend with the architecture of Palazzo Poli; the basin simulates the natural elements such as rocks and water, at the same time interacting with the light effects created by the real water, exhibiting the same fluidity of the liquid matter. The marble statues themselves come together in a refined confusion composed of the false rocks. Everything is dramatized, made rhetorical, blurring the boundaries of what is nature or natural and what is simulated by sculpture.

In this mythical place, therefore, Marcello and Sylvia bathe in an osmotic space between reality and virtuality that once again alludes to the *forma urbis* of the whole city. Ultimately (and unsurprisingly), Marcello's seduction game does not work and in fact the last image of the sequence shows a model of the fountain without water, as if the flowing of imagination had suddenly dried up. The fictional element, the model, appears in the instant when the imaginary geography of Rome and the monumental fountain lose their ability to bind the protagonists to the invented. A city like Rome survives on its evocative status, and as such it is possible to extend its opaque semantics to the whole world, having as the only border, in Fellini's poetic geography, the shoreline and surface of the sea, an expanse without any system of signs that can mark its territory. Like a map of the medieval world, Fellini's Rome is surrounded by an indistinct and infinite ocean; indeed it is here – at Ostia, the end of his immediate world – that Marcello ends his Roman journey in *La dolce vita*.

Satyricon and the Impossibility of Linear History

Years later, in his *Satyricon* (Fellini, 1969),[28] Fellini's conception of Rome's historically fictionalized image beyond it becomes much more literal (or visual). The boundaries of the ancient Roman Empire for its citizens were the limits of world, while the city coincided with the entire extension of its domain. Fellini intended to represent the Roman Empire using the fragments of Petronius's novel, and quite significantly the choice of an incomplete work helps to reveal the director's poetic intention. In *La dolce vita*, contemporary Rome was a confused entanglement in which significant references are difficult to articulate, albeit it remained a city. Imperial Rome, on the other hand, given its extraneousness from our culture, could be described only in terms of fragments. The author's immersion in its system of signs is equivalent to an alien losing his way, and arriving on an incomprehensible planet, which coincides moreover with mysterious geographies of the unconscious. Fellini himself, discussing *Satyricon* in his book *Fare un film* (Making a Film), supplies a useful key to his work. After suggesting that the filmmaker should work like an archaeologist, reproducing unearthed fragments of a past world in her/his own fragmented narratives, he continues:

> Il film dovrebbe far intravedere un universo dissepolto, proporre immagini quasi offuscate dalla terra, un film rotto nella sua struttura diseguale: episodi lunghi e ben articolati, altri come più lontani, sfocati, irricostruibili nella loro frammentarietà. Non un film storico, ma un film di fantascienza. La Roma di Ascilto, Encolpio, Trimalchio, più remota e fantastica dei pianeti di Flash Gordon.[29]
>
> (A film should allow us to glimpse an exhumed universe, propose images that are part-obscured by the earth, and be fractured by its unbalanced structure: long and well articulated episodes, others more distant, unfocused, impossible to reconstruct because

of their fragmentariness. Not a historical film, but a science fiction. The Rome of Ascilto, Encolpio, Trimalchio: more remote and fantastical than the planets in Flash Gordon.)

In other words, the ancient human and anthropological universe is almost impossible to reconstruct, therefore shooting a film about it is like producing science fiction. The universe of Rome is so fictional that it could be situated either in the past or in the future. As striking as this image of Rome is, it has little consistency: the urban geography is even less pronounced than in *La dolce vita*, and as a result his protagonists appear to move through the city in an even more dazed and confused manner than Marcello (or even Wanda and Ivan).

The director elects to represent the reality of Rome and the Empire ironically through the ultimate collection of images: a museum that appears in a brief but effective scene in the movie, when Encolpius meets for the first time the idle poet Eumolpus. Fellini's museum is not a physical place, but, as often happens in his films, a metaphor for his cinema. It is one where the various and bizarre works on display unite in a specific constellation of fragments that we conventionally use to consider historically the Classical Age, an age so conventional that even for the ancient protagonists of the film it has already passed and is becoming forgotten. The museum does not constitute the epiphany of historical consistency, but rather a deposit of pieces that forge, not without a poetic complexity, inter-actions and extemporaneous links both between them and with their viewers (profilmic and non). *Satyricon* itself is a museum of sorts, that overall displays a non-linear but wavelike temporality. The protagonists of the film, in a final *mise-en-abyme* after a long and vain journey in the imaginary of Rome, mutate into a part of this imagery for the following centuries. The final scene sees all of them, after many vicissitudes, transformed into a fantastic fresco, impassibly exposed against the open sea. Once again the Fellini-esque city extends in space and time, while its characters become fragments of this temporality whose only possible boundary is the indistinct chaos of the sea.

'Toby Dammit' and *Roma*, and Fellini's 'Roman Ideology'

If *Satyricon* dealt with Rome as discourse on the idea of the classic, the earlier 'Toby Dammit' (1968), adapted from Edgar Allan Poe's eponymous story and transposed to contemporary Rome, addresses more directly the relationship with the urban form. It is worth noting that little of Poe's original story remained in this adaptation, except perhaps for the climactic decapitation. The short film can perhaps instead be thought of as a notebook for themes to be developed more fully in his later film *Roma*. Fellini's attention is concentrated on the post-modern city life. As I have suggested, in *La dolce vita* Rome certainly does not perform the function of a straightforwardly passive background, but in 'Toby Dammit' the 'background' details of Rome's daily life, its traffic and the jet set, are the foregrounded interests of the director. Terence Stamp, a fading British actor who arrives in Rome to film the first 'Catholic Western', is quickly plunged into a nightmare. The urban architecture almost disappears, the *forma urbis* is instead intimated by disturbing lights and by the grotesque details of blurred and mysterious forms. The visceral, almost cannibalistic elements of Rome are evoked through a funereal atmosphere in which the actor wanders around, constantly drunk or dazed. The only recognizable landmark is the Colosseum, which appear for a short moment as a symbol of the eye of the existential vortex that will ultimately swallow Dammit's life and body.

Maybe Rome is a Kafkaesque hell, or perhaps it is a secluded place that is impossible to enter or to exit; what is important for Fellini is to show how Dammit can only wander around without understanding the meaning of the mysterious or even demonic apparitions he meets. Characters are grotesque shadows, and the few shots of the city do not seem to give any idea of space. Rome is formless and the protagonist will literally lose his head, unable to control his self-destructive impulses. The favoured means of transportation in Rome, the car, is useless to Dammit. His Ferrari is always speeding in a false movement that does not seem to take him anywhere, prisoner in a suburban area that remains apparently endless and centreless.

The post-metropolitan area of the Castelli Romani seems to be both inside and outside the city, an enclosed and claustrophobic space which is at the same time formless. Comparing it to the great classics of urban dystopia such as Kafka and Orwell's stories, included in the great archetype of the labyrinth, the Castelli in Toby Dammit, seen from the protagonist's point of view, is labyrinthine, but also, to use Bauman's metaphor, 'liquid'.[30] We are in a space of mediation between identity and otherness. Reinterpreting the archetype of Rome according to Jameson's and Harvey's urban theorization, the presence of a kind of dialectic with the outside world is apparent: the postmodern metropolis is decentralized and relocated to an area that continually seeks to include inside spaces of otherness, opened, according to Jameson, to schizophrenic experiences.[31] In Fellini, this dialectic mediation is limited to the psychological sphere of the protagonist, to his human experience. Dammit is defeated in his existential life and Rome is the perfect concretization of such defeat.

In the final sequences, the protagonist plunges into a nightmare produced by prolonged point-of-view shots from the front of the car, showing an open space that is evidently recreated in studio: the only way out of his existential (and spatial) stalemate is death, and indeed the actor throws his car towards a crashed bridge in an impossible attempt to reach the other side, beyond which stands the young girl, almost a literal quotation from his friend Mario Bava's B-movie, *Kill, Baby Kill* (Mario Bava, 1966). There is a very clear and symbolic continuation here between the sweet girl, the salvation for Marcello in *La dolce vita* who stands, unreachable, across the ridge in Ostia, and this equivalent girl who has become demonic and wicked, corrupted through the passing of time. Immediately after Dammit's decapitation, Fellini gives us the only long shot of the film: a collapsed bridge leading to a straight road that is entirely inaccessible. This is the linear path through the heart of the city that has become impossible. 'Toby Dammit' and *Satyricon* too thus mark a very interesting point in the trajectory of Rome in Fellini's vision, where the straightforward linearity of history or of the urban landscape are no longer simply deprioritized, but rather rendered impossible through the fragmentation of vision.

According to Fellini, the urban experience does not coincide with the dialectic of openness and the inclusion of the other, but rather with an endless movement, where the outside appears only in the ambiguous forms of horizon, distant lights and enveloping darkness. The city does not open itself to otherness, rather it can only expand to infinity, like the immense hinterland south of Rome. Rather than being in a dialectical space, we are in the dark body of metamorphosis.

Fellini further develops the idea of the substantial impossibility of knowing the essence of Rome in a film that bears the name of the Eternal City itself, *Roma*. This is a culmination of Fellini's 'Roman ideology' that had been evolving through his earlier films. As in 'Toby Dammit', the city first impacts upon the foreigner or the provincial as he arrives at the station or in an airport, and is immediately introduced to a section of Rome's radical alterity in which the gaze is eternally lost. Toby Dammit arrives at a grotesquely crowded and clearly falsified Leonardo Da Vinci airport (located near Ostia), in which, according to the ambiguous Father Spagna, one has to walk for miles. In *Roma*, the entrance sequence chosen by the director records the Grande Raccordo Anulare, the ring road that surrounds the city. Fellini constructs the path of his crew (who appear profilmically too) towards the centre, following a spiral movement: a centripetal vortex dragging all traffic inwards, culminating in the final paralysis of the traffic jam in front of the Colosseum (see Figure 2.1 on p. 54). In comparing the filmed sequence to the original script, what emerges is that the entrance sequence into the town through Porta San Paolo has been omitted.[32] Fellini, refusing to show the moment in which the circular motion around the Raccordo changes into linear motion towards the centre, suggests that the visual spiral coinciding with the city map has neither a beginning nor an end. The path towards the centre breaks up repeatedly in a series of surreal visual details, in grotesque and hyperbolic scenes. The film slides in a reverie, accumulating mismatching images and sounds. The visual excess becomes a lack of meaning and thus the traffic jam in front of the Colosseum can easily be interpreted as a paralysis of the imagination. Similarly, the arrival of the young provincial boy at Termini station, shot mostly from a subjective point of view, accumulates a number of different

Figure 2.1: The traffic jam in front of the Colosseum, in Fellini's *Roma*.

sensorial stimuli: smoke, odd characters, advertising, art and various means of transportation.

One quite striking observation to be made of *Roma* in this context is that the mediating character, the presumed double of the young Fellini, at some point disappears from the diegesis. Divagations and memories from the director's unconscious are no more attributed to a supporting character, and his hermeneutic challenge of the city becomes no longer personal but collective. The *forma urbis* here coincides with the mindset, but the mind is prisoner of its unconscious alterations. Any notion of mapping is dissolved and the monuments of the city do not mark anything except their own identity as mysterious floating archetypes. The subsidence into unconsciousness is visualized in the sequence describing the excavation of the underground metropolitan train line. References to *Satyricon* are evident: the workers find the ruins of a Roman villa with beautiful and well preserved frescoes and statues. But what should be the essence of the classical, the rediscovered image of the Great Mother and the deep archetypes that Fellini, fascinated by Jung, imagined emerging in the urban texture, dissolve like a dream in front of the eyes of the spectators when the modern, damaging gusts of air enter the ancient room.[33]

Once again it seems that Fellini, contemplating this labyrinthine and multidimensional universe, associates the only possibility of a relationship with the city as being that of a liberating escape. In the closing sequences there is a group of bikers whose lights illuminate and animate the static, empty squares of Rome, before getting lost in the dark of night, through the monumental access to Via Cristoforo Colombo, towards the recurring symbol of the sea.

Conclusions

For a long time, Fellini's approach to Roman iconography was not adopted into a communal visual repertoire that ranged from the traditional oleography of genre film to the search for a non-place, harbouring a deep otherness in the manner of Pier Paolo Pasolini. Perhaps the only director of that generation who illustrates coherency with the Felliniesque discourse about Rome was Michelangelo Antonioni. Antonioni's *L'eclisse* (1962) had, a decade before *Roma*, read Rome and its architecture as a set of metaphysical signs, and most of the recurring images of the city show only the EUR, where twentieth-century rationalism and the classical vocation of Roman architecture overlap. Even if Antonioni's approach to the image is very different, the two directors are in consonance with respect to the playful and paradoxical emotions with which this metaphysical Rome leaves the visitor.

Yet among the deepest insights of international twentieth-century filmmakers, the multilayered nature of cities remains forcefully prevalent, making the city similar to a small world. If cinematic Rome is the whole world in its cinematic representations, it coincides also with the minds of its inhabitants, it constitutes the effort of every individual to conceptualize her or his relationship with existence through the creation of a complex geography. This aesthetic and existential complexity is not limited to Rome: it is only necessary to think of the role that Paris played for Jean-Luc Godard and François Truffaut, New York for Woody Allen and Martin Scorsese, or Los Angeles for David Lynch and Michael Mann.

The relationship between life and urban space, however, identifies a conflictual relationship between people's experience and their ability to attribute sense to the reality, almost always expressed though a dialectic between inside and outside. The plurality of stimuli that a metropolis offers immediately constitutes infinite openings for new images of the world, but they can also suggest a disharmony which translates into a chaos, paradoxically claustrophobic in its breadth. According to Fellini, Rome is so difficult to interpret that it can become, as in 'Toby Dammit' for instance, a nightmare from which it is impossible to escape, yet where it is similarly impossible to feel at ease. Roman flâneurism is a melancholic, if not horrific, experience, based on a growing feeling of defeat. Pier Paolo Pasolini, another major auteur of this generation, attentive to his relationship with the city, identified in Rome the sign of a crisis of the entire bourgeois civilization, exploring the border areas, outskirts he saw open to the experience of an existential epiphany, revealed in the almost prehistoric space of the *borgata*.[34]

Fellini's achievements become a starting point for new directors. If Rome is a limited space with no possible exit point, it is also a space that is eternally rearticulated, therefore with infinite centres and full of existential opportunities. The work of Fellini, especially after 'Toby Dammit', is powerfully attracted by so fragmentary a human experience that it cannot be reduced to unity. The world exploded – or perhaps it has never been intact – and Rome is an ideal mental landscape that cannot or will not attempt to reorganize its fragments. Interestingly, Fellini sees the city of Rome as the perfect allegorical site of modernity, at least during his own contemporary era. Rome is in pieces because the world is in pieces.

It remains difficult to think of Fellini as a particularly postmodern author. Perhaps he was lacking an explicit theoretical framework to be defined as such. But of course the director understood and performed a completely new way of approaching the subject of reality that can be traced out in the shift, for instance, from *Lo sceicco bianco* and *La dolce vita* to 'Toby Dammit' and *Roma*. His fragments live in configurations that the subject produces sequentially both in its memory and in its historical present. In his films, there is therefore a gradual shift towards a representation that is disconnected from unifying restraints, even merely conceptual constraints, typical of the postmodern sensibility.

3 CENTRE, HINTERLAND AND THE ARTICULATION OF 'ROMANNESS' IN RECENT ITALIAN FILM

Lesley Caldwell

Introduction

This chapter describes some aspects of the suburban expansion of the city of Rome with particular attention to the typical emphasis that has anchored its critical discussion to a rigid model of centre and periphery. A division between Rome and its edges has been in place since antiquity, but the differentiation became increasingly significant in the period after 1870, the siting of the national capital, and the beginning of the historic city's transformation from a town of some 200,000 inhabitants to the largest Italian *comune* (municipality), with a population today of more than 2.5 million. I make use of cinematic examples *Caro diario* (Dear Diary, Nanni Moretti, 1993) *Velocità massima* (Maximum Velocity, Daniele Vicari, 2002), *Romanzo criminale* (Crime Story, Michele Placido, 2005)[1] to describe the specificity of present-day Rome and the search for representations that address its contemporary spatial complexity.

Past and Present

Rome exhibits traces of two millennia of settlement that remain visible in its palimpsestic, vertical ordering of successive pasts. In constructing the ancient city and then in elaborating the papal city, these pasts have consistently exploited the occupation and re-occupation of space (the Pantheon), the use and reuse of materials (St Peter's Basilica) or the borrowing of forms (the Baptistery of St John Lateran). To give an illustrative example: in the Basilica of San Clemente, as Dorigen Caldwell writes,

> the visitor is led vertically into the past. The church closest to street level dates from the twelfth century but was constructed on a pre-existing fourth century basilica, itself built on top of a first century 'titulus' associated with Clement, an early succes-

sor to Peter. The lowest level houses a Mithraeum, reminding us of the overlapping cults of late antiquity, out of which Christianity emerged triumphant.[2]

The lower levels of the Basilica, excavated only in the nineteenth century, make available a more extensive vertical ordering than that encountered by earlier Romans and visitors. This history gives one indication of how the past is reshaped and expanded in the experience of the city now: a past that is immediately evident in its synchronic organization, which in turn provides a familiar inventory of images stretching back over centuries. This diachronic axis nevertheless today proposes an equally strong claim to being a key characteristic of the post-Second World War city and its representations.

In 1870 Rome was contained within the Aurelian Walls, and its centre located near the church of Sant'Ignazio. Of the new populations that migrated into the newly appointed capital city, the majority remained within that boundary, encircling the original nucleus; there were also some developments around and beyond the northern gates of Porta Pia, Porta Salaria and Porta Maggiore.[3] The first wave of building in and outside the walls was managed by private interests with foreign capital, as a resolution to the urgent problem of housing the influx of labourers required to build the new capital. Nevertheless, hastily assembled shanties and a widespread use of available outside spaces – porticoes, the stairs of churches – were quickly established as preferred alternatives. After these shelters were forcibly closed, housing was officially provided only in one-floor shanties with common facilities.[4] When a public housing body (the Istituto Case Popolare, ICP, or Institute for Popular Housing) was finally established in 1903, it began to construct housing projects within the walls at San Saba and Testaccio, but before 1920 official 'borghetti' (small clusters of houses) were also set up along the consular roads to the east, at Centocelle and Torpignattara on the Via Casilina, and at Quadraro on the Via Tuscolana. Other settlements followed the line of the Tiber at Tor di Quinto and Valle and Forte Aurelia; each of these catered for the continuous influx of migrants from other areas of Italy in search of work.[5] A pattern of official and unofficial housing beyond the walls was repeated and intensified under fascism, and consolidated and further developed in the post-war period, particularly in the years of the economic boom (1958–65) and in the wake of the public housing initiatives of the seventies and early eighties.

The balance of population between the city of 1870 and the new *quartieri* that circled its historic centre was inevitably redrawn, and as early as the 1920s it was the area beyond the walls that accounted for the majority of the city's population.[6] Between 1871 and 1951 Rome's geographical area increased fourteen-fold, and by 2001 only 4 per cent of the population lived in the historic centre.

A nostalgic invocation of earlier lifestyles and a lament for a Rome that is no longer what it once was has historically distinguished much cultural work on the city, and this continues to provide a fundamental element for any understanding of the comparative slowness in establishing an alternative image repertoire of the city. The postcard picturesqueness of central Rome remains a problem in contemporary representations and, in the cinema, many directors have chosen to avoid the iconic monuments. Nevertheless, the tenacity with which some narratives continue to provide a nostalgic account of the present has contributed to a somewhat anachronistic vision of the modern city and its concerns.

Several films released in the immediate post-war period provide consistent reference points for discussion of the city through its ruins, ancient monuments, the papacy and Baroque architectural splendour. This partially concerns the quality and genre of the films themselves, their cinematic exceptionality, their status as continuing accounts of present day. The city falls prey to the lament for another Rome, one that may be preferred but is increasingly out of step with contemporary life. In her introduction to the special issue of *Parolechiavi*, 'periferie' (suburbs), Mariuccia Salvati draws attention to the comparatively recent loss of Rome's surrounding countryside, the Ager Romanus, as one possible factor in the recurrent, strong references to the history, tradition, urban space and the presence of an archaic past that shaped the work of artists who were only recently citified ('inurbati') themselves.[7] This encounter with a rural–urban split is one important dimension of the historic centre–periphery division that has organized much cultural, artistic and professional discussion of the city. While the relation between different areas, zones and sectors is common to discussion of any city, the persistence of a circular-spatial reference for Rome is worth dwelling on since it has so repeatedly subsumed transformations common to the growth of any city in terms of infrastructures: housing, the development – or lack of it – of industry, transport, services, decentralization and sprawl. Together with the city's consular roads, which function as its main arteries, the framework of a circular form of growth that mimics the walls has often produced an oppositional, dualistic approach to discussions of the city.

Continuity and discontinuity are constant factors in the study of any city, yet their negotiation remains a problem of representation as well as one of urban planning and political policy. When the architect Aldo Rossi described the Roman Forum as 'an urban artefact of extraordinary modernity', he emphasized the parallels between its original and contemporary uses in delivering its proximity to us: '[p]eople passed by without having any specific purpose, without doing anything, it was like the modern city where the man in the crowd, the idler, participates in the mechanism of the city without knowing it, sharing only in its image'.[8] He argued that since 'an inherent characteristic of the city is its permanence in time',[9] this was not a misplaced concern with ancient Rome, but a fundamental characteristic of the modern city which appropriates what is there, making it its own.

Growth and Expansion

'Roma per fortuna ha un piano. Anzi due', (Luckily Rome has a city plan. In fact, it has two), Paolo Avarello announces ironically in his account of post-war urbanization.[10] In relation to Rome's expansion in advance of the Olympics in 1960, the two plans to which Avarello refers are the 1931 *piano regolatore* (henceforth, master plan) and its 1942 variant. Since the first master plan of 1883, Rome has been the focus of more than a century of planning policies, most of which remained unrealized. Historically, one reason for this lack of implementation was the initial decision of the new city administration to privilege entrepreneurial activity in construction as offering major economic returns, but without accompanying this policy with any concerted attempt to provide the essential infrastructures vital to the organization of the new capital. The construction trade – one of Rome's few industries and a major source of employment – has been marred historically by the tradition of exploiting and selling land without recourse to planning laws. A reluctance to curb speculative building activity stretched through the twentieth century, reaching its height in the 1960s. Despite these legal questions, all official plans have since come to endorse retrospectively the previous decisions, ignoring illegal activity and focusing planning initiatives elsewhere. This has significantly shaped the modern city. Renato Nicolini, the architect who was in charge of the culture section of the city council from 1976–85 and was responsible for the 'Estate Romana' (Roman Summer) project, a sustained cultural programme aimed at revivifying the city, argued that the emphasis on planning and housing was the most serious mistake in Rome's development. In his view, it tied the city to what he terms an 'emergenza abitativa' (housing crisis),[11] an essentially local imperative that ultimately extended the national priorities of fascism and hindered Rome's development as an international city.

The earliest significant directions of expansion of the city were east and north, then later south-east, along the old consular roads. Conversely, the 1942 master plan, which enacted the proposals of the GUR ('Gruppo Urbanisti Romani', Group of Roman Urban Architects), emphasized development towards the south-west, the route to the sea. This was repeated in the 1962 plan, then further extended and consolidated in the 2003 plan, and finally made law thanks to the left-leaning councils of mayors Francesco Rutelli (originally in the Green Party, 1993–2001) and Walter Veltroni (a central member of the Democratic Party, 2001–8). The 2003 plan envisages an administrative reorganization which amplifies the historic centre (*centro storico*) to include a much wider area, to be known as the historic city (*la città storica*). The latter is distinguished by geographical extent and range, and including the rivers, the railway network and an axis that runs from EUR in the south to Flaminio in the north via the Forum in the centre. The plan is also committed to the polycentric city (*la città policentrica*), which extends into the Lazio hinterland and aims to build upon a changed understanding of the relation between centre and outskirts, so as to accommodate an area that already goes beyond the municipality's administrative boundaries into the authority of the province. It moves away from the model of a small historic centre to a larger inner city and it anticipates a regional reorganization that takes account of the current situation and its future trajectory. It acknowledges the changed contours of Rome. An increasingly large urban area has absorbed the former small towns that ringed the city in the past, incorporating them into a continuous urbanized sprawl whose essential infrastructures of roads, electricity, water, gas, transport and communication links are increasingly allocated among different public authorities and private initiatives.

In his work on regional urbanization, Edward Soja argues that, due to the transformation of the traditional urbanization process over the past forty years, the dualism of the urban–suburban model as applied to large cities has become increasingly irrelevant.[12] In arguing that density convergence and changing patterns of communication and activity across whole regions erode traditional distinctions between city and suburb, Soja offers an account that conforms in many respects to the continuing regional growth in the Roman hinterland. A model of the city defined by the common European pattern of a walled city centre and successive waves of settlement outside it, and economically sustained by the tourism of heritage sites, is increasingly less compatible with the growth of the enlarged metropolitan area tutored by the province and the region of Lazio, and endorsed by the idea of the polycentric city envisaged by the 2003 master plan. All three of the films which are discussed below incorporate this extended terrain in their representations of modern Rome.

The Periphery

The notion of the Roman periphery as formed of concentric bands which are increasingly distant from the historic centre, and which contain isolated nuclei, is tied in particular to the post-war period; however the initial exploitation of economically unpromising countryside in reality began with two earlier, related policies of the fascist regime. These were the establishment of the official *borgate* – the first at Acilia, near Ostia, in 1924 – and the clearances (*sventramenti*) of swathes of the city centre in a programme aimed at the isolation of its ancient monuments in the pursuit of a 'romanità' (romanness) that would parallel Mussolini's Rome[13] with that of the empire. These policies resulted in the enforced rehousing of great numbers of inner city dwellers to new settlements that ringed the city at distances which were exaggerated by the lack of facilities, transport and essential services. Twelve areas in total were developed,[14] most of which were devoted to housing those uprooted from the centre by these drawn-out policies which continued until the early 1940s. Settlements of more than 5,000 residents were compelled to include access to domestic water and services, and as such later developments were built more densely and for larger populations. Residents of the larger *borgate* thus had a curious advantage over smaller settlements like Val Melaina: the *borgata* of *Ladri di biciclette* (Bicycle Thieves, Vittorio De Sica, 1948), where water had to be brought from the well.

Inner city clearance and the establishment of settlements in far-flung areas of the hinterland can thus be read in terms of ideological politics that were specific to that time and place. In fact, some clearance of inner city areas had begun even before the advent of fascism[15] and moreover initiatives of this kind can be easily associated with the modernization processes of all major cities, so that continuities can be perceived between Mussolini's plans and the projects of planners in the preceding governments as well as those of the post-war liberal democracy. Ciacci identifies two important initiatives, the isolation of the 1911 monument to Victor Emmanuel, now known as the Vittoriana, and its positioning at the entrance to the new Via dell'Impero (1932), now Via dei Fori Imperiali; and the demolition of the mediaeval buildings between the Tiber and Piazza San Pietro in the construction of Via della Conciliazione. The post-war government continued both of these plans, and Via della Conciliazione and Via Gregorio VII were opened in 1950. As Ciacci observes, 'projects successively become part of a new, at times alternative, political programme, which usually adopts the shell, transforming its meanings and confusing their attribution in the collective memory'.[16] Similar policies continued in the post-war period in both public and private sectors under the pressure of the large influx of population and the increased demand for housing. Renato Nicolini,[17] for instance, argues in favour of distinguishing the inevitable moves towards making Rome a modern city from the squalid corruption of its immediate post-war administrations.

The 'Classic' Modern Periphery in Rome

The urbanist Italo Insolera has described the *borgata* as 'a piece of the city in the middle of the countryside that is not quite one or the other',[18] and this inbetweenness captures the essential quality of the settlements available to those seeking somewhere to live (often camping out) in a variety of structures beyond the city centre. It is moreover captured in many of the first cinematic representations of the *borgate*. *L'onorevole Angelina* (The Honourable Angelina, Luigi Zampa, 1947), *Ladri di biciclette, Totò cerca casa* (Totò Looks for a House, Mario Monicelli & Steno, 1950), *Europa '51* (Europe '51/No Greater Love, Roberto

Rossellini, 1952), *Ai margini della metropoli* (At the Limits of the Metropolis, Carlo Lizzani and Massimo Mida, 1953), *Il tetto* (The Roof, Vittorio De Sica, 1956), *Le notti di Cabiria* (Nights of Cabiria, Federico Fellini, 1957), *La notte brava* (The Good Night, Mauro Bolognini, 1959) and *La giornata balorda* (A Crazy Day, Mauro Bolognini, 1960) all focused on deprived, outlying areas of the city with a tenuous link to an elsewhere, the centre, featuring as part of their strong social critique narratives. Such texts continue to provide invaluable evidence for mapping Rome's contours and their transformation.

Writing in 2000, Salzano begins his article on the periphery nostalgically:

> Ricordo com'erano le periferie delle nostre città, mezzo secolo fa. Erano luoghi lontani dalla città. Le periferie erano oltre le mura, oltri i sobborghi legati alla città vecchia dalla crescita di poche case, allineate lungo una strada. Erano, prevalentemente, in campagna: la interrompevano con i quartieri popolari di casermoni a molti piani abitati prevalentamente dagli operai e dai contadini immigrati, o con le casette dei vari stili impiegati dagli architetti del regime (fascista) o da quelli della democrazia, oppure ancora (soprattutto a Roma) nei tuguri e nelle baracche di legno, lamiera e carrozzerie sfasciate.[19]

> (I remember what the peripheries of our cities were like half a century ago. They were places far from the city. They were beyond the walls, beyond the little towns that linked with the old city through the growth of a few houses lined up along a road. They were mainly in the country, interrupting it either with the popular districts – big multi-storey public housing inhabited mainly by workers and peasant immigrants, or with smaller housing units of various styles designed by the architects of the (fascist) regime and later by those of the democrats, or, especially around Rome, in hovels, or in shanties made out of wood, sheet metal or smashed up cars.)

This is the vision of the periphery of post-war Italian cinema promoted above all by poet, novelist and director Pier Paolo Pasolini, whose images remain an enduring evocation of a mythic Rome 'beyond the walls'. His cinema and his writing, like the monuments of the ancient and papal cities, are now fixed references in the inventory of images of Rome. The ruins of the aqueduct in the terrain inhabited in such a presumptive way by the characters of his film *Mamma Roma* (1962)[20] was an everyday matter for the titular protagonist, her son Ettore and his friends, as it is for those who live nearby now. This particular emphasis of normality, as well as the fact that Pasolini depicts it in referencing the long tradition of painting and drawing the Roman *campagna*, draws attention to the potential impact of location and its particularity for the lives of generations of Romans shaped by the material condensation of historical experience in their immediate environment. Despite the increasing uniformity of global cultures, the intense particularity of local living remains a paradox of all contemporary cities, especially of Rome. In something of a similar vein, as I will show, the films which I discuss below insist on their 'romanità' in their deployment of the *further* extended city, whether registering those areas that could be anywhere (or anywhere in Italy) or in those that universally signify 'Rome'.

The 'mythical topography'[21] of Pasolini's films and writing provides a way of looking, a powerfully enduring image repertoire that, even at the time of their production, was soaked with nostalgia.[22] Pasolini himself ceased depicting the city after the second half of the 1960s, but his elegiac lament for a popular Rome embedded in the most marginal sectors of the population, which he viewed as carriers of the values of a pre-modern civilization, had cemented an image of the Roman periphery as an interstitial space that paradoxically challenged (and continued to challenge) Italian society more generally, despite celebrating, through its intense concentration on the specificity of certain sites, the actual city and its inhabitants. In his work the dynamic spaces of the periphery are protagonists in their own right, and their fluidity supports and confirms the characters and their placement within shots through filmic techniques and choices whose most immediate allusions are pictorial. Pasolini's early film techniques drew upon a determinedly Italian visual past and its associations in order to represent a specifically *modern* past, linked to growth and progress, to the capitalist development he so forcibly decried.

The periphery in these films extends from the official *borgate* of the thirties to the hastily assembled illegal post-war dwellings along the railways and the aqueducts, and to the social programmes of the public housing body INA Casa (*Istituto Nazionale Abitazioni*, National Housing Institute), established by a law of 1949 and in operation for fifteen years. INA Casa employed most of the major architects of the time in the construction of housing for workers in a distinctive style. It aimed to emphasize the district as a community, a collectivity, a sort of little village,[23] and its architects made consistent use of a style that was concentrated in the detailing of windows, doors, gates and lampposts, a latter-day version of rationalism with particular stylistic architectonic features. It referred to a recognizable artisanal style in housing developments, sometimes dubbed 'neo-realist', which aimed at well-made self-sufficiency. Pasolini critically connects Mamma Roma's deep wish for one of these new homes to the destruction of Ettore, and ultimately to her subsequent despair.[24]

Mudu comments on the extreme segregation of populations and the relative inaccessibility of the periphery encountered in actuality, and in Pasolini's writings and cinema.[25] Reaching the centre represented a journey to another existence, one whose difficulty exaggerated a definite condition of marginality that was significantly but not exclusively geographical. Living beyond the centre at that time was shaped by lack: of running water, of roads, of work and of transport. Transport was private until 1911, when the municipal company was established; but, extraordinarily, this was only extended to the areas of the region in the 1970s. The motorway circling Rome, the GRA (Grande Raccordo Annulare, literally Great Ring Interchange), was built between 1951 and 1955, but at that time only five bus routes arrived at this new boundary and the car was not yet the most common form of transport.

Rome's development has always included an incursion into an agricultural area, but the city boundaries, even when they were marked by the Aurelian Walls, have always included considerable unbuilt-upon, semi-rural land, often close to the city centre. Even in 1981 it was estimated that such land equated to over half of the whole urban space, and indeed many traces of countryside or bare land continue to exist within and especially beyond the Aurelian Walls, making Rome one of the greenest cities in the world.[26] Culturally, a conception of the periphery denoting marginality through geographical distance and separateness emphasized a lumpen or semi-rural underclass, poverty and various temporary forms of housing. In the introduction to his recent collection *La città fuori le mura: Roma come non l'avete mai vista*, Giuseppe Cerasa writes,

> Tor Bella Monaca, Corviale, Laurentino 38, Tufello, Magliana: per anni, per troppi anni sono stati sinonimo di violenza, di criminalità. di degrado. E poi, ancora emarginazione, separazione della città storica, dai suoi riti, dal suo fascino, terre di nessuno. Per troppo tempo regno di stereotipi e preconcetti. Solo lande da conquistare.[27]

> (Tor Bella Monaca, Corviale, Laurentino 38, Tufello, Magliana: for years, for too many years these were synonymous with violence, with criminality, with degradation. And moreover with marginalization, separation from the historical city and from its rites, its fascination; they were no man's land. For too long they were dominated by stereotypes and prejudices. Just land to be conquered.)

Cerasa's volume offers an affectionate, differently inflected, contemporary account of the Roman outskirts, one committed to this larger and inclusive Rome and to the changed status of previously marginal areas in the overall map of the city. In a very useful manner the volume's contributions definitively challenge the old image of these quarters as *not* the city, as *not* a part of Rome; for the contributors the periphery *is* Rome.

A Different Director; A Different Rome

In 'On My Vespa', the first chapter of the episodic film *Caro diario*, director and protagonist Nanni Moretti rides around a deserted Rome in August, looking at what he says he likes most: houses, and neighbourhoods ('la cosa che mi piace di più di tutto è vedere le case, vedere i quartieri'). This expression of interest, alongside his ruminations in front of apartment blocks of different periods that link housing to the specific districts in which that it is found, links the home to a socio-economic and geographical topography. This recalls Aldo Rossi's identification of the central aspect of the city, its permanence, as comprising monuments *and* housing. Rome is internationally familiar as a city of monuments, but what Moretti presents is a Rome of houses, streets and a few random people that he comes across in various places. No connections exist between the zones visited outside of the protagonist's preferences. Many of his choices are areas that few tourists visit, indeed few Romans either, unless they actually live there. In ranging from Via Dandolo and Monteverde, to Villaggio Olimpico, Tufello, Casalpalocco, doubling back along the walls on the Janiculum hill and through the large Piazzale Clodio, to the river, to Moretti's preferred bridge, the film gathers an unfamiliar Rome of built-up areas and green spaces. Moretti's favourite neighbourhood, Garbatella, a formerly working-class district originally conceived on the model of the garden suburb, appears twice (in fact this neighbourhood provides a significant location for *Romanzo criminale*, which I return to below). The Vespa ride takes him to Spinaceto, a sixties public housing project about 10 km from the centre along the Via Pontina, that was developed on a site chosen because the land already belonged to the council. Although the urgent need for public housing had been given further impetus by the passing of law 167 in 1962,[28] the projects themselves began during the 1970s: Spinaceto, designed for 165,000 inhabitants, and, as Moretti notes, reflecting the film's localness, notorious as a place from which to escape; Corviale, a famous horizontal development begun in 1974 (not visited by Moretti) and Vigne Nuove (1972–9), a high-rise area to the north (shown as a tower block from low-angle). Considerable distance separates these initiatives from each other and from the centre. Like Spinaceto, they were areas with a reputation as 'quartieri ghetto italiani' (Italian ghetto quarters),[29] though as Mudu illustrates, this definition requires considerable qualification since the neighbourhoods rather constitute 'una periferia molto articolata' (a very complex periphery).[30]

Over 20 km from the centre along the Via Cristoforo Colombo, which corresponds to the fascist regime's Via Imperiale, designed to unite Rome with the sea, Nanni arrives at Casalpalocco. This area was designed in 1958 but built between 1961 and 1975, having previously been sanctioned by the Rome council as the first private initiative conceived as a residential area for the middle class. 'Passing these houses there is the smell of tracksuits worn instead of clothes, a smell of videocassettes, guard dogs in gardens and take away pizza in cardboard boxes', says Moretti, asking 'but *why* did they come out here thirty years ago?' The local resident getting out of his car looks around, and responds, 'the green, the peace and quiet'. Nanni is sceptical. 'The green ... well ... yes ... you came here, what, about thirty years ago right? '61?', The man agrees, 1962, and Nanni continues, 'but thirty years ago Rome was a marvellous city ... here is different, it's different even now ... Rome *then* was *beautiful*. This is what scares me ... dogs behind gates, videos, slippers!' This is the dread of the suburbs and what it implies, but as Roger Silverstone's work on understanding the unspectacular but massive growth of suburbs internationally points out, 'for millions, and mostly by choice, the city was too much to bear. It was a place to leave'.[31]

This episode of *Caro diario* wanders from place to place, and much of its pleasure lies in this cinematic meandering around a loved, clearly familiar hometown. At the end of the episode Moretti reaches the site of Pasolini's murder, at that time neglected and overlooked, representative of the traditional Roman outskirts in its desolation, neglect and poverty. We see a straggle of houses along the road, empty spaces, bamboo, the sense of a former non-place that has become notorious, a place that evokes both Pasolini himself and the periphery of the 1950s that he made famous.

The contrast of associations, especially cinematic associations, in Moretti's evocation of his city and its surroundings offers a different account of Rome, where the sense of the city overrides the opposition between centre and periphery through a mosaic of dwellings and the spaces between them. Whether the far-flung inhabitants of Vigne Nuove, Spinaceto or Casalpalocco are to be called 'Romans' forms part of a very large debate on the contours of the city, on the relation between periphery and centre, on the use of the *città diffusa,* the 'dispersed city'[32] and, with a different emphasis, the question of belonging to a place, of being at home.

The second episode of *Caro diario,* 'Islands', shot in the Aeolian islands off the coast of Sicily, elaborates further the lives of individual Italians and of Romans of a certain class and outlook, in other words people not dissimilar to the director himself. If it is the spatial disposition of the city that carries successive periods of recent history in the first episode, the second part of the film uses the customs and habits of a particular group to relate not only to the physical environment, but also to individual lives and to how autobiographical memory carries the characteristics of a city, whether its bearer currently lives there or not. This too forms part of a broader history and the sense of permanence and consistency that Moretti's portrait of his city develops through its physical presence in episode one and its absence as physical location, but insistent presence as a way of life, in the second episode. The third episode, 'Doctors', returns to the city and narrates the director's own personal history in his encounter with the medical establishment and his cancer. Though 'On my Vespa' foregrounds the city's built environment and its landscape, Rome is not only inscribed in space and the physical environment but in the way the particular subjectivities of its citizens are tied both to place and to the extra territorial links that comprise the attachments of a group. *Caro diario*'s three-part structure should be considered as a whole which offers an account of the city, of its director and of the life of its 'real' citizens, who are rooted from the beginning in Rome's periphery.

Later Encounters

The axis to the sea, which was one planning priority from the 1940s, provides the focus in two more recent films, *Velocità massima* and *Romanzo criminale.* Both films illustrate how location and place anchor Rome as cinematic city *now* by taking for granted the existence of the city beyond its familiar monuments and its historic residential quarters, thus showing some ways of seeing and living it in a contemporary light. How 'romanità' is secured in the social relations among Romans and their identification with specific zones of the city form indispensable parts of both narratives, such that the impact of place in shaping the collective life of the city emerges between the characters and the wider networks of which they form a part. Daily experience and the organization of self and subjectivity is narratively constituted in and through distinctive locations in the city's south and south-west hinterland in the first film, and in that area's links with the historic centre through crime and the state in the second. In both films, the protagonists are young white males, placed within a rhetoric of 'ordinary people'. In Vicari's very local film these men are united by their passion for the car; in Placido's it is crime and the desire for the domination of Rome which unites them.

Velocità massima

Daniele Vicari's first feature-length film after some success as a documentarist stars Valerio Mastandrea as Stefano, owner of a garage near Ostia, and an enthusiast for souping up cars and racing them illegally. The location of these races is the EUR, the district to the south of Rome projected by the fascist regime as the site of the 1942 international exhibition (EUR Esposizione Internazionale Roma). EUR was envisaged as separate from Rome, but since the 1960s its expansion toward the city has engulfed it within the metropolitan area. It is now a wealthy middle-class suburb and location of many government offices and museums. In the narrative, Claudio, a young man whose father wants him to work in the family car-wrecking business, leaves home and goes to work for Stefano, who in turn uses him and his computers skills to help him do up a Ford Sierra, which they then race at EUR and win. Claudio meets Giovanna, an exgirlfriend of Fischio, the reigning champion of the competitions and an ex-lover of Stefano too. When Stefano sleeps with Giovanna once again, Claudio walks out, after destroying the car they have both worked on so devotedly.

In an interview about his film, Vicari, a Roman himself, commented on continuity and change:

> Una cosa che ho ho messo in rilievo nel mio film è che Roma è cambiata profondamente ma con degli elementi di continuità: cioè i ragazzi che vanno a correre con le macchine all'Obelisco sono i nipotini di Accattone, esprimono la stessa identica cultura e sottocultura, e l'ex sottoproletariato urbano con tutto quello che ne consegue: volontà di affermazione sociale anche feroce, un atteggiamento godereccio nei confronti della vita spesso portato alle estreme conseguenze ... ma c'è una differenza gigantesca: questi hanno (spesso, non sempre) un sacco di soldi.[33]

(One thing I stressed in my film is that Rome is profoundly different, though there are elements of continuity: for instance, the guys who race their cars round the Obelisk are the grandchildren of Accattone. They express the same cultural and sub-cultural identity, of the former urban lumpen proletariat with all that implies: a ferocious wish for social confirmation, a pleasure-seeking behaviour in relation to life that is often carried to extremes ... but there is one huge difference. They often, not always, have lots of money.)

Vicari identifies continuity and a difference between his male protagonists and those of the past, both cinematic and actual: on the one hand there are their origins, their values and their language, on the other money, cars and the city's decentralized development. The characters of *Velocità massima* never really go into the centre, not because it is inaccessible or difficult, but because their lives are, and importantly *can comfortably be*, centred elsewhere. The material bases of life and living are there; the centre does not represent a significant other that shapes an imitation of itself in a straggle of isolated shanties, distinguished by the lack of amenities and services, in a zone that is irrelevant and neglected in itself and in relation to the city.

The Scipione garage, run ineptly by Stefano, is in the Ostian hinterland. The film's main characters, Stefano, Claudio and Giovanna, live and belong near the coast; they interact in and with its ambience of bamboo and sea, dirt roads and fields, and Ostia itself, its nightclubs, its beaches, its bathing establishments. This is where Giovanna occasionally works while fantasizing about travelling and going to university. It is an essentially local terrain from which they venture forth along roads of all kinds, driving and testing cars. The men's lives, and indirectly the woman's too, are focused on the car; money, cars and those who drive them provide the cement of the lives and the tenuous relationships of the group, and their 'esistenza cruda', in Vicari's words. The geographical focus of this life is EUR and the illegal car races around its obelisk, a 45 m high reinforced concrete *stele* adorned with 92 m high relief marble panels celebrating the work of Marconi and others, begun in 1939 according to a design of Arturo Dazzi and completed only in 1959, in time for the Olympics (see Figure 3.1 on p. 70).

The history of Dazzi's memorial is the common history of most of the buildings planned for EUR, an area, despite its location, quite unlike the historic periphery of Rome. The original project was halted by the war and completed gradually during the post-war period, thanks in particular to its attraction to the middle class and to the location of a range of government bureaux there. In the original design by the architects Marcello Piacentini and Adalberto Libera in the late thirties, EUR was conceived according to the model of a roman castrum, organized by a series of *piazze* and intersecting roads, to be linked, through archaeological sites and Via dell'Impero, with the centre at Piazza Venezia.

Vicari speaks tellingly of himself, his film, and a different Rome when he says,

Figure 3.1: The obelisk dedicated to Guglielmo Marconi in EUR (Arturo Dazzi, 1959).
Photograph: Dan Holdaway. Reproduced with the kind permission of the photographer.

Vedendo i film (di Pasolini) mi sono stupito di quanto fosse profondo il suo interesse per il mondo delle borgate: il suo sguardo poetico si sovrapponeva all, esistenza cruda di queste persone. Non ho scoperto le borgate attraverso Pasolini. Pasolini, cioè un grande intellettuale, si era interessato al mondo in cui io vivevo. I suoi lavori però, non hanno influenzato *Velocità massima*. Il mio è un film plebeo non è un film di un intellectuale che riflette sulla periferia.[34]

(seeing Pasolini's films I was struck by the depth of his interest in the world of the *borgata*. His poetic gaze was superimposed on the crude existence of these people. I didn't discover the *borgata* through Pasolini. Pasolini, a great intellectual, was interested in the world I lived in. But his works haven't influenced *Velocità massima*. My film is a plebian film, it isn't the film of an intellectual who reflects on the periphery.)

Velocità massima is perhaps not an exceptional film as Pasolini's *Accattone* (1961) undoubtedly is, but it does offer a frank, unromanticized account of Roman men who live in the outskirts and the choices that govern their existence.

Romanzo criminale

Romanzo criminale, Michele Placido's eighth film and his first major, international success, dramatizes the story of the *Banda della Magliana,* a group of local criminals who took control of Rome's drugs, gambling and prostitution circuits, constructing links with the Mafia and the Camorra, as well as with certain arms of the state, the secret services, and with terrorist and fascist groups. The written description with which the film begins, 'in the middle of the seventies, a gang of delinquents set out from the periphery in order to conquer Rome', explicitly adopts the sense of the periphery as other, as *not* Rome. They come *from* Magliana, the area to the south of the centre between the Via Portuense and the airport at Fiumicino which is notorious for being completely illegally built (below the level of the Tiber) during the housing speculation of the 1960s.

The prologue in fact begins in EUR, under one of its most well-known images, the water tower nicknames the *fungo* (mushroom), built in 1959 and used by Antonioni in perhaps the cinema's most famous encounter with this district in *L'eclisse* (1962). A group of teenagers steal a car and head off along the Via Cristoforo Colombo to the sea where they are apprehended by the police. The boys grow up to be the gang's three leaders, Libanese (Pierfrancesco Favino), Freddo (Kim Rossi Stuart) and Dandy (Claudio Santamaria), and the film follows their personal lives and their careers as Rome's criminal bosses with links to several important events of the decade, including the killing of Aldo Moro (1978) and the bombing of the Bologna railway station (1980). Dandy falls in love with Patrizia, a high-class prostitute, through whom the police pursue the gang, and with whom the Commissario Scajola (Stefano Accorsi) also has an affair. While Libanese concentrates on the ambitions of the group through contacts with the Mafia and the state, Freddo falls in love with Roberta, his brother's teacher, and tries to leave the gang to be with her. The killing of both Libanese and Roberta sees Freddo's return to avenge their deaths, in a campaign in which both Dandy and he himself are ultimately killed.

The film ranges over the geographical terrain of the whole city, but it always returns to the centre as the locus of power: the power of the gang and the power, official and otherwise, of the state. Classic images of Rome's *centro storico* – ruins, steps, churches, the open space of the piazzas (filled with cars at that time) – and the anonymous administrative blocks emphasize a Rome of government intrigue, state corruption and links with power bases with roots elsewhere: Sicily, Naples, Milan. State officials and senior police are seen inside central ministries with spectacular views out towards the Forum or Trajan's market, or in the streets near these places of work around a central complex of the Forum, Piazza Venezia, the Vittoriano, the Campidoglio, the Viminale and Piazza Argentina. The meetings with the Camorra and Cosa Nostra bosses, on the other hand, take place outside Rome.

In an early sequence the gang leaders, Libanese and Freddo, are shot walking from Trastevere, where Freddo has just been released from prison, across the Ponte Sisto into the city, with St Peter's in the background. Rome is their territory, but the familiar pieces of the Western collective memory owe little to their artistic and tourist histories, and everything to their links with the intricately interwoven networks of criminality, police, government, politics, mafia. The city centre's appearance signifies the institutions of contemporary power; indeed the bringing together of organized crime, politics and the secret servants of the state always takes place in the *centro storico*. The film's own incoherence around the links between its criminals and the state personnel of the special services is a faithful replica of the actual situation: the interlocking networks of those years are still under investigation though there is some evidence for the band's links to the Moro case.[35]

Familiar, central sites function as the locations for significant events and killings: one of the gang is rounded up in Piazza Farnese, another on the Isola Tiberina, open public spaces where passers-by are drawn into gangster-style events or police round-ups that have more than a passing acquaintance with the American cinema. The knifing of the former boss, 'Il Terribile', on the Spanish Steps (see Figure 3.2 on p. 73), is a brief and very stylish sequence that takes place in the piazza itself as it is crossed by a swerving car, a glimpsed panorama, tight framing that concentrates on the approach of the killers, a diagonal take on the stone of the steps themselves (omitting their famous backdrop, Trinità dei Monti and the Pincio), a chilling exchange of words before the knifing, and the leisurely walk away from the body by the killers.

The streets of Trastevere, the most consistently photographed popular area, feature repeatedly, especially at night. Libanese is knifed to death here, in a vespasiano after he leaves the nightclub owned by the gang. He staggers into the piazza of Santa Maria in Trastevere before falling to the ground, framed in death

Figure 3.2: The last breaths of 'Il Terribile', between Libanese and Freddo on the Spanish Steps in *Romanzo criminale*.

against its basalt cobblestones. Luca Bigazzi's photography records a Trastevere that remains insistently Roman, making an irrelevance of its many tourists and its Anglo-American residents – today the largest migrant group in Rome, and already a significant presence in the 1980s. The local nature of business and criminal affairs is shown through their links with older aspects of inner-city Roman life which continued to exist in parallel with an inner-city life that is increasingly dominated by the gentrification of the rich, the foreign and, in this case, the criminal. The growing peripheral condition of those Romans who have remained in Trastevere, part of the considerable influx of working-class people made homeless in the 1930s by the inner-city *sventramenti* on the other side of the river, is here inverted: its historic popular 'romanness' is given visual and narrative precedence. Placido plays on a geographical juxtaposition of the different forms of power: central, state power located around the Forum and the Capitol, and its more popular, criminal variant located across the river in Trastevere.

A similar 'popular' association anchors Freddo's first meeting with Roberta when he goes in search of his brother in Garbatella, the formerly exclusively working-class district in the south-west of the city, so beloved of Nanni Moretti. Designed and mostly built in the 1920s to an enlarged plan by the architects of the regime, Gustavo Giovannoni and Marcello Piacentini, as part of the public building projects undertaken by the ICP, and initially designed to house the workers of the industrial zone of the same area, Garbatella was almost immediately extended from the original plan of predominantly small houses in the local 'barocchetto' style in order to include bigger apartment blocks. These were designed by Innocenzo Sabatini, the architect who had contributed to the working-class district of Testaccio and who would go on to have a hand in part of the Donna Olimpia complex (Pasolini's *grattacieli*) on the other side of the Tiber, begun in 1932.[36] Roberta and Gigio's homes are made of a distinctive reddish ochre brick, one of the *alberghi suburbani* (suburban hotels), further accommodation for those evicted from the centre that extended the original plan for the 'garden' suburb. This sequence visually echoes the scene of killing on the Spanish Steps, with Freddo and Libanese once again sitting on textured travertine steps. (See Figure 3.3 on p. 75.)

The use of this most common Roman stone in combination with *laterizio*, the narrow Roman brick, is one of the distinctive signifiers of the colour and texture of Rome. It has been employed, and remained visually familiar, over an extended history, and it was frequently exploited by early twentieth-century architects at San Saba, Testaccio and Garbatella, and later in different modalities in post-war developments. The contrast of colour has been increasingly reproduced in less expensive surfaces like concrete painted in the same colour tones. These associations are strongly evoked in this sequence in Garbatella, thereby

Figure 3.3: Freddo and Libanese sitting in Garbatella in *Romanzo criminale*.

mapping a very different but continuous set of Roman connections that tie the film and the gang's origins to their *romanness* through the visual links between the classic city centre and its suburbs.

Bigazzi exploits the colours and textures of travertine and brick here as he does in the big scenes of killing and revenge in the centre. For Freddo's own killing, he returns to the 'Madonna dei Pellegrini', the Caravaggio that hangs in the church of Sant'Agostino to which he had first been introduced by Roberta. There he avenges both her death and Libanese's by assassinating the gang member, Ciro, who had betrayed them. The church interior is lit by shadows and strong lighting effects, mimicking the manner of the painter, and not only the subject of the painting but also Caravaggio's own low-life links provide another resonance. Freddo, framed against the stone façade, kills Ciro at the entrance to the church, and its steps then provide the site of his own shooting by a government sniper from the building opposite. Freddo falls onto the same stone and is framed against it.

Sequences such as this, which take place in the *centro storico*'s public spaces, ruthlessly appropriated by crime and criminals, make the city's monuments a picturesque but incidental backdrop to criminal and political intrigue, even as they engage the spectator in a calculated involvement in the fabric of the city through colour and texture. Remarkably free of people, both known and unfamiliar locations in these public spaces, streets, buildings and monuments are semanticized through the film's light, sound and colour. The city in *Romanzo criminale* acts as signifier of the tensions of a historic period through the film's location of the city's ruthless exploitation by the criminal gang in Rome's monumental, everyday splendour. Despite Placido's references to De Palma, Scorsese, Leone and to the Visconti of *Rocco e i suoi fratelli* (1960), the film remains emotionally and cinematically local, Roman, grounded in the city of its protagonists. The streets, the colours and textures, the monuments of the past, the houses on the coast, the roads and the vegetation all signal late twentieth-century Rome, the city as locus of corrupt power that today gestures back to the earlier films of Francesco Rosi and Elio Petri, Italian directors who made the corruption of modern Italy their focus.

Conclusion

Rome has always been a city of migrants, and the classical Roman periphery was first constituted of those who came from other areas of Italy. It was added to by those forcibly uprooted from the inner city and later by those who moved out through choice. The most recent waves of migration have been from other countries, and the outlying districts of Rome today are inhabited by various national groups, where encounters with local Italians produces high levels of racism, prejudice and fear of difference. In many respects those who have some form of concrete accommodation are the more privileged, since sleeping rough in both central and more distant areas – railway platforms, river banks, under bridges and, before policies were introduced that closed off access, the surrounding land of monuments, churches and Rome's abundant green spaces – is as common now as it was in earlier eras. Yet for these people location and distance from the centre is only one aspect of their marginality. Other contributing factors include belonging or non-belonging, homelessness, illegality, clandestinity and the search for work. The reality of diverse migrant groups often still incorporates a dichotomy between life in the outskirts, for instance for domestics and carers, who live at a distance, but work closer to or in the centre. Travel and the time it takes remain important indicators of a peripheral condition, though the marginal population is also located in the empty spaces of the historic centre: along the banks of the Tiber,[37] in disused factories, in the unbuilt spaces that have distinguished Rome's development. In this, the twenty-first century repeats the patterns of earlier urbanization. In Rome, the enforced imposition of living in particular areas is replicated today in the *case di accoglienza* (housing shelters).

Distance is just one aspect of a study of metropolitan Rome now, although it has diminished in importance since the characteristics of what was traditionally associated with each pole of the centre–periphery opposition have been rendered increasingly complex over time. The sheer growth of the population and its distribution, the kinds of housing and services constructed, the presence or absence of links between the historic centre and the surrounding, smaller urban centres that have been absorbed into the administrative area of the Rome council have together contributed to a different account of centrality and marginality, and of urbanization more generally. But if the metropolitan area traversed by Moretti on his scooter now includes a wide range of types of buildings, conveniences, access and cultures that may be called both urban and suburban, where a way of living has actually been chosen, other areas in the Roman conurbation maintain a similar status to that of earlier periods in accommodating groups of migrants.

The Rome of Placido and Vicari is inhabited by young white men, often with money, whose lives are also defined by the capacity to choose. These men converge on and circulate around a large diverse metropolitan area, assisted by the ubiquity of the car, and yet the city centre is still not primarily peopled by them or people like them. If the reorganization of Rome to exploit its major industry, tourism, threatens to make Romans themselves marginal, except for the affluent and the very rich, these films nonetheless capture one aspect of Roman lives now, in both wealthy and working-class areas. All three films offer an account of aspects of the city through a mise-en-scène that highlights the relation between inhabitants and locations, some continuity in attitudes and values, and between 1950s Rome and Rome today. In revisiting the earlier cinematic periphery in colour, the invoking of Rome and its boundaries in recent film immediately establishes a dialogue, an interrogation of the classical post-war accounts of the city, because of its articulation of difference.

4 TOPOPHILIA AND OTHER ROMAN PERVERSIONS: ON BERTOLUCCI'S *LA LUNA*

John David Rhodes

I mentioned to a friend that I was going to try and write about Bertolucci's *La luna*, a film shot mostly in Rome and released in 1979.[1]

He said, 'But that's a terrible film. It's so *literal*. It knows everything it's doing'. I said that *that* was what I was going to try to write about. He replied, 'Then you'll just be explaining why it's a bad film'. Although I might admit to loving this film, I can also admit that it may in fact, *be* a bad film: for instance, it seems a series of parts, rather, perhaps, than an integrated (not to say organic) whole. But my own partiality towards it extends from its own – its own partiality. In part, what I want to explore here is partiality itself, the cathexis, prioritization and, finally, the fetishism of parts of films, of parts of Rome, of parts in films where parts of Rome become visible, often fleetingly. *La luna* is hardly a film about Rome. But in watching it, we are thrown about and around Rome; we are made to lurch from here to there and back. Something feels important about where and when Rome appears, or is made to appear (both happen) in this film. I sense that Bertolucci, who was not a native Roman, but who lived there during his adolescence and early adulthood, knows what he is doing *with* Rome in *La luna*, but also that the film's images of Rome are doing more than he knows.

When a film is located and shot on location in a specific place – and especially a place like Rome – then that place might weigh heavily on the film's narration; the background can arrest us, can press into the foreground, make us wonder why a scene is being shot here and not somewhere else, make us wonder if this location matters and why. Siegfried Kracauer touches on a film's emplacement potential to overturn perceptual and narrative priorities when he considers the effects produced when a spectator is absorbed by a film's 'small unit' of materiality:

> The moment disengages itself from the conflict, the belief, the adventure, toward
> which the whole of the story converges. A face on the screen may attract us as a sin-

gular manifestation of fear or happiness regardless of the events which motivate its expression. A street serving as the background to some quarrel or love affair may rush to the fore and produce an intoxicating effect. Street and face, then, open up a dimension much wider than that of the plots which they sustain.[2]

Elena Gorfinkel and I have proposed that Kracauer's is 'an account of a spectatorship that is both distracted and overcathected'.[3] This experience of looking closely, but perhaps at the wrong thing, offers a useful heuristic for discovering what films might have to tell us about the cities (or non-urban locations) in which they were shot. Sometimes we may find ourselves noticing something that seems only contingently there in the image; other times film's affinity with contingency may have lulled us into not noticing or not taking seriously a particular film's intentional use of a place or space – places and spaces that are, like the film image itself, products of intention and contingency.[4] Looking at a film's explicit or implicit use of locations may be a way of reinserting a film back into a thicker historical context, but it can also be a means of reanimating that context (and perhaps the film, as well) so that what we get is more than a richer sense of the history that gives rise to the film and to which the film responds. The investigation of a film's locationality allows us to capture or recapture the film's theoretical address to its historical context: its embrace or refusal of what was given, its questioning – and not simply its documentation – of the world that was before it.

In what follows I hope to offer some thoughts not just on Bertolucci's Rome – as interesting as that may be – but also on the way that an understanding of this encounter between filmmaker and city (as overdetermined as we suspect it may be) can tell us something about what it means, today, to think about places through filmmaking and filmmaking through places. Rome and Bertolucci's engagement with it in *La luna* offer themselves as exemplary sites and practices within which to trace an itinerary towards a theoretical understanding of this problem. And in tracing this itinerary, I hope also to suggest some of what might be at stake in thinking of Rome as a site and product of postmodernity.

*

In previous work that focused on the films of Pier Paolo Pasolini, I explored Rome as a curious and complex site of the modern and the modernist.[5] My curiosity about Rome extended initially from the fact that other cities, cities more emblematically modern, had served as the basis for many of the most exciting and persuasive theories of modernity. Here we think of Paris, Berlin, New York City – those ur-sites of modernity. Asking what sort of modern city Rome was seemed to be a way of figuring out what sort of modernist director Pasolini was. His brusque editing patterns, his boring, long travelling shots, his insistence on situating historically oppressed bodies in relation to historically produced sites of social exclusion (or pseudo-inclusion): these traits are intimately linked to Rome's immense and irregular growth in the post-war period, a time in which the city's periphery expanded outwards in outcroppings of both sub-artisanal handmade domestic architecture (what have been called *le borgate* in Italian), often made from pilfered or scavenged building materials, and large-scale speculative real estate developments. The precursors of the history of these post-war constructions were the fascist *borgate*: cheap mass housing built in the late 1920s and 1930s to re-house a working-class urban population that had been expropriated and displaced by Mussolinian monumental urban redesign and major archaeological excavations. The excavation and redesign of Rome's centre – the *sventramenti*, or 'disembowellings' of the city – necessitated the intense nodal development of the city's edges. This development, however, in both its fascist and post-war phases, was always piecemeal, awkward. Rome's urban modernity was, in many senses, measured in the long, dusty distances that were travelled arduously by foot or on wheezing buses by Rome's least fortunate. Or else it was registered in the large open spaces that had been newly cleared by Fascism's ideologically overdetermined archaeology. The most startling example of such archaeology is the Via dell'Impero (now the Via dei Fori Imperiali), which was made by razing several densely settled neighbourhoods, so as to connect visually, materially and symbolically Mussolini's headquarters on the Piazza Venezia with the Colosseum (metonym of the authority of Italy's ancient Roman past). The experience of Roman urban modernity, therefore, encompasses both a constantly expanding periphery and central zones of radical evacuation. Its texture is rather different, for instance, from the dense verticality of New York, or the technological modernity of Berlin. Modern Rome's condensed history of displacement and destruction – a history notable, as well, for the relative lack of more daring forms of modern architecture – offers itself as a powerful location from which to think and re-think the modern, in relation both to an experience of emplacement and an experience of the cinematic.[6]

Perhaps the nature of Rome's modernity is not so different from the account of London's modernity as it is explained by the narrator of Patrick Keiller's *London* (1991): perhaps Rome, never having been sufficiently modern, was 'already postmodern'.[7] If, however, the postmodern has tended to be thought in relation to places like Los Angeles, Las Vegas or delirious New York, then thinking Rome as postmodern strains the conceptual and textural features we attribute to the postmodern.[8] The palimpsest could be turned to as a figure that would organize an image and understanding of Rome as postmodern. However, Rome's hyperbolic and extravagantly literal palimpsestic nature, and the fact that its tissues, erasures, voids, superimpositions and incorporations have been a distinctive feature of the city since long, long before modernity make us question how far we can go with this metaphor; it might be too seductive. If Rome's palimpsest is not peculiarly modern, much less postmodern, then we might question this term's usefulness in thinking about what is peculiar about Rome's postmodernity (assuming its peculiarity is something we are interested in in the first place).

Another much-remarked on feature of postmodern experience might usefully be brought to bear on Rome: that of spatial confusion, of our 'unmappable' relation to totality that so preoccupies Fredric Jameson in his notorious encounter with the Bonaventure Hotel in downtown Los Angeles. In this scene (for truly this passage of theory has the flavour of narrative fiction), Jameson proposes that the 'postmodern hyperspace' embodied by the Bonaventure 'has finally succeeded in transcending the capacities of the individual human body to locate itself, to organize its immediate surroundings perceptually, and cognitively to map its position in a mappable external world'.[9]

Bill Brown has suggested that this passage is a recapitulation of Dante losing himself in the *selva oscura* at the beginning of the *Divine Comedy*, and has traced not only Jameson's well-known and acknowledged debt to the planner Kevin Lynch's book *The Image of the City*, in which a theory of the mappable city is put forth, but has also emphasized Lynch's debt to early modern Florence. If, for Lynch, a place like Jersey City has what he calls 'low imageability'[10], this is because of its lack of coherent shapes, strong organizing landmarks. Lynch's research allows him to suggest that '[m]uch of the characteristic feeling for Jersey City seemed to be that it was a place on the edge of something else'.[11] Jersey City is contrasted unflatteringly (and as Brown notes, unfairly) with Florence, which Lynch calls 'a highly visible city'.[12] In Florence, according to Lynch:

> Every scene is instantly recognizable, and brings to mind a flood of associations. Parts fit into parts. The visual environment becomes an integral piece of the inhabitants' lives ... [T]here seems to be a simple and automatic pleasure, a feeling of satisfaction, presence, and rightness, which arises from the mere sight of the city, or the chance to walk through its streets.[13]

Brown observes that 'there is a disorienting history at the heart of the orientation that Lynch and Jameson pursue, for the construction of medieval Florence can be understood as the prefiguration of a certain modernist endeavor'.[14] Florence's visual clarity inspired not only Lynch's (late modernist) vision of the 'imageable' city, but also the work of modernist designers and planners like Le Corbusier.[15] In other words, it is a pre-modern experience of visual clarity (one taken, moreover, from classical Roman, axial planning, a context Brown does not mention) that informs the experience of the modern city. The postmodern will be that which has failed to be adequately pre-modern, therefore never truly modern. Its postmodern formlessness extends from a deficit of premodern form.

Where does this leave Rome – modern Rome or postmodern Rome?[16] On the one hand we have the *sventramenti* that cleared the way for Rome's automobilized boulevards that cut through the centre of the centre of the city; their connection of visible monuments one to another would seem to be the very epitome of a 'visible city', however weirdly enervating they are at the same time for those who walk their lengths and widths. On the other hand we have the neighbourhoods that remained untouched – especially the area around what was known as the medieval *abitato*; these neighbourhoods constitute one of the most difficult to picture, most spatially confusing and unmappable chunks of city space in the west.

Modern Rome has often been understood and experienced as a city of unmappable confusion. Here is the novelist Elizabeth Bowen in her book *A Time in Rome*, describing her struggle with her 'Nuovissima Pianta' di Roma during her stays in the city in the late 1950s (the chapter from which I am quoting here is entitled 'The Confusion'):

> Again and again, while I was out walking, I turned aside into cafés; over some tiny table the Pianta could be draped like a limp cloth – in such pauses I could at least establish where I was not, or how far from where I had hoped to be. Rome seemed an often-shaken kaleidoscope …

> I lost my way on leaving the Pantheon, my second afternoon. In a hurry to keep an appointment better not made, I believed myself headed for the Corso, when, without warning, the Largo Argentina, excavated temples, trees, theatre, taxi rank and all, burst upon my horrified gaze. Nothing should have been wrong with the Argentina: simply I had had no idea of Rome's containing anything of the sort.[17]

Bowen laments, a little later: 'The Colosseum, I could have sworn, had shifted its position since last I saw it; I wasted a morning in angry search for it'.[18] This is, of course, a common experience for the tourist, even perhaps for the odd Roman unfamiliar with a particular neighbourhood. Obviously a kind of lost-ness is not specific to Rome, to Bowen's encounter with it, nor is it specific to Jameson or postmodernism. But in thinking the postmodern, the point is not the absolute novelty of a spatial or sensual experience, but the way in which that experience is related to a 'cultural dominant' that, in Brown's terms, can 'exemplify postmodernity once (the experience of) it is rendered properly allegorical'.[19] Rome's confusion – a result of its palimpsest of ancient, medieval, early modern, baroque, nineteenth-century and finally fascist attempts to shape it – might offer us a way of thinking about the city in relation to the postmodern, might clear a path out of or into the confusion of the postmodern text, or a way out of or into postmodern modes and methods of textual analysis. I want to see if I can test these theoretical and critical intuitions by turning to Bertolucci's *La luna*, a film that might seem like an unlikely object for these considerations, but that is, as we shall see, all-too-conveniently suited to my purposes.

*

Perhaps the problem with Rome is not only that it cannot be 'imaged' (in the sense of 'cognitively mapped'), but that it is also too imaged, over-represented, saturated by representation. Rome, in effect, might be merely a sequence of images. This is a familiar complaint, of course, about the postmodern: that it is nothing other than an endless proliferation of images, a 'society of the spectacle'. Bowen found her map confusing because of its 'would-be attraction' in which 'principal monuments' are represented on the map as drawings. These occlude and confuse the actual street plan: 'Outside facades blot out, each time, the street-network in their vicinity, so that ways of approach to them or departure from them cannot be traced'.[20] These maps narrate a (post-war) touristic Rome, one that is less a unified urban whole and more a series of disconnected sites. The city is reduced to a ground against which festishized monuments appear. Thus, fetishism of a place actually prevents the mastery of the city's whole, its inter-connectedness and interrelatedness. (Such a fetishism produces a kind of castrated blindness.)

In the case of Bowen's 'Nuovissima Pianta', the image that is meant to anchor, orientate and produce spatial (historical, cultural) knowledge – to produce mastery, in other words – is in fact an obstacle to mastery. A city that can produce for and impress on its inhabitants (or visitors) images of itself will be a city that, in Lynch's terms, can be mastered. But imageability and mastery, as Bowen shows us, has an uncertain relation to the image itself.

In an interview about one of his more recent films, *Besieged* (1998),[21] a film set in Rome, but that is fairly reticent (obtuse?) about its setting, Bertolucci describes the fleetingness of images of Rome's familiar landmarks in terms that directly invoke the problem of mastery:

> You just have a glimpse of the Spanish Steps when Shandurai reads the letter on the terrace, between the drying sheets. You see behind the two towers and the obelisk of the Spanish Steps. I've been very economical with the Spanish Steps because it's so much an image on postcards … [W]hen she opens the windows … at the beginning of the film, you see the Steps outside. You don't know what Steps they are, but people living in Rome, they would know. The way I show the Spanish Steps is like a game going back to Freud's little grandson who didn't cry when his mother left him. He would throw a wooden spool tied with string over the edge of his crib and then pull it back. It was like exercising in abandoning, and being abandoned.[22]

Bertolucci's comment suggests that there is more happening here than the paying of a compliment to the odd Roman spectator's sense of civic identity. This analogy suggests the way in which the image of the city is either too much or too little, and that film will need to mediate this relation so that the film is not overwhelmed by obviousness or folded into abstraction (the film could be just anywhere, not specifically in Rome).

The fort-da analogy also suggests something unsettling about dealing with Bertolucci: his self-consciousness – of his own methods, of their relation to psychoanalysis, of his choice of locations, bodies, gestures. Bertolucci's work, especially when read in light of his own commentary on them, might risk suffering from an excess of intentionality – of organized, self-conscious labour that is too easily discovered in or verified by the films themselves. In fact, it is difficult, and, I think, almost impossible to separate Bertolucci's articulate (at times overbearing, irritating) self-consciousness from the same quality that we sense in the films themselves and see especially in a film like *La luna*. Understandably, we hesitate in saying much about artworks that already seem to know so much about themselves. Bertolucci's films are as self-conscious about their debt to (or conversation with) psychoanalytic method as they are about their use of location. This sort of self-consciousness, as the anecdote I cited at the outset of this essay illustrates, has frequently been regarded as a weakness of his work, especially of *La luna*.

In another interview, one given in 1978, the year in which he was preparing *La luna*, Bertolucci commented,

> In general my films are constructed according to a stratification so mysterious to me that I could never separate the political from the psychoanalytic, linguistic, the means of production, etc. I feel that it's all mixed together. It seems to me that my films are all about finding the way out of this labyrinth, this chaos of politics and psychoanalysis.[23]

The labyrinth is (as Bertolucci is all too aware here) the controlling figure of his *Strategia del ragno* (The Spider's Stratagem, 1970), a film set in the small city (or town) of Sabbioneta, an example of seventeenth-century 'ideal city' planning methods in Emilia-Romagna.[24] The labyrinth also features (as both motif and in terms of form) in *La luna*, which is, of course, primarily set in Rome, but whose locations include Brooklyn, Parma and the seaside south of Rome (Sabaudia). These two films, *Strategia del ragno* and *La luna*, have much to connect them. Striking in *Strategia del ragno* is the fact that the film takes place in a town so clearly designed that becoming lost would seem to be completely out of the question. As Eamon Canniffe has written, the problem in Sabbioneta was probably that of *never* being *invisible*, never being lost: 'Living within a frozen urban spectacle, the inhabitants as both audience and actors could be expected to comply with stage directions, be they theatrical or social'.[25] *Strategia*'s labyrinth is metaphorical: it is a labyrinth history (and desire, and historical desire), not actual city form. The rigidity and legibility of its urban form are used as counterfoil to the illegible history that has taken place in its streets, theatres, public squares and private dwellings. In *La luna*, however, locating ourselves in *space* seems to be a more pressing concern than locating ourselves in time.

Strategia del ragno narrates an impossible search for a father. *La luna* narrates another search for a father, but also a literal love affair of a son and his mother. Caterina Silveri (Jill Clayburgh), an opera diva, escapes to Rome with her son Joe (Matthew Barry) following the unexpected death of her husband, who we later learn was not Joe's real father. Joe, apparently left to his own devices as his mother rehearses for and delivers a series of opera engagements, loafs around Rome and stumbles into heroin addiction. Caterina attempts to cure or over-whelm his addiction through a variety of seductions. Following a trip to Parma where she visits her former voice teacher and where she is followed by Joe, she reveals to her son the identity of his paternity. Joe, his father, and Caterina all finally assemble at the Baths of Caracalla where Caterina is rehearsing a new production. While this sketch of the film's story indicates its erotic excesses, it does little to indicate the film's elaborate visual style, its intense melodramatic acting, and its metacinematic allusiveness. Its use of locations is imbricated in all of these elements of excess.

La luna's treatment of Roman geography is both elliptical (in the film's abrupt cuts across locations separated by considerable distances) and legible – sometimes at the same time. The labyrinth theme is made present by the film's self-conscious quoting of *Strategia* (whose title self-consciously nods in the direction of the Ari-adne myth), as well as its too-overt staging of symbols and names associated with the myth of King Minos's labyrinth, and the thread provided by Ariadne that gave Theseus the means by which to defeat the Minotaur and find his way back out again. In *La luna*'s prologue, we are given the 'thread' of this theme, an actual image of the infant Joe (who, as an adolescent will be our protagonist later in the film), tangled up in yarn, as he stumbles towards a character – Joe's grandmother, we would correctly assume – played by Alida Valli, who also plays the mysterious woman at the centre of the *Strategia del ragno*. Bertolucci confirms in an interview with Richard Roud that this yarn could be read as a symbol of the 'umbilical cord' connecting the child to the mother. In the same interview he also confirms that the mirror we see in this scene is, in fact, a nod to Lacan's theory of the 'mirror stage'.[26] We are also given a character named Arianna (Italian for Ariadne), a beautiful young woman who befriends Joe and apparently initiates him into sex and heroin and whose appearances punctuate the film.

The problem with these references – to myth, to psychoanalysis, to Bertoluc-cis's own work – is that they seem to make sure that in this film we will never be lost *enough*. Not only does it boldly make self-conscious reference to patterns of myth and psychoanalytic interpretation (itself organized around myth, of course), but the film also makes excessive reference to Bertolucci's own previous filmmaking, mostly by way of repetitions of shot set-ups, instances of staging, camera movements and the like, in addition to the numerous repetitions of Bertolucci's ongoing thematic preoccupations. T. Jefferson Kline, who has traced many of the film's auto-citations, suggests that the film operates 'as though Bertolucci had transposed the figure of repetition ... to the level of his entire oeuvre'.[27] Bertolucci, of course, already knows this. He says: 'A film about incestuous fantasies has to be traversed by this violently autoerotic and incestuous movement that is behind self-quotation'.[28] It is exactly this hyperbolization of self-consciousness in *La luna* that has turned off so many commentators. Robert Kolker, perhaps the most exasperated of any commentator on this film, suggests that *La luna* 'embarrasses the viewer with its excess'.[29] Much of this embarrassing excess involves Bertolucci's flagrant, profligate self-quotation. Kolker worries that these gestures, unlike Bertolucci's established practice of allusion to *other* filmmakers elsewhere in his work, indulge the 'self-indulgence' of viewers familiar with the director's work.[30] Kolker, acknowledging the 'vulgar psychologizing' that such a move risks, suggests that 'these allusions were a way for the filmmaker to comfort himself, to provide a retreat from the trauma of *1900*'.[31] (*1900* was a commercial and critical failure; its production costs had run out of control, and there were enormous disputes between Bertolucci and the production companies who funded the film over the length of the film's theatrically released cuts.) Kolker's suspicion that the film was made 'for the solitary pleasure of its maker'[32] gives way finally to the conclusion that 'of all Bertolucci's works since *The Grim Reaper*, *La luna* has the least political subtext'.[33] Clearly auto-citation amounts to a gratification that, while it may leave a 'critic' (like Kolker) 'breathless with his own pedantry',[34] can amount to little more than a form of self-abuse: we could call this mutual masturbation.

I find intriguing, however, Kolker's anxious, condemnatory pairing of *La luna* with *The Grim Reaper* (*La commare secca*, 1962),[35] as Bertolucci's 'least political'. These two films, more than any others in the director's oeuvre, I would argue, are preoccupied with the texture of Rome's urban spaces. *Partner* (1968) and *Il conformista* (The Conformist, 1970) are both set in Rome, but in these films the melodrama (personal or historical) overwhelms the 'mere' interest in Rome *qua* Rome that I think we see in *La commare secca* or *La luna*. *La commare secca* was Bertolucci's first film, made from a treatment given to him by Pasolini, his neighbour and mentor. *La luna* marks, moreover, an explicit return to Rome, following the success of *L'ultimo tango a Parigi* (Last Tango in Paris, 1972), set in Paris, and the disappointment of *1900* (1976), set in Bertolucci's native Emilia-Romagna.

La luna's first view of Rome could hardly be more touristic: a view from the Janiculum. Rome lies before us, an image. The camera, however will leave this view of the city to follow the movement of a black limousine and teenaged skateboarders as they roll, cruise and tumble down the Paseggiata Gianicolo, past the Pontificio Collegio Pio Romeno (the Romanian seminary which was built in 1934 just after the completion of this sinuous street that leads up to the fascist-era monument to Anita Garibaldi). In this return to Rome, we begin by making a descent from Bertolucci's first Roman neighbourhood, Monteverde, where he lived until the early 1960s on Via Giacinto Carini, in the same building as Pasolini. This sequence follows seamlessly from the prologue that opens the film (in which we are introduced to Joe, Caterina and her husband Douglas, we witness Douglas's death and funeral, and are offered major, overt allusions to *Last Tango* and *Il conformista*; for the latter see Figure 4.1 on p. 89), and in it we are suddenly in Rome. The visual motif that links the departure from the funeral and our movement (across a single cut) to Rome is the black limousine: first the one that drives Caterina and Joe out of the cemetery as fellow mourners stare, and this second one crowded full of teenagers, laughing and getting high while the boys on skateboards weave around and in and out of its path. Rome is thus a kind of afterlife, a dead place. And yet, it is also a city of young people who seem possessed by a narcotic, somnolent vitality.

Like all of the sequences in this film in which we move through Rome, this one is effected through ellipses that are both spatial and temporal. The ellipses in this sequence, however, do not remove us from central Rome and they only abbreviate the duration of a continuous action, or narrative unit. We move from the Passeggiata (when we first see Joe in Rome, reading while skateboarding), then inside the limo, where we find Joe and glimpse through its window the ruins of the Forum (in what I think is a process shot), and then we are given a wonderful, circular tracking shot of that most-photographed of Roman obelisks – the one supported by Bernini's elephant in front of Santa Maria Sopra Minerva – and next we are back inside the car (we glimpse Trajan's market through the car window), and then, when Joe asks the driver to stop the car (who is this driver?), we cut to a downward tilt that deposits us and Joe (and Arianna) in Piazza Cavour.

This trajectory is at once disorientating and all too orientated. The languid movement of camera, bodies and automobiles displaces the displacements of the editing's abrupt erasure of distances between places. The moving shot of the Bernini obelisk would seem to suggest its relation to a point of view; however, clearly, it is a view that is offered to the spectator via the camera, unmoored to subjectivity – for certainly it is clear that the shot does not suggest the point of view of the teenagers in the car. As we, the spectators of the film, see this shot we also see ourselves seeing, because we might recognize it – although it does not figure in Kolker's catalogue of auto-citations – as an allusion to one of the most elaborate sequences in *Strategia del ragno*. I mean here the scene of a showdown between Athos Magnani and the statue of his eponymous Oedipal nemesis. Here the monumental marker (a 'fake' statue, placed in front of the 'real' church of San Rocco in Sabbioneta) commemorates the pseudo-martyrdom of Athos senior, a fascist collaborator whose crimes were kept secret so as not to contaminate the

Figure 4.1: Intertextual auto-citation in *La luna* (nodding in the direction of *Il conformista*).

myth of his (and the town's) resistance to the regime.[36] Athos junior encounters the bust by chance soon after his arrival in Sabbioneta, where he has come to trace his origins. At this first encounter with the statue, Athos seems to register and then ignore the statue; the film, however, introduces it to us by means of a close-up tilt shot, one that connotes and performs visual absorption and through whose agency we read the inscription on the plinth. This public sculpture – which we find castrated, its eyes whited out, in its second, more sustained appearance in the film – is a blind marker to the metaphorical labyrinth of Athos senior's and the town Tara's secret. But it is also a too-obvious marker of the film's Oedipal mythographic allusions, just as Sabbioneta's too-obvious axial planning would, as I said before, prevent one from ever being truly lost inside its *cinquecento* walls.

This condensed and displaced view of this bust in *La luna*, in which it now appears as Bernini's obelisk, is difficult to parse. A solution, however partial or suggestive, to the shot's enigma could be assayed by looking into the history of the obelisk itself, now the object of so many postcards, the site of so many tourist photographs. It is the last work completed by Bernini for Pope Alexander VII and was completed in 1667.[37] This whimsically serious urban marker, shown in Figure 4.2 on p. 91, compresses and combines a long history of iconography. The elephant, symbol of divine wisdom, carries, seemingly effortlessly, the weight of profane, pagan, Egyptian illumination. Unlike the obelisks erected by Pope Sixtus V at Piazza del Popolo, Santa Trinità dei Monti, San Giovanni in Laterano and elsewhere, this obelisk is less a marker of spatial orientation and urban form (it is not the terminus of a long-distance prospect), and more a monument to the personality of Pope Alexander VII, who, with more limited means than his *cinquecento* predecessor, sought to enrich, organize and make grand Rome's urban core, in particular a number of areas in neighbourhoods near Santa Maria sopra Minerva, some of which serve as principal locations for *La luna*. Rather than a marker of 'mappable' urban space, then, we might see the elephant and obelisk as more a cryptic image, meant to locate us ideologically and to initiate the observer, who already knows *where* she is, into some knowledge of *what* this *where* is. The elephant is a monument to selfhood, one that sought to glorify the achievements of Alexander VII's papacy.[38] Whether singling it out, as Bertolucci does, in this, his 'return' to Rome is meant to appropriate to himself this self-aggrandisement in serious or mocking terms remains an open question.

The shot-counter-shot sequence that registers the encounter between the bust of Athos Magnani senior and his living son is handled in circular panning movements. And yet the object of the camera's vision is also always moving, so that the movement is doubled. In *La luna*, Bertolucci (and Vittorio Storaro, the film's cinematographer) cannot make Bernini's elephant and obelisk move, the way he could make move his prop of a statue move in *Strategia di ragno*. So the camera in *La luna* traces its own, lonely arabesque, as it slides across the surface of the intransigent real.

Figure 4.2: Bernini's elephant in *La luna* (nodding in the direction of *Strategia del ragno*): being too well-located in Rome (and in Bertolucci's work).

In the elliptical passage from the Janiculum to this obelisk and in the circular shot that glides around it, the editing loses us, or rather *disperses* us across Rome. But then no sooner does it do this than it knowingly gives us something known (a landmark in Rome, a landmark in Bertolucci's career): the film relocates us on the flattened, palimpsestic surface of the image of Rome's own palimpsestic surfaces. Being lost; being too found: here two experiences of the postmodern seem to be laminated onto the same transparent support.[39]

This sequence ends on the Piazza Cavour, which Bertolucci explains he chose because it was one of those 'bits of Rome' featured in the film that were 'not the usual ones', and that would produce a sense of Joe's having been 'completely uprooted' and of Rome as 'an exotic, colonial city'.[40] While it's quite likely that few casual tourists will have fetishized Piazza Cavour's Palazzo della Giustizia, many will have changed buses there (in front of the Cinema Adriano); most will have at least glimpsed it from the north end of the Via Zanardelli (and wondered, perhaps, what is *that*?). If the intention were, really and truly, to offer us another Rome, why then does the film go to such lengths to let us know (twice) that Caterina and Joe live in a flat in central Rome's most celebrated and fetishized baroque piazza, the Piazza Santa Maria della Pace?

Our movement towards this tiny but immensely famous piazza commences in a scene set at one of the former limits of the city (now comfortably in the centre): the Porta Settimiana, a gate in the Aurelian Wall in Trastevere. In a rooftop terraced restaurant, Caterina has thrown Joe a hapless birthday party that Joe sullenly submits himself to before sneaking off to shoot heroin with Arianna. In a generational inversion of the primal scene, Caterina discovers them and forces Joe to leave the party. Joe, either out of genuine neophyte confusion or due to a heroin-induced stupor, seems not quite to know which way is which and walks north along the Via della Lungara, not the fastest way back to where we will soon learn he and his mother live. A series of elliptical edits, very much like those analysed above that initiate us into the film's negotiation of Roman urban space, takes us first somewhat further along the Lungara (already past the Villa Farnesina), then back along the Lungotevere, towards and across the Ponte Sisto (more familiar), then to the Piazza Farnese (all too familiar, and where the camera revolves around Caterina much as it did the elephant and obelisk) and finally, to Santa Maria della Pace, which we see via a travelling shot that does not include the characters (though we do seem to hear their footsteps). Even with Joe's initial wrong turn, this is a plausible route home, from the relative semi-obscurity of the Porta Settimiana to the legibility of Santa Maria della Pace (see Figure 4.3 on p. 93).

While Bernini's elephant and obelisk was one of the last projects executed under Alexander VII's papacy, the Piazza Santa Maria della Pace was the first. The church had strong Chigi associations[41] and was a significant place of worship for officers working in the law courts nearby.[42] When Alexander VII assumed

Figure 4.3: Santa Maria della Pace in *La luna*, next to Caterina's flat: a Rome that is too known?

the papacy, its facade was plain, and the street leading to the church, the Via della Pace, was only 7 m wide. There was no piazza as such in front of the church. Given that 'no one of social standing' 'could allow himself to be seen except in a coach',[43] the church's situation was less than ideal. Pietro da Cortona was charged with devising a plan for the renovation of the church and its surrounding space. His solution became one of the jewels of Roman baroque urban design. In addition to the construction of the church's novel facade, da Cortona's plan required the destruction of the Casa Santa (a home for indigent widows) on its left and shaved back the hospital attached to Santa Maria dell'Anima on its right.[44] The project, thus, participated in not only Rome's 'edification' but also in the city's constant cycle of *sventramento* and displacement.

The complex of the whole was meant to bring legibility and splendour to this little corner of the abitato, while also promoting the smoother circulation of horse-drawn traffic. While it is tempting to think of the whole of the complex in rather diminutive terms as a 'gem' of urban theatrical design, the plans were ambitious and at one time included the extension and straightening of the approach to the church all the way down the Via Parione to the Via del Governo Vecchio.[45] It was, in Richard Krautheimer's terms, 'a key element in what was to become Alexander's remapping of Rome'.[46] And as Jorgin Merz documents,

> The intention to create a unified scheme is underlined by the fact that Alexander VII drew up a legal document and placed an inscription on the wall of the palace to the left of the church to guarantee the preservation of the piazza in perpetuity.[47]

The church, in other words, would be exempted from the conditions that made possible its creation. Merz, whose interpretation of these interventions is somewhat more sharply worded than Krautheimer's, argues that Alexander 'was expressing his domination over the city by laying out Piazza S. Maria della Pace'.[48]

Like the shot of the elephant, here, Bertolucci deposits us in the too-familiar (a miniature Piazza San Pietro, the final design of which was overseen by the same pope). Not only is this a 'known' Rome, it is a Rome designed with knowing, mastery, imageability in mind – a Rome designed to correct the medieval, labyrinthine and illegible density of the abitato.[49] In other words, I am trying to suggest here that we entertain a productive alignment (or intersection?) of Bertolucci's too-knowing, too obvious auto-cinephilia and the appearance of a Rome that is also already seen, already known, one that has, in fact, always been predicated on its known-ness and on its giving to be known.

By contrast, if we think back to Bertolucci's first film, *La commare secca*, apart from a desultory visit to the Colosseum, the most remarkable and identifiable urban structure that this film pictures (repeatedly) is not a monument, but a piece of infrastructure, the Viadotto della Magliana, which connects Magliana with EUR on the other side of the Tiber. Of course, this semi-refusal of the centre was typical of Pasolini (Bertolucci's teacher), but also of Michelangelo

Antonioni, and was, moreover, a feature of neorealism's anti-touristic approach to shooting in Rome. Early on in *Accattone* (1961),[50] Pasolini's first film and one on which a young Bertolucci acted as director's assistant, we are teased by some remarkable and extended location shooting at the Ponte Sant'Angelo. This spectacular location succeeds the film's very first shots, taken in the unspectacular and, certainly for most spectators in 1961, nearly impossible-to-locate environs of Pigneto, a *borgata* south-east of the Esquiline, nestled inbetween the Via Prenestina to the north and the Via Casilina to the south. In moving, within the film's first few minutes, from suburban obscurity (Pigneto) to urban fame (the Ponte Sant'Angelo) Pasolini seems to be rehearsing the touristic gaze at Rome, one familiar to Italian and international filmgoers, and one that, following this scene, he will almost never repeat. The move from obscurity to legibility to obscurity (we return to the *borgate* following this scene at the Ponte Sant'Angelo) seems to be saying: let me show you what you think you want and what I refuse, henceforth, to grant you.[51] The withholding of familiar images of Rome's centre and the displacement to lesser-known areas in Rome's periphery are emblematic features of what we might call the 'modernist' phase of Italian art cinema in the early 1960s. Italian art cinema's modernism is characterized, we might say, by a love affair with Rome's periphery, not its centre.

La luna, then, stages a return to a Rome that isn't exactly a return, because it is a *turn* to a Rome that Bertolucci had mostly avoided in his earlier films shot in the city, especially in his first and most Pasolinian film, *La commare secca*. In *La luna* when Joe wanders off from the Piazza Santa Maria della Pace and into Testaccio in an opiate daze, he traces his course with a piece of chalk casually pressed to the surface of the walls he walks beneath. But there is no need for this Ariadnean thread, because we, in a sense, already know our way around. We, like Bertolucci, have been here before: in *Accattone*, whose eponymous protagonist dies just a couple hundred metres from the bar on Via Galvani (backed up against the Monte Testaccio) where we are not surprised to be hailed, along with Joe, by Accattone himself – that is, by an unnamed character played by the actor Sergio Citti, who is evidently still haunting the neighbourhood (Figure 4.4 on p. 96). Citti's character makes an awkward attempt at picking Joe up; Joe would rather imitate John Travolta's dance moves from *Saturday Night Fever* (1977) while the Bee Gees play on the bar's jukebox. Or else he would rather concentrate on consuming his gelato which Citti's character has bought him as a prelude to a seduction that does not take place.

There is no getting lost. Joe's chalk mark is a tautological sign of a Rome that is populated by its images of itself. Our problem will not consist in finding our way back, but in finding our way out – in finding something that we didn't already know. This is a film that is traversed (in Bertolucci's own words) by the perversity of the director's own auto-erotic cinephilia – which is both made manifest and grounded by a symmetrical and analogous topophilia, a cathexis of places that are themselves the objects and products of emplaced cathexes.

Figure 4.4: The re-appearance of Accattone (Sergio Citti) in *La luna*.

Then, of course, there is the film's story's perverse incestuous sexuality, in which mother and son refuse to move from the too-known precincts of Oedipal desire. Surely we would be foolish in hoping to find something new here. At the level of story and in its use of locations, the film literalizes an attachment to the same, to the known. In other words, it literalizes a condition of the *familiar*. But if we, as spectators, take pleasure in the sights of these well-known landmarks ('Ah, that's Santa Maria della Pace!'), then surely we risk – with Bertolucci, with Caterina – a dangerous perversion that we had better avoid.

The film might be seen to invoke something of a scrape with perversity like that described by Freud in 'The Uncanny' in which Freud finds himself '[s]trolling one hot summer afternoon through the empty and ... unfamiliar streets of a small Italian town', only to end up unintentionally in a red light district.[52] Despite his best efforts to flee from and avoid 'the narrow street' in which '[o]nly heavily made-up woman were to be seen at the windows of the little houses', Freud helplessly and unintentionally returns there twice more before finding his way back to the safety of a more salubrious piazza.[53] This anecdote's narration of the 'unintentional return'[54] traces an experience of an unfamiliar place becoming increasingly and unpleasantly familiar. More often Freud's examples of uncanniness elsewhere in the essay exhibit an experience in which something that was once familiar is experienced as unfamiliar. Freud's story of peripatetic urban uncanniness is slightly different (in that the unfamiliar is becoming too familiar rather than the other way round), but 'produce[s] the same feeling of helplessness' that the subject experiences in other uncanny episodes.[55] In *La luna*, as I have suggested, we are never as lost in Rome as Freud is in his small Italian town. However, the recurrence of so many familiar sights – whether these are urban landmarks or allusions to Bertolucci's earlier work – is upsetting, if only because we must confront the critical problem of what to do with so much familiarity, if we are not simply to write it off as critics like Kolker have done.

So much familiarity *is* a bit (maybe extravagantly) perverse; it would be useful, therefore, to consider the subject of perversion itself. Perversion is a mode of over-investment, of investment in the wrong thing. The fetishist, for instance, has taken too much pleasure in the wrong object (be that a foot, a pair of lips or one's own son). For the psychoanalyst and psychoanalytic theorist Robert Stoller, perversion is a technique, a method of overcoming: 'it is the reliving of actual historical sexual trauma', however, in the reliving, 'trauma is turned into pleasure, orgasm, victory'.[56] Trauma, for Stoller, thrives on risk, but not any real risk, rather what Stoller calls 'a *sense* of risk'. The risk cannot be too great. 'One can only have the impression of risk'.[57]

This sense of an intensely controlled repetition that carries with it a 'sense of risk' might sound a lot like Bertolucci's project in *La luna*. In fact, Kolker's suggestion that the purpose of the film's auto-citational poetics was to find a refuge from the 'trauma' of *1900* coincides strikingly with Stoller's thesis. I think this

account of perversion, however, might describe not only his auto-erotic fascination with his own oeuvre, but also the spatial logic, perhaps even the spatial
politics, of the film. This connection may then, finally, return us to the question
of postmodern Rome.

*

Just as Caterina cannot help but choose as an erotic object the object nearest to
hand (her son, the would-be centre of her world), so does *La luna* circle around
a series of monuments and places that are rather too convenient. Even our trips
to the places that are peripheral to the centre – like Testaccio, for instance – are
not in the periphery, per se. We might be forgiven, initially, for thinking that
Bertolucci has gone all *Roman Holiday* on us. But the decision to stick close to
the centre tells us another story.

According to historian Vittorio Vidotto, between 1951 and 1997, the
population of the *centro storico* declined from 424,000 to 142,000.[58] Today, the
number of full-time inhabitants in the *centro storico* (roughly the area between
the Piazza del Popolo and the Campidoglio) is only 50,000, around half the
number of tourists staying in this same area at any one time.[59] The profitability
of charging higher rents for flats in the city centre or converting palazzi into
alberghi that would accommodate the demands of the tourist industry has
forced out the traditional inhabitants of the centre (with the exception, perhaps,
of some wealthy families who have managed to keep hold of flats in a handful
of noble *palazzi* still owned privately). This process has been as effective as the
sventramenti in displacing Romans from the *centro storico*.

Whereas, in Pasolini's cinema, the truth content of his historical moment
lay at Rome's periphery, by the time of *La luna*, the best evidence of what had
become of Rome lay instead back in the fetishized centre: its large flats occupied
by wealthy Americans, its piazzas given over to trade in recreational drugs. Even
the appearance of Trastevere and Testaccio – those semi-peripheries – remind
us, from our vantage point today, that they are exactly the areas that would, in
the decade following *La luna*'s release, be colonized by gentrifying sons and
daughters of the middle classes who were no longer able to afford flats in Rome's
centre. Whereas the sites of Rome's centre had been exploited by Hollywood
productions of the 1950s, the subsequent products of Italian art cinema (again,
chiefly Pasolini and Antonioni in their extension and renovation of a project
initiated by neorealism) forced us to look elsewhere. This looking – or forcing
others to look – had a politics. It was the periphery that told the true story of
what Rome (and the world) had become. That lesson (one which Bertolucci also
enjoined us to observe in *La commare secca*) had long been observed by the late
1970s. The periphery-as-image no longer, perhaps, promised the same explana-

tory, revelatory power. And besides which, having become image and become naturalized as such, the periphery's status (as image) entered into an exchange economy. The political programme that claimed the periphery for our attention also had the effect of claiming the periphery *for Rome*. Having been a site of alterity, it had become only an assimilable part of the whole. If the periphery were no longer peripheral, perhaps the centre becomes the place from which to observe what Rome had to teach about its – and our – place in the world.

The politics of looking and living in the centre were inflected, moreover, by other forces in 1979, the year of *La luna*'s release. This moment inherited and extended the post-war period's radical proliferation of images, during which Rome circulated as an image and was increasingly overpopulated by images (in inverse proportion to the actual human population living of Rome's centre). *La luna* also appears at the end of the *anni di piombo*. The Italian state's response to this violence was a radical escalation of surveillance of public and private spaces.[60] Meanwhile, the increased trade in illegal drugs, which serves in *La luna* as a major symbolic and plot device, was the cause of even more policing of Rome's streets. (*La luna*, by the way, chooses to associate, rather romantically, the trade in heroin with the seemingly lone, entrepreneurial Arab boy, Mustafa, omitting, of course, the major role played by the Mafia in the drug trade).

Moreover, this is exactly the period at which Italian television, as a result of its gradual deregulation in the mid-to-late 1970s and early 1980s, came to adopt the 'mixed system' of public and private broadcasting that ushered in a situation and a period in which, as Michael Siegel has written, 'television began to saturate the rhythms of everyday life.'[61] Broadcast hours doubled, and twenty-four-hour-a-day programming was introduced for the first time. In Siegel's words: 'The consumerist images of mass culture, via television's vast and ever increasing reach, were moving beyond the screen to become a part of the very fabric of the everyday life – of its practices and objects, its concepts and experiences.'[62] The circulation of images in and through Rome (and the rest of Italy) meant that a regime of images threatens to absorb the city (and absorb it as an image), as it absorbs the attention of its spectators.

In other words, *La luna*'s spectacular turn to Rome's centre is not an empty, pictorial, apolitical gesture, a masturbatory love-fest. This turn is, I want to suggest, the very grounds of the film's purchase on the historical, on the political. However, it is the film's perverse core – its inability to do more than repeat itself, to re-enact the formal mastery of Bertolucci's triumphs, its near refusal to locate itself anywhere or picture anything but the centre – it is this *centrally* perverse attitude towards Rome and towards image-making that make visible this politics. In this sense, it does do something new; it is not *Accattone*, nor is it *Roman Holiday*.

*

Bertolucci's auto-cinephilia, his self-love, his re-mastering of the trauma of the career low embodied by *1900*'s commercial and critical failure (if we are to follow Kolker's perhaps dubious account), is also predicated on an implicitly (unconsciously) acknowledged topophilia. Knowing where we are, taking delight in our knowledge ('I know that place!') is a perhaps a defense against, or mastery of something that does go missing as the 1970s give way to the 1980s. Bertolucci would comment, perhaps ironically (that is, both meaning and not meaning what he says): 'Really, I think the goal of a movie is pleasure. That's why I say the eighties look much better than the seventies'.[63] Perhaps we should – probably going against Bertolucci's intended meaning – place the accent on the word 'look'. Perhaps 'looking better' does not merely signify depoliticization *tout court*, so much as it signifies the need to reassess the way in which politics will have to reckon with the look, with looking.

It is Rome's too-imageable spaces – not in and of themselves, but as they appear at a particular historical moment – that give us the evidence of the historical conditions that characterized Rome in the year that *La luna* was released. Thus, while Kolker can only see *La luna*'s perverse auto-cinephilia as hopelessly apolitical, perhaps we can look to the film's topophilia as a means of understanding the political charge of its cinephilia. The problem here – in postmodernism, or in postmodern Rome – is not just that everything is simulation, is not actually lived, or lived directly (pace Debord, pace Baudrillard, et al.), but that everything feels like it has *been lived already*, and thus presents itself to us not as 'just' an image, *but as an after-image*. And yet at the same time, we are still left with the material fact of Rome, of a place, with some sort of life (who are we to say if it is 'real' or not?) still being lived, or enacted inside its contours. Maybe this is the real terror of the postmodern, whether in Rome, or elsewhere: of never being lost, of being too placed, too imaged, of being too known, of knowing too much.

In closing I want submit as evidence the all-too-knowing pleasure of the film scholar, knowing that too much has been said, and therefore looking to the places of films and the emplacement of film, hoping that here, in the irreducible material real of the film, maybe the film's evidence (of place) will be evidence of something forgotten, or else something not forgotten because not yet said, because not yet known, only looked at, but not seen.

5 MARCUS AURELIUS AND THE ARA PACIS: NOTES ON THE NOTION OF 'ORIGIN' IN CONTEMPORARY ROME

Filippo Trentin

Premise

In April 2008, Rome's administrative election ratified the victory of the right-wing coalition after almost twenty years of left-wing administration. This political change brought two Roman monuments to the centre of public attention. Soon after his election, the new mayor stated: 'we'll move Richard Meier's museum for the Ara Pacis from Rome's city centre to its periphery.' The structure to which he was referring, an 'international-style' building composed of glass, travertine marble and white concrete, had been blamed for having 'disfigured' the historical centre of Rome. At the same time, a group of his supporters were celebrating the victory of his election atop the replica of the Marcus Aurelius equestrian statue located at the centre of Piazza del Campidoglio, the heart of Rome's political power for more than 2,000 years. The continued public attention on these two landmarks of 'classical' Rome proves their enduring legacy even after a millenary history. How can one define these public sentiments? Is this an attachment to a tradition that is still relevant to our times, or is it simply a conventional and traditionalist gesture lacking any deeper meaning?

Introduction

The two global cities that are most often taken as the quintessential postmodern locations are the phantasmagorical urban imageries of Los Angeles and Las Vegas. In an effort to visualize the images of the postmodern cityscape, we would indeed probably call to mind the stylistic pastiche of Las Vegas, in which visitors can walk around reproductions of the Venetian Grand Canal, of the Parisian Tour Eiffel or of the Manhattan skyline. Or perhaps we would envision a network of commercial strips scattered with billboards, parking lots and casinos, intersecting one another in a harmonic chaos, which Robert Venturi once defined as 'the commercial vernacular' of America.[1] Or, following Fredric Jameson, we could linger on the glassy and glossy surface of the Westin Bonaventure hotel in Los Angeles, with its depthlessness and its aspiration 'to being a total space, a complete world, a kind of miniature city'.[2] Or, stretching our view to the whole urban form of the postmodern city, forcing gaze beyond human limits, alongside geographer Edward Soja we might attempt to imagine it in terms of a 'sprawling, decentred, polymorphic, and centrifugal metropolis, a nebulous galaxy of suburbs in search of a city'.[3] Pushing our imagination even further, we could even enter into the timeless space of that utopic–dystopic Los Angeles which is Disneyland, the perfect allegory of hyperreality, according to Jean Baudrillard,[4] or as Marc Augé has argued, the quintessential 'non-space'.[5]

Synthesizing all these perspectives, the space of postmodernity would emerge as a surface of scattered billboards, glassy buildings and replicas of famous monuments connected to each other by a network of junctions that run around a sprawling and decentred urbanscape, surrounded by amusement parks. A scenery in which the subject, using Jameson's words, 'has lost its capacity actively to extend its pretensions and re-tensions across the temporal manifold and to organize its past and future into coherent experience'.[6] Thus, in the postmodern cityscape the diachrony of time appears to have been overtaken by the synchrony of space, and the phallic verticality typical of modernity (New York), is replaced by a vacuous horizontality (Los Angeles).

No place would at first sight appear more remote from this imagined, prototypical postmodern cityscape than Rome. With its history displayed in an exceptional series of monuments ranging from its ancient classical ruins, its medieval churches, Renaissance roads and Baroque fountains, to its modern restructuring; from its 'piemontesizzazione' at the end of the nineteenth century to its fascist rationalization in the hands of Mussolini and Piacentini during the 1920s and 1930s, to the uncontrolled growth of its peripheries in the second half of the twentieth century, Rome displays in its image an inevitable, diachronic flow of history. In Rome, pastiche – the stylistic language of the postmodern, for theorists such as Jameson and Linda Hutcheon – seems to not have taken root, and the symbolic value of its classical tradition appears as the cultural dominant of its long architectural history.

In Rome, the weight of tradition and the paradigmatic legacy of the past continue to haunt the present, and while the city's modern development produced a rigid detachment between its centre and its periphery, its postmodern course appears to have radicalized this dynamic. If on the one hand Rome's periphery has expanded in an immense sprawl which goes from the Bracciano Lake to Ostia and to the Castelli Romani, on the other hand its historical centre basically remained untouched from the end of the Second World War until now. This decision, which was taken as a reaction to the traumatic destruction of entire neighborhoods by the fascist regime (the so-called *sventramenti*, or evisceration) during the 1920s and 1930s, seems to have preserved Rome's city centre from any postmodern mutation. Thus, the *topos* of Rome as the 'eternal' city which circulated in Western cultural imagination for centuries (think, for example, of the Grand Tour travellers and intellectuals such as Gogol, Stendhal or Goethe) has been able to survive until contemporary times.[7]

In an attempt to challenge this *topos*, my thesis here is that, far from being the expression of eternal values stemming from a fixed classical *origin*, the ancient stones, statues and monuments which are disseminated around Rome's historical centre are undergoing a change of meaning which responds to an essentially post-modern mutation of the concept of history. Michel Foucault splits the concept of origin into two different meanings: (1) origin intended as an immobile and pure beginning which usually follows the perception of its fall in the linear flow of time (the German *Ursprung*); (2) origin intended as the onset point which produces 'a profusion of entangled events' in the reticular flowing of history (the German *Herkunft*).[8] Here I draw on Foucault in order to investigate the way in which classical relics perform history and produce space in the cityscape of con-temporary Rome. I will do so through an analysis of two classical monuments which have been in the spotlight in the last two decades: the equestrian statue of Marcus Aurelius and the Ara Pacis Augustae. Through an 'archeological' reading (in Foucault's sense) of these monuments and a critical discussion of their recep-tion, I will attempt to capture the symptoms of a specifically postmodern attitude towards time and history from a Roman perspective. I will argue that the 'muse-umification' of the Marcus Aurelius equestrian statue, and the new museum for the Ara Pacis designed by Richard Meier exemplify two opposite yet complemen-tary tendencies within Rome's postmodernity. That is, the necessity to fabricate a myth of origin which leads to the 'simulacrization' of tradition, as exemplified by the Marcus Aurelius case; and the capacity to re-activate a channel of com-munication with tradition via the deconstruction of the myth of the origin, as demonstrated by the construction of the new museum for the Ara Pacis. It goes without saying that for Rome this myth of the origin is constituted by the attach-ment to its classical tradition as origin of its cultural identity.

The Replica of the Marcus Aurelius Statue:
Simulacrization of the 'Classical'

On 20 April 1979, during the most dramatic years of the so-called *anni di piombo* – less than a year after the kidnap and murder of the president of the Christian Democratic party, Aldo Moro, and one year before a bomb exploded at Bologna's train station killing eighty people – a bomb made of 4 kg of trinitro-toluene exploded on the Capitoline Hill in Rome. Fortunately no people were killed or injured, as a strong thunderstorm had prevented tourists and passers-by from stopping in the square at the time of the detonation. The explosion damaged some of the buildings in the square – specifically, the gate of the *Palazzo Senatorio*, the arch and the column located at the left of the palace and the marble pedestal of the equestrian statue of Marcus Aurelius at the centre of the square. Traumatized by the possibility of losing the 'symbol' of Rome's civic value, the Italian cultural authorities decided 'to provide a screening' – using medical terminology – of the statue of Marcus Aurelius in order to test its state of conservation. On 17 January 1981 the statue was moved from the square to the San Michele Institute for restoration, also in Rome.[9] The screening consisted of a series of chemical, radioscopic, ultrasonic and climatic tests, as well as surveys on the technique of construction, the alloy and the thickness of the metals of the statue. The results showed that the statue had been relatively unaffected by corrosive phenomena caused by to its open-air position, but rather more substantially by the inexorable aging of an object with almost 2,000 years of history. For this reason, local and national cultural authorities decided to move it into a museum.[10] On 11 April 1990 the statue of Marcus Aurelius was returned to the Capitoline Hill, and placed this time inside a small room on the ground floor of the Capitoline Museums instead of its previous position in the centre of the Piazza del Campidoglio. It found its final arrangement in 2005 inside a new room designed by the architect Carlo Aymonino (see Figure 5.1 on p. 105). However, on 15 April 1997 a perfect copy of the Marcus Aurelius was positioned at the centre of the square in order to fill the void left by the 'hospitalization' and the subsequent museification of the original one (see Figure 5.2 on p. 106). The copy was the product of an enormous deployment of financial and technological means, with final cost reaching two billion lire (more than one million euro). This was necessary to cover the expenses of 'cloning' the original, via an innovative photogrammetric model as the basis for the casting of the new statue.

Statements from Walter Veltroni, contemporary Italian minister of culture, and from then Mayor of Rome, Francesco Rutelli, shed light on the reasons behind the decision to mould a perfect copy of the ancient statue. For the former, placing the copy in the Capitol was necessary so as to 'restituire alla sua dimensione una piazza finora mutilata' (reinstate the form of a mutilated square); while for the latter,

questa è la migliore copia possible ... Io certo mantengo l'opzione della città perché possa tornare l'originale. Ma ci sono dubbi sulla sua salvaguardia, a cui si aggiungono altri rischi in un momento in cui certi protagonismi demenziali spingono a lanciare sassi. È enorme la responsabilità di porre all'aperto il bronzo più antico del mondo.[11]

(this is the best possible replica ... Of course, I do not exclude the possibility that the original statue can be relocated in the square, but there are still doubts about its preservation, and moreover its protection currently, in a moment when certain demented individuals have taken to inane acts of vandalism. Putting in the open the most ancient bronze statue in the world is an enormous responsibility.)

Figure 5.1: The original Marcus Aurelius equestrian statue inside the Capitoline Museums. Reproduced with the kind permission of Andrea Puggioni.

Figure 5.2: The replica of the Marcus Aurelius equestrian statue at the centre of the Piazza del Campidoglio. Photograph: Ireneo Alessi. Reproduced with the kind permission of the photographer.

However, not all reactions were positive. According to the former director of the Central Institute for Restoration, 'Questa faccenda del Marco Aurelio è uno scandalo ... per il decoro, il buon gusto, la cultura, il nome di Roma' (the Marcus Aurelius affair is a scandal ... an attack on decency, good taste and culture, the name of Rome),[12] and, for the supervisor to Rome's archeological heritage, 'la copia che c'è ora è pessima: io dico che non si può fare un mondo 6 nto, le cose devono stare al loro posto', (the copy is of a terrible quality ... I say that we should never make a fake world, things have to stay in their own place).[13]

As these reactions demonstrate, behind the scenes of the Marcus Aurelius case, on the one hand the 'conservative innovators' emerged, those who supported the museification of the statue in order to preserve it from the passing of time, and attempted to make it immortal for the future generations. On the other hand the 'guardians of tradition' materialized, those willing to keep the statue in its 'original' location in order to preserve the genius loci of the Piazza del Campidoglio and the authenticity of the statue itself. However, despite their formal differences, both the 'conservative innovators' and the 'guardians of tradition' seem to share the same perspective towards history and tradition. What is shared by the conservatives' fear of losing the statue and the guardians' sense of horror for the copy is an obsessive attachment to a monument perceived as the immobile root of a fixed 'Roman' identity. The deployment of financial and technological means in order to musealize and then replicate the statue betrays the signals of an intimate fear of losing something which goes beyond the statue itself, and that rather has something to do with the symbolic value of a tradition which is considered as the binding root of a fixed tradition. If, as Foucault says, *Ursprung* indicates a notion of origin as 'an attempt to capture the exact essence of things, their purest possibilities, and their careful protected identities',[14] then both the 'guardians' and the 'conservatives' – with their attachment to a purist, ideal and immobile conception of origin – seem to share a common conception of history as *Ursprung*. In the linear flow of history, what has to be protected is the preservation of the origin, an attitude which appears confirmed by the fact that a few months after the arrangement of the Marcus Aurelius copy in Piazza del Campidoglio, Rome's cultural ministry decided to replace a series of ancient statues located in its public parks with their copies, in order to save them from acts of vandalism.[15]

However, as the history of the Marcus Aurelius statue itself demonstrates, monuments do not stay 'in their own place' eternally. The meaning of any work of art is not fixed in a specific point in time, but it constantly mutates throughout history. The apparent immutability of statues conceals the fluid metamorphosis of their symbolic meaning.

*

The bronze statue representing the emperor Marcus Aurelius riding a horse was probably erected in order to commemorate Rome's victory over the Germans in AD 172, or that over the Marcomanni and Sarmatians in AD 176.[16] The victorious emperor wears a *tunica* and the senatorial shoes, and originally under the horse's right leg was the figure of a kneeling barbarian, though this was lost during the Middle Ages. As Julia Lenagham argues: '[t]he image expresses Marcus Aurelius' military prowess (understood from the emperor's dress and the defeated barbarian) and his firm political control (the restrained horse and gesture), obtained and sustained through military strength.'[17] In Marcus Aurelius's face, ancient Roman citizens could probably read values such as steadiness, rectitude, pietas and morality.

The statue was preserved during the fall of the Empire and the first period of the Middle Ages only because it was generally believed that it represented Constantine, the first Christian emperor, and not Marcus Aurelius, a pagan emperor. Documents from the eighth century shows that the statue was located in front of the Basilica of St John Lateran; papal acts from the tenth century shows that it was used to hang traitors to the popes.[18] At that time the Lateran was the seat of the Catholic Church, and consequently the epicentre of medieval Rome. During this time, no precise iconographical interpretations of the statue were accepted by the papacy, which preferred to interpret it as a testimony of the continuity between the universalism of the Empire and that of the Catholic Church.[19]

During the fifteenth and sixteenth centuries, Rome underwent a series of major urban changes. After the end of the exile of the Curia to Avignon (1305–78), Pope Nicholas V (1397–1455) began the new urban planning of the Catholic capital, which he hoped would bring back Rome to the splendour of its glorious past. This project was supported by almost every subsequent pope, above all Pius II and Julius II, and continued throughout the Renaissance.[20] In this period the focal point of Rome was the Vatican, where Pope Nicholas V decided to concentrate all his resources to renovate it as the Papal Residence after the Avignon schism. A few decades later, Pope Paul III (1468–1549) also focused on the Capitol (the location of the Ancient Roman Senate), in order to exhibit the Catholic influence over the civic centre of the city. For this reason, he appointed Michelangelo to design a new project for the site.

On 18 January 1538 the Marcus Aurelius statue was moved from the Lateran to the Capitol. The decision was taken by Pope Paul III under the supervision of Michelangelo, who designed the new pedestal for the statue and projected the restoration of the Capitol square. The second displacement of the statue demonstrates how, during the Renaissance, it no longer represented its classical meaning of steadiness and military prowess, nor its medieval sense of civic justice, but had acquired a new symbolical meaning. As Lucilla De Lachenal argues:

il gesto dal lui compiuto con la mano destra (ed interpretato – com'è noto – per tutto il Medioevo quale simbolo di comando e di autorità suprema ed assoluta, perfino sul piano giuridico e giudiziario) veniva a stemperarsi – di riflesso – in un segno di clemenza, sino a diventare addirittura quasi simbolo foriero di pace.[21]

(his right-hand gesture (interpreted – as has been noted – during the entire Middle Ages as a symbol of supreme and absolute command and authority, even in the juridical and judiciary way) became toned down – as a historical reflex – in to a sign of mercy, thus almost becoming a sign of peace').

In the Renaissance reading of the statue, the figure of the ancient emperor represented a Christian champion of virtues, and his right arm was no longer pointed against a barbarian enemy, but was rather a sign of the eloquence and domination of the papacy over the civic dreams of the city's independence from the Church. As Cristopher Frommel argues, Michelangelo's reading of the Marcus Aurelius 'stressed the hierarchical nature of papal power ... It marked the architectural defeat of republican autonomy'.[22]

In light of this new interpretation, it is the aspect of the figure itself which appears to metamorphose into something different. Michelangelo's choice to make the statue the focal point of the square is an extremely important gesture that physically depicts the centrality reacquired by 'classical' art in the sixteenth century. Michelangelo's Piazza del Campidoglio is able to embody the primary characteristics of the Renaissance: namely, a central perspective built through the re-interpretation of classical style. The legacy of classical tradition, embodied by the Marcus Aurelius statue, was thus re-elaborated in a 'modern' way, and the rearrangement of the statue can be considered the very symbol of Renaissance Rome.

*

The history of the Marcus Aurelius statue seems to suggest at least four paradigm shifts, or better, four different mutations of the statue itself. The erection of the statue, which occurred sometime between AD 172 and 176, symbolized the submission of barbarians to the power of Rome and the military authority of the emperor himself. The first movement of the statue, from an unknown location of the Roman Forum to the Lateran, aimed to stress the continuity between the universalism of Imperial Rome and that of the Christian city. Its second movement, from the Lateran to the Capitol, aimed to mirror the primacy of Renaissance Rome over classical Rome. The identity of the emperor was not important at all for either Pope Paul III or Michelangelo, and they decided to put the statue in a position where it could look forward towards the new Christian centre of Rome, the Vatican, while at the same time symbolically showing its back to the centre of the ancient city, the Forum. Finally, the museification of the statue and the decision to place a replica of it at the centre of the piazza determines the postmodern mutation of the statue into its own simulacrum. Its contemporary meaning appears indeed to be the fetishization of a past era, considered otherwise to be the fixed origin of the city's contemporary identity. Hence, the fourth and final displacement of the statue from the Capitol square to the museum appears to testify to the postmodern paradigm shift of the statue, which Jean Baudrillard vividly described as 'extermination by museumification'.[23] In this regard, to understand more clearly the way in which the Marcus Aurelius statue has been framed by Rome's cultural administrators – origin as fixed root – it is useful to return briefly to Baudrillard's discourse.

By looking at the interventions on two other ancient relics, namely the Lascaux caves in southern France and the mummy of Rameses II in Egypt, the French philosopher shed light on a certain (postmodern) attitude towards time and history. After their discovery in 1940, the Lascaux caves – which contain mural drawings dated back to the Upper Paleolithic era – were closed to the public in 1963. Twenty years later, in 1983, a perfect replica of the caves was inaugurated at a 200 m distance from the original ones. The aim was to preserve the originals from the decay brought about by the continuous influx of tourists. According to Baudrillard, such a duplication leads to the loss of the original as well. The case of the Lascaux caves illustrates a process of de-semanticization that can be read onto the Marcus Aurelius statue, too, which similarly undergoes a loss of meaning:

> It is in this way, under the pretext of saving the original, that the caves of Lascaux have been forbidden to visitors and an exact replica constructed 500 metres away, so that everyone can see them (you glance through a peephole at the real grotto and then visit the reconstituted whole). It is possible that the very memory of the original caves will fade in the mind of future generations, but from now on there is no longer any difference: the duplication is sufficient to render both artificial.[24]

A similar fear of losing a sign of our historical origin is illustrated for Baudrillard by the decision to move the mummy of Rameses II into El Cairo's Egyptian museum, an event which happened in 1974. For the philosopher, the internalization of the mummy from its tomb to the museum represents the mummy's passage from its original symbolic meaning, based on ancient Egypt's medical and religious precepts, to our own symbolic order, based on scientism:

> For mummies do not decay because of worms: they die from being transplanted from a prolonged symbolic order, which is master over death and putrescence, on to an order of history, science, and museums – our own, which is no longer master over anything, since it only knows how to condemn its predecessors to death and putrescence and their subsequent resuscitation by science ... We need a visible past, a visible continuum, a visible myth of origin to reassure us as to our ends, since ultimately we have never believed in them.[25]

Thus, overlapping with both the duplication of the Lascaux cave and with the museification of Rameses II's mummy, the Marcus Aurelius case appears to signal the simulacrization of Rome's ancient relics. The contemporary museification of the statue attests to the lethal condemnation of the 'classical' form, while its subsequent duplication in the square testifies to the accomplished change of semantic meaning of classicism. Today the statue seems indeed to have mutated its meaning, from vernacular Roman style to empty quotation of a past that is important to visualize because it remains as the only proof of a fixed and immobile concept of historical origin (*Ursprung*). This paradigm shift seems also to reveal the re-appropriation of the statue claimed by the political supporters of the mayor elected in 2008 as gestures mimicking the survival of this conservative idea of the classical past. There is no spirit in the statue because its duplication does not seem able to generate any further meaning than blind attachment to a crystallized idea of tradition. As these examples demonstrate, the work of art which follows the postmodern paradigm of the simulacrum undergoes a semantic shift from representation to simulation. It is not a mere discourse of copy and original, but the overturning of the original into something else. The word originality is no longer relevant, it is a category from another historical age. The original Marcus Aurelius statue is a *simulacrum* as well as the copy. The gesture of replicating the 'classical' equestrian statue is a demonstration of its incapacity to signify anything outside of itself, and this gesture appears as a simulation that renders both, the copy and the original, as *simulacra*.

The New Museum for the Ara Pacis Augustae: Deconstruction of the 'Classical'

The inauguration of the new Museum for the Ara Pacis, which occurred on 21 April 2006, represented an extremely important moment for Rome. The building, a parallelepiped made of steel, glass and travertine and designed by Richard Meier, was indeed – and still remains – the first building erected in Rome's historical centre since the 1940s (see Figure 5.3 on p. 112). Perhaps because of this highly symbolic meaning, the controversies and the disputes provoked by this project have no precedents, even in the usually animated Italian cultural–political debate. Before and after its inauguration architects, art historians, political leaders, Roman citizens and cultural authorities participated in an engaged and often aggressive debate on the purposefulness of this monument.

These judgments ranged from the incitement of students to the statement 'mettere una bomba sotto l'Ara Pacis' (put a bomb under the Ara Pacis)[26] of a politician and art critique who also publicly burnt a small-scale model of the same building, to the electoral promise of the prospective mayor 'volerla smontare e trasferire in periferia' (to disassemble it and move it to the periphery) if elected.[27]

Figure 5.3: The Museum for the Ara Pacis, designed by Richard Meier. Photograph: Ireneo Alessi. Reproduced with the kind permission of the photographer.

This is a statement which not only demonstrates a visceral hatred for the new monument, but also states the candidate's hierarchical subordination of the periphery to the centre. Other declarations, among which that of then Prime Minister Silvio Berlusconi, highlighted the 'monstrosity of the monument', describing it as 'a rape', 'a horror', an 'ecomonster', 'una ferita nel centro storico di Roma' (a wound in Rome's historical city centre)[28] or compared it to a 'pompa di benzina texana' (Texan petrol station).[29] According to these critics, the new architectural structure not only ruined the memory of a monument of classical Rome such as the Ara Pacis, but it had also led to the destruction of Vittorio Ballio Morpurgo's shell for the monument, commissioned by Mussolini and erected in 1938, which for many architects and urbanists was a perfect example of Italian rationalism. Some other commentators focused on the fact that Richard Meier, being American, should have never been allowed to design a contemporary building in central Rome because of his lack of knowledge of the city's history.[30]

What all these allegations seem symptomatically to reveal to us, again, is the existence of an unresolved problem concerning the relationship between past and present in contemporary Rome. Despite the intrinsic value of the building itself, something which will be more thoroughly analysed later on, such furious and outraged reactions to the erection of a modern building appear to be the symptoms of a Roman phobia for the 'impurity' of the modern, in that it does not 'respect' the precepts of the city's classical tradition. Just as the decision to replicate the ancient statue of Marcus Aurelius and of 'hospitalizing' the original statue in a museum was made in the name of Rome's tradition, the fuming reactions to the erection of this modern building are pronounced in the name of a fixed and immutable notion of the city's history.

The angry calls for the demolition of Meier's museum, the irritated requests to move it from the centre to the periphery and the invalidation of Meier's project for ethnical reasons – the scandal of an American architect designing something in Rome! – are cries of intolerance which suggest the entry of Meier's Museum of the Ara Pacis into a grey area located at the margins of dominion. That is, the exceptional place where all the untolerated minorities are pushed. For the guardians of classical Rome, what is worth safeguarding is a pure idea of tradition, something which Meier's building is supposed to have put under threat. However, as in the case of the Marcus Aurelius statue, an 'archaeological' history of this monument supports the argument that no historical relic is the pure testimony of an idealized tradition, and that meaning is something which mutates throughout time – using Foucault's distinction, origin as *Herkunft*.

*

The Ara Pacis Augustae was built in 9 BC in order to celebrate the acquired state of peace of the Empire, after Augustus had established definitive control over the provinces of Gaul and Spain. The altar was originally located in the *Campus Martius*, a sacred area where fifteen years earlier the emperor had already built his Mausoleum. As Augustus himself wrote in his *Res Gestae*:

> When I victoriously came back to Rome from our battles in Gaul and Spain, dur-
> ing the time when Tiberius Nero and Publius Quintilius were consuls, the Senate
> ordered that it was necessary to celebrate our victories. Thus an altar was erected in
> order to celebrate the new state of Peace. The Senate decided to put it in the Campus
> Martius and ordered that magistrates, ministers and Vestal virgins celebrated sacri-
> fices in it every year.[31]

After Augustus's death, the project of constructing a holy area dedicated to the memory of the emperor began to teeter and fade away, eventually leading to the submergence of the altar, which was buried under metres of detritus for almost 2,000 years. As Paola Favretto argues, a major contribution to the loss of the monument was the political and cultural distance felt by the new generations in relation to Augustus's era.[32] In short, in the eyes of the Roman citizens who succeeded Augustus, the reason for the altar's construction, its floral decorations and its figures transmitting a sense of Olympic peace, were something difficult to make sense of and to understand, as they were perceived as symbols of a 'Golden Age' of the Roman Empire which was progressively fading away.[33]

The first relocation of some fragments of the altar occurred in 1859, after res-toration works of a building located in Piazza San Lorenzo in Lucina. However, due to the difficulties of excavation and to the lack of interest of the papacy for these relics, no further action was attempted. The German archeologist Friedrich von Duhn was the first to recognize these relics as the remnants of the Augustus altar in 1879. As a consequence of this clamorous discovery the international scientific community pressured the Italian government to attempt a recovery of the relics. However, the lack of financial means of the young country postponed the beginning of the recovery until 1903, when a new inspection took place. It was only in 1937, during the years of Mussolini's most intense effort to revive the pomp of the Roman Empire for propagandistic reasons, that the relics of the Ara Pacis started to be retrieved.

The occasion was given by the imminent celebration of the bi-millenary anni-versary of the birth of Augustus, which in the eyes of Mussolini should have ratified the rebirth of the ancient Empire in fascist Italy. The dictator decided to locate the new monument in the nearby Piazza Augusto Imperatore and appointed the architect Vittorio Ballio Morpurgo to design a project for the altar's cover. Mor-purgo was asked to follow Mussolini's idea to 'revive' the classical antiquities in order to ideologically support the fascist empire. Given that the Augustan year would have expired on 23 September 1938, the architect had less than a year to project, design and realize the cover for the altar. For this reason, and due to the lack of financial resources of the fascist state, the cover ended up being a simplified version of the original plan, while the fragments of the altar were assembled with concrete and placed on the top of a copy of the original base.

In this new arrangement, fascism revealed its despotic and demagogic nature: to make space for the new square, Mussolini decided to demolish more than 120 buildings in the adjacent area, compelling the former residents to move to the sub-urbs.[34] Morpurgo's shell in reality appears very distant from the best examples of Italian rationalism such as Adalberto Libera's design for the Post Office in Rome (1932) or Giuseppe Capponi's building for the Faculty of Botanic and Chemistry at 'La Sapienza' University (1932–5); it rather synthesizes the most rhetorical characteristics of fascist architecture: pompous rationalism, authoritarianism and demagogic use of tradition. The fascist pavilion endured for sixty years but for many reasons, above all the inadequate structure of the old shell built by Morpurgo, in 1996 the mayor of Rome decided to hire Richard Meier in order to plan a new museum for the altar. As mentioned before, the inauguration took place on 21 April 2006, and represented the first important architectural intervention on the surface of central Rome since the age of Mussolini.

The choice to appoint Richard Meier as the designer of the new shell illustrates the efforts of Rome's public administration to address the development of the contemporary city on the democratic side of the rationalist tradition. Meier's project for the Ara Pacis Museum seems to reveal the attempt to deconstruct the idea of classical tradition as pure origin. While the altar remains the material fulcrum of the museum itself, Meier's building appears ultimately to propose the idea of a decentred space in which the ancient altar is the pretext for an urban intervention aiming at creating a more osmotic and fluid relationship with the surrounding space and with Rome's classical tradition. First, the materials used by the American architect – porphyry, travertine but also plaster, steel and glass – are a mixture of traditionally Roman and contemporary hi-tech materials. Second, the form of the building is a modular intersection between a de-structured classical temple and a modernist building in the style of Le Corbusier. Third, it communicates with the square around it through the use of white plaster, and with the two eighteenth-century churches in front of its entrance through the construction of a square which faces them. Moreover, it illuminates the ancient altar with natural light and makes it visible from both sides of the cover through two transparent glass windows. Finally, the fountain positioned at the left of the square aims to recall the old Ripetta harbour, which was located in front of the actual monument and was demolished at the beginning of the twentieth century during the first wave of Rome's modernization. In other words, Meier's museum for the Ara Pacis appears to re-elaborate Rome's classical legacy in a creative and playful way, treating it as the symbol of a fluid and multi-stable identity (*Herkunft*) rather than as pure origin (*Ursprung*). Thanks to Meier's museum for the Ara Pacis, we are able to visualize an interstice which breaks into the empty centre of Rome, while at the same time challenging the historicist notion of history which supports this paradigm.

Meier's interpretation of the Ara Pacis seems thus to move from Morpurgo's authoritarian rhetoric to an organic dialogue with time and space. The apparent decision to side with Mussolini in keeping the altar under a cover – an event which signals the regime's interpretation of classical tradition as immobile origin of a phantomatic Roman identity – is accompanied, in Meier's structure, by the attempt to deconstruct the idea of classical tradition as pure origin. If Morpurgo's cover put at the centre of attention the altar as symbol of a fabricated and immobile origin, Meier's project announces a desire to rethink this fixed concept. It appears to re-elaborate Rome's classical legacy in a creative and playful way, treating it as the onset moment of *Herkunft* rather than *Ursprung*.

The dialectical movement from the structured form of Morpurgo to the genealogically deconstructed one operated by Meier seems thus to suggest a movement from what Foucault described as 'Traditional History' to 'Effective History':

> Traditional History ... is given to a contemplation of distances and heights; the noblest periods, the highest forms, the most abstract ideas, the purest individualities ... Effective history, on the other hand, shortens its vision to those things nearest to it ... it unearths periods of decadence and if it chances upon lofty epochs, it is with the suspicion – not vindictive but joyous – of finding a barbarous and shameful confusion.[35]

If Morpurgo's building proposed a conservative idea of history in which classical antiquity is considered the founding moment of a glorious past which has continuously to be re-evoked in its purest form, Meier's project seems able to propose a creative engagement with history thanks to its deconstruction of the past. Thus, in light of Meier's building, classical tradition is liberated by the chains of an oppressive and rhetorical conception of history, in that its decentralization seems to invalidate the universal tendency of 'classical' art. In this respect, the re-elaboration of the 'classical' operated by Meier's building appears to stage history and tradition in terms of 'the rhythmic form' of Western culture rather than as the fixed root of an immobile idea of origin.[36]

Conclusion

In conclusion, the space of postmodern Rome appears opposite and at the same complementary to that of Las Vegas and Los Angeles. While the idea of centre is still dominant both in spatial and historical terms – and this appears to distance Rome from the quintessential American postmodern cityscape – the way in which history is staged and performed suggests a tendency towards compression and a certain difficulty to order past and present into a coherent experience, which ultimately characterizes Rome as a postmodern location. In Rome, the legacy of 'classical' tradition has reached a crossroads where two different postmodern tendencies emerge. They are the crystallization of historical time into a purist idea of origin – the *simulacrization* of tradition into its mythology – and the re-elaboration of tradition into a different shape – its deconstruction.

In light of this, we can thus attempt to formulate an answer to the questions that arise regarding the meaning of the persistent legacy of classical tradition in contemporary Rome. The concept of history stemming from the simulacrization of the Marcus Aurelius statue and the reactions which followed the inauguration of Meier's building seem indeed to signal the persistence of a traditionalist and purist idea of origin in contemporary Rome, which corresponds to Foucault's definition of it as *Ursprung*. However, while the way in which the statue has been arranged demonstrates a historicist attitude towards the past which ratifies a condemnation to death of the creative spirit of classical style, the new arrangement for Augustus's altar indicates a possible way to re-interpret tradition via its deconstruction. The perfect reproduction of the classical form in the Marcus Aurelius copy and the fear of losing the original statue are indeed counterbalanced, in Meier's project, by the attempt to 'translate' the classical tradition into a shape which re-activates a channel of communication between past and present (*Herkunft*). In this reading the concepts of *Ursprung* and *Herkunft* acquire a deep importance, as opposite ways of dealing with the 'weight' of the past. In Rome this weight is heavy, and contemporary interventions on the ancient surface of this city are forced to respect the city's classical past, yet the incapacity to deconstruct a pure and idealized concept of origin essentially risks, and will continue to risk, marring Rome's future.

6 A POSTMODERN GAZE ON THE GASOMETER

Keala Jewell

A colossal piece of industrial architecture, Rome's 'gasometro' (gas holder, or gasometer) stands out as a dissonant element on a skyline of historic cupolas and ancient ruins – the emblems of a long-lived and powerful urban civilization. Sited adjacent to the Tiber River, beyond the Aurelian Walls in the Ostiense area, its height, girth and location endow this geometric cage with an iconic status in a cityscape devoid by law of skyscrapers (see Figure 6.1 on p. 120). Built in 1937, the circular metal tower has been invested, in the context of the larger gas factory or in depictions of the isolated structure, with evolving cultural significations: photographic, artistic, filmic and literary representations of this Roman landmark have detailed its birth, expansion, fall into ruin. The latter occured when the edifice no longer stored gas and lost its mechanical functional by the mid-1960s. By the 1990s, urban renewal in the Ostiense zone endowed the building with new symbolic meanings as it came to stand metonymically for the 'ex-industrial' area and era. The building established itself firmly in the collective memory of architects and Roman citizens alike as a sign of 'the contradictions that characterized urban development'.[1] This chapter focuses on a selection of emblematic paintings and literary works in order to bring into focus the gasometer's iconic status while at the same time it asks two questions central to a longitudinal approach. First, what features and meanings might be forgotten or bracketed in evolving representations? Second, how is this familiar structure worked into cultural discourses that produce contemporary perceptions of, or gazes on, industrial Rome?

Given the context of a volume on postmodern Rome, I will also be asking how we might attach postmodernity to this landmark. The gasometer does not automatically have an obvious status as a postmodern cultural product, first because of its high modernist origins, and, second, because Rome itself is hard to peg as a global mega-metropolis organized into a postmodern template. The city is monument dense, and the gasometer has itself become a monument.

Figure 6.1: The Gasometer in Ostiense, Rome. © Francesca Brocchetta – Fotolia.com

Nonetheless, the edifice can symbolize Rome's new directions in the twenty-first century, when the city is no longer identified as either classical or ecclesiastical. Fernando Proietti wrote in *Il Corriere della Sera* of a 'simbolo di una Roma sospesa tra passato e presente' ('symbol of a Rome suspended between past and present').[2] The complex meanings attached to the building circulate along sometimes surprising and multiple pathways. During the festival of La Notte Bianca ('Sleepless Night') in 2006, a Roman artist, Angelo Bonello, transformed the circular tower's grid into a stunning light show. He used kilometres of optical fibre cable to create a monumental, flashing piece of environmental art, the 'Luxometro'. That festival makes the city's treasures freely accessible to its citizenry for twenty-four hours. So boldly featured, the gasometer demonstrated Rome's openness to international-style urban innovations. Mayor Walter Veltroni presided over the Luxometro's triumphal opening moments and spoke fondly of an 'industrial structure' with a unique beauty. In the same breath, he linked it to the local citizenry as 'part of its historical identity'.[3]

The Ostiense neighbourhood that was once home to industrial workers, vendors working in the marketplaces and artisans, has over the past two decades become a fairly pluralized zone, hospitable to renovation and to new inhabitants that include immigrants as well as students and professionals. The Roma III University has led a not uncontroversial urban renewal project that is concomitant with a commercialization and museumification of the Ostiense area.[4] Defunct industrial sites and the old main market have become university or exhibition spaces – most notably with the old electrical plant that now houses statuary holdings of the Capitoline Museums in the spectacular Museo Montemartini and with the Macro Museum of modern art in the old slaughterhouse buildings. The gasometer is enmeshed in this large-scale urban planning effort in a part of Rome that was selected for urban renewal promoted by both the Rutelli and Veltroni mayoral administrations and evident in Rome's 'Piano regolatore generale' of 2003.[5] In this outlook, 'historic' Rome has to include what is beyond the walls, and Ostiense has been a testing ground for the policy that tries to forge ties between neighbourhoods within and without the walls.[6] That said, a large portion of the gasworks compound is currently an eco-monster loaded with contaminants that will be difficult and expensive to remove. The integration of ex-industrial sites into the city fabric is fraught with obstacles, some of a cultural rather than physical nature.

The gasometer's cultural meanings in fact have shifted several times since its erection in 1937: first it was an icon of industry in the 1930s, next it had an intermediate status as the signifier of dying industry once river transport was abandoned along with the river port, and, finally, it took on the sense of a post-industrial icon. Each historical layer of representations does distinctive cultural work and participates in the negotiation of a sense of 'Romanness'. These representations with their differing histories can enter into conflict, and they do not necessarily support unitary 'Roman' identificatory processes; they may support divisions. A postmodern gaze on the gasometer shows that the transmission of the cultural meaning of 'modernity' is not a process that unfolds in a linear way to provide a clear sense of some self-updating of Romanness over time. A weave of representations can, however, give us a sense of how Rome's limited industrial past works its way into postmodern identifications.

Origins: The 1930s

The gasworks compound grew up in the Ostiense area on the east Tiber bank, near its city port, early in the twentieth century. The gas-metering tower is contained within a larger facility for manufacturing city gas that dates originally to 1910 and was designed by Ulderico Bencivenga.[7] The compound eventually came to include four separate gasometers. The factory grounds were from the beginning a small city unto itself, with rail lines and aerial transport systems, extensive processing and storage areas, silos, cranes and docking stations on the

Tiber – though not all of this is still visible. The compound was part of urban development that included the Magazzini Generali (warehouses), Mercati Generali (central marketplace) and several other factories. This industrial area slowly became more integrated into the city during its general expansion in the interwar years. Ostiense, a relatively far-flung and unbuilt zone, provided room for expansion in the direction of the sea and commerce and was serviced by a railway line. The area opens out along the direction of the fascist era 'Via del Mare' to Ostia and was linked to commerce along the river – a crucial means of transport when there was no trucking.[8] The tallest gasometer (114 m) was the last of four to go up and is the one that carries the weight of symbolization into the future. Built during the fascist drive for industrialization and modernization, the airy structure was once the support of an enormous storage tank that was part of the manufacturing of coal gas for domestic and municipal distribution. The telescoping tank was filled up with fresh gas produced on a twenty-four hour cycle so that the flexible storage container for the gas would expand vertically up the metal tower overnight and by day's end the flexible tank would have been empty, and would have sunk onto the horizon, leaving only the frame tower visible. This constant movement provided a spectacle of action. Cooking gas flowed out to all the connected stoves in the city. Finally, instead of having to build a fire to make your morning coffee, you could flick on the city gas.

The gasometer was specifically, we must note, part of fascist policy that pushed for economic and political gains from the energy industry.[9] The gas factory, 'nero e pulsante' (black and pulsing), provided vivid evidence of fascist progress.[10] Fascism promised increased wealth and comfortable modernity for the masses that used gas and benefitted from illumination of the city. The energy push was not, however, unchallenged even from within fascist quarters.[11] The energy sector was in the later 1930s the subject of policy strife over 'autarchy', the drive to make Italy self-sufficient in terms of its resources. Mussolini declared his new policy in 1936 during the Ethiopian War. Coal had to be imported, however, to make coal gas. Therefore this kind of gas production would not have conformed to the principles of independence from foreign energy sources. Despite this, coal continued to be heavily imported, and the fires kept burning.[12]

The gas factory, surrounded by walls, underwent technological enhancements and enlargement in a part of the city that also harboured displaced populations from urban demolitions in the historical centre of Rome during fascist years, for example La Garbatella. The dislocations were part of urban planning in the 1930s and set out in the *Piano Regolatore* (urban master plan) of 1931. In terms of social policy related to industry, urbanization and population displacement, the growing numbers of gas workers were organized into a company community with material and social connections to the energy enterprise. Distinct measures to foster a sense of unity among the 'gasisti' were adopted. The grounds contained housing and a small church where, for instance, children of staff would celebrate first communions.[13] A space of social belonging countered the uprooting of populations from downtown. The Ostiense area demonstrated how the fascist state might favourably reorganize the city's social fabric. The city governments from Unification forward, along with the Ecclesiastical hierarchy, had resisted the industrialization of the city in part because of a reluctance to foster the growth of a potential socialist presence, of workers ready to revolt. The Garbatella area, along with the older Testaccio neighbourhood, became a positive example of a working class not connected to manufacturing but instead to service-related industries.

Painterly Views on the Gasometro

Roberto Melli painted the gasometer and its surroundings as an emblem of a distinctly fascist-era 'terza Roma', (third Rome) (see Figure 6.2). Completed in 1938, this work of art shows us that the structure was immediately empowered to signify. The painting illustrates what Fran Tonkiss has observed about cities: 'Urban space provides a stage for an official geography of authority as well as for the mobilization

Figure 6.2: *Il gazometro a San Paolo* by Roberto Melli (1938). Reproduced by gracious permission of INA Assitalia S.p.A.

of alternative politics.'[14] In this case, official geography commands the viewpoint. Melli, importantly, wrote an art column for the fascist-leaning *Quadrivio* (a journal that, starting in 1934, used anti-Jewish and 'anti-international' rhetoric that later was turned against Melli himself). The gaze onto the cityscape in the painting is from slightly above the rooftops in order to feature a broad horizon. The industrial, commercial area expands into the distance. Melli positions the gasometer strategically at dead centre. Multiple, circular smokestacks and numerous low buildings appear as ancillary forms to the main attraction at eye-level. Industrial machinery is clearly active, with the visible storage tank half full on its daily cycle of inflation and deflation. We witness industrial productivity in action in the curling, grey smoke that cuts diagonally across the sky. The smoke is light and breezy, and not dark as in factory paintings by Umberto Boccioni and Mario Sironi. Melli prefers a cohesive perspective over the fractured spatialities of early futurist painting (in pre-war years). The gasometer towers over a neat, rectangular grid of medium-sized, commercial buildings viewed close-up. Mathematical perspective reigns. The represented space gives a clear geometry, a proper demarcation of buildings and a proper hierarchy of spaces with industry – in the figure of the gasometer – on top. The low end of the tall edifice sits exactly on the horizon of the city in order to foreground a vertical monumentality. The exposed metal gridwork of the support tower creates a functional, criss-cross pattern over a blue sky. If not the ideal Renaissance city so familiar to us in the Italian painterly tradition, this piece of city is idealized and Italianate in ways that surely are meant to evoke an illustrious artistic inheritance. Melli had links to the 'Scuola Romana' in terms of his 'tonal' style, in which colouring was a distinctive element of composition. Following fascist architectural styling for a 'Roman' look, we see a modern Rome that does not appear to be overly distant or different from the ancient city's characteristic styles and colours – with its light-toned marble arches and earthy brickwork. Melli's city resembles antiquity even if there is no representation of the ruins of the ancient city per se on the canvas.[15] While it is true that industrial Ostiense looks new, productive and dominating, it is not being presented as totally different from the ancient city.

Another artist, Renzo Vespignani, offered a quite different gaze on the gasometer. Vespignani painted the subject many times, and his works demonstrate that Melli's city portrait was not uncontested. Tensions inherent in reading the urban site were evident, in fact, from the start. Public opinion was reluctant to see the tower as majestic instead of monstrous. Archival documents at Italgas give an inventory of critical views that led to building delays, with one simply saying that the structure's dimensions are 'imbarazzanti' ('embarrassing').[16] And a large number of literary and artistic texts represent the edifice negatively, providing evidence of critical outlooks on the modernization of Rome. Vespignani's *Periferia con gasometro* (Periphery with Gasometer, see Figure 6.3 on p. 125), painted in 1946, takes this approach. Interestingly, Vespignani was one of the

Figure 6.3: *Periferia con gasometro* by Renzo Vespignani (1946). © DACS 2013.

founders in 1956 of *Città Aperta*, a publication concerned with urban culture. In his painting, we can quickly read the cityscape as outskirts not only because of the title but also because windows crowd into a tight pattern that stretches visually across a number of eight-story buildings. Romans called these 'grattacieli' ('skyscrapers'). The gasometer structure does not appear as particularly Roman, Italian, productive or planned. The view is from street level but the block of buildings is spatially remote and isolated from the viewer. The empty space at the canvas front signals the presence of the street, but the block seems to float in an undefined yellowish haze. The painted surface seems to flow around the buildings. There is no mathematical perspective and nothing volumetric about the architecture of the buildings. They look two-dimensional and inhospitable. The right side of the gasometer lines up exactly with the edge of the block of buildings to create one long, black line on the canvas from the road up into the sky. Vespignani's composition subsumes the tower into the city block. Smokeless, the structure's functionality disappears just as the gas service goes unnoticed. Vespignani destabilizes Melli's view of the gasometer as industrial and monumental. It is not an emblem of industrial power and progress, nor does it function to anchor a Roman identity in that way. There is no 'Roman' colouring, no marble and brick. The colours are nearly expressionist. Thick paint of an expansive blue-grey palette appears in the proliferation of small, square windows. The repetition of forms and colours is dominant, and architectural detail is absent. Vespignani declares the un-Roman quality of his city painting in the following words:

> Ho sempre dipinto una città priva di lineamenti storici, la periferia, il villaggio univer-sale e claustrofobico che riassumeva tutte le città: Roma uguale ad Amburgo, Parigi, Napoli, Berlino. Nebulosa di esistenze minime e criminali, un mondo inaccessibile.[17]

> (I have always painted a city lacking historical lineaments: the outskirts, the universal and suffocating village that summed up all cities. Rome is equal to Hamburg, Paris, Naples, or Berlin, each place a nebula of minimal and criminal existences, an inacces-sible world.)

Although at the time that the painting was executed Vespignani clearly chose not to make his gasometro 'Roman', many decades later his paintings did come to be considered symbols of Rome. The irony of this appropriation is evident in a description we read in a press release from the owner of *Periferia con gasometro*, the Banca Nazionale del Lavoro:

> Singolare fu la scelta di Vespignani che elesse a simbolo della Roma del dopoguerra il Gasometro, oggi uno dei luoghi più movimentati della Capitale, allora desolato e sconosciuto.

> (Vespignani made the unique choice to raise the gasometer – today one of the capi-tal's liveliest areas but at that time desolate and unfamiliar – to the level of symbol of post-war Rome.)[18]

As we know, the gasometer was far from 'unfamiliar'. The Ostiense area was bombed during the war, so the adjective 'desolation' may be apt historically, but the gas compound was fully functional and necessary to the city's economy, and it was visible from around the city when Vespignani painted it. Only when the gas factory ceased its main functions in around 1965 would it begin to be in a sense 'unknown'. The statement from BNL that the gasometer is particularly a symbol of Rome flies in the face of Vespignani's statement that he paints a 'universal village'.

Pier Paolo Pasolini's Ostiense

If Melli evoked Rome in the context of the fascist recourse to a re-born Rome, and if Vespignani eschewed that in favour of a Rome at one with European city 'outskirts', the writer, poet and film director Pier Paolo Pasolini drew Rome's industrial area in Ostiense into his own distinct weave of representations. Paso-lini and Vespignani were like-minded observers of a newly modernizing Rome in post-war years. Both were specifically concerned with the socio-historical dilemmas facing the outlying city, and in this sense we could call them both 'neorealists'. The working class in industrial Ostiense was the subject of many neorealist works of literature, art and film, where the desperation of the poor is referenced and where Rome appears as far from beauteous, long-lived or ideal. In general, disparate encounters in these ex-industrial areas in these years (familiar from films such as *I soliti ignoti* (Big Deal on Madonna Street, 1958), *Il ferroviere* (The Railroader, 1956), *Un giorno in pretura* (A Day in Court, 1953), *La banda degli onesti* (The Band of Honest Men, 1958), Alberto Moravia's *Racconti romani* (Roman Tales, 1954), etc. do the crucial work of growing, we might say, the new Romans, of identity-building in the post-war years. The gasometer figures large, coming to epitomize an impoverished, dirty, decaying Rome in some, if not all, of its representations. For example, in Moravia's *Racconti romani*, in the story 'Scherzi del caldo' (Hot Weather Pranks), a man who lives on Via Ostiense escapes from a large, irritable family during a hot afternoon. He travels along the Tiber, along a path 'tra campi brulicanti sparsi di mondezze' ('between swarming fields strewn with garbage') and comes upon the gasworks compound.[19] In Moravia's story, the gasometer appears as a dead, skeletal object cut off from any other city 'horizon':

Il Tevere ... pareva, anche per il colore fangoso, una fogna allo scoperto. Il gasometro che sembra uno scheletro rimasto da un incendio, gli altiforni delle officine del gas, le torri dei silos, le tubature dei serbatoi di petrolio, i tetti aguzzi della centrale termoelettrica chiudevano l'orizzonte così da far pensare di non essere a Roma ma in qualche città industriale del Nord.[20]

(Partly for its muddy colour, the Tiber looked like an open sewer. The gasometer, which looks like a skeleton left by a fire, the gas factory's furnaces, the towers of the silos, the pipes of the petroleum tanks, the pointed roofs of the thermal power station – all these closed off the horizon.)

Here Ostiense gathers scorching industrial and human wastes at once.

Pasolini echoes this depiction and factors it into his discourse on Roman identifications; these derive from the particular ways that his characters are made to occupy and circulate in city spaces – the *borgate* or industrial areas. Early Roman prose and poetry depict young men in troubled neighbourhoods caught in historical transformations, including the Ostiense area. Pasolini was turning his gaze to the cultural behaviours of disenfranchised groups in the context of destructive building speculation in post-war Rome.

It is important briefly to note the background to Pasolini's thinking. The Ostiense area suffered from bombing during the Second World War and then from unregulated growth. Pasolini's texts, and especially *Alì dagli occhi azzurri* (Blue-Eyed Alì, 1950–65), bring two strands of symbolization together and both of these mobilize Ostiense's population and territory. On the one hand, these works lament modernity's real destructiveness in terms of material and cultural social fabrics. The poverty of the Ostiense area, which Pasolini called 'periferia' (outskirts), is a historical fact of the 1950s, when the industrial activity of the area declined there and across the river on the Monteverdi side of the Tiber (a setting of Pasolini's novel *Ragazzi di vita* (Roman Ragazzi, 1955). Any compact industrial working class was dispersing. Farmers who had lost employment in rural areas came to populate Roman outskirts and struggled both economically and with urban identifications. On the other hand, Pasolini brings to the forefront positive associations of Ostiense's populace with the social history of Roman working classes before, during and after the fascist period and into the 1950s. The 'gasisti' in particular had maintained trade-based identifications. Pasolini depicted the variety of working people and artisans in the areas around the Protestant Cemetery in Ostiense in his poem, 'Le ceneri di Gramsci' (Gramsci's Ashes, 1957). This association of Ostiense with a Roman working class – in the Testaccio and Garbatella zones as well – provided the material for the author's characterizations in novels and films. John David Rhodes refers to this kind of weaving together of disparate strands, here the physical degradation of Ostiense mixed with a theme of resilient working people, as 'poetic syncretism'.[21]

Pasolini's treatment of Ostiense echoes Moravia's dark portrait in the parts of his writing that treat the losses stemming from negative modernizing trends in Rome. Like Moravia, Pasolini did not represent the gasometer as a stand-alone object with iconic status. It appears as one fixture of an urban texture. The landscape is often subsumed into a city that has become physically 'sick'. When the author depicts the striking new phase of the city's history, with its blight of highrise apartment buildings, he narrates illness and physiological decay:

> Dietro Monteverde tra le occhiaie quadrate dei più orribili palazzi d'Italia, piccole scatole da scarpe sull'orizzonte imbevuto di sporcizia, tramontava il sole, rosso come le guance di un tisico, e colpiva strappandolo dal buio di topaia o di carrozzone dei silos, del gasometro, delle gru, un ponte arancione. Di là dal Tevere di un verde marcio, col buio, cominciarono a scendere le mignotte.[22]

> (Behind Monteverde, the sun was setting over the dark, squaring eye-sockets of the most horrible palazzi in Italy, over shoeboxes sitting on a horizon sopping with garbage. As red as the cheeks of consumptive patients, the sun struck a bridge of orange and ripped it from a rat's den, from the parade of silos, the gasometer, and cranes. On the other side of a rotten-green Tiber, whores began to descend together with the night.)

Here the new part of the city is deathly: the whole built and natural landscape is being consumed, and the sinking sun can bring forth only a spectrum of fiery shades. The gasometer and industrial ruins are a rodent's abode. Importantly, though, city dwellers will travel there because the riverbanks provide a refuge despite the deathliness. The banks below the gas factory attract prostitutes and their clients to what Pasolini calls the 'teatro della grande Amata' (the thea-tre of great love-making).[23]

This way of depicting the city space and its occupants' ways of living in the city stems from the author's attention to circulation in its spaces, to people's move-ments within its hidden parts. Pasolini observes movements based on the kinds of work and commerce that unfold in city zones, and sex workers, their clients and their circle of companions are writ large. In this evening Ostiense, prostitution is not clearly relegated to particular buildings as other jobs may be, belonging to markets, factories or compounds. Sexual commerce at night is out of doors. Young city dwellers in Pasolini move constantly across the Tiber bridge to gather on both riverbanks in their daily and nightly dealings, some love-related and oth-ers subsistence-related. In this way, Pasolini sets up a 'rootless' cast of characters, unanchored in traditional workplaces and in familiar categories of class. In one story, for example, Ostiense boys have buried a cat alive and periodically return there to monitor its death throes over some days. This syntax of movement in space leaves out the central position of the block-long dwellings and warehouses of Melli's and Vespignani's paintings. Tonkiss uses Michel de Certeau's thought to describe how city dwellings create a 'grammar of movement' and, in de Certeau's formulation, 'gaps in the spatial continuum'.[24] The characters in Pasolini's stories and poems are irregular, they follow no established route; they are temporary and nocturnal, especially in the section 'Squarci di notti romane' (Lights of Roman Nights). These spaces, though fragmentary, are producing lives and identities even if they do not resemble those of the Testaccio, Garbatella and Ostiense work-ers of yore. Returning to Tonkiss's formulation, Pasolini deploys representations of urban space in a way that is functional to his imagining of a 'different' Roman population, one that suits 'the mobilization of alternative politics'.[25] Rhodes observes that Pasolini tints the Roman urban fabric with a paradoxical 'sublime' quality and that 'the periphery cannot be dismissed as merely ugly, or beneath contempt. Instead, we begin to see it as something awesome, of great importance, impossible to understand, perhaps, but also to ignore.'[26]

Poems of Deindustrialization[27]

Once we have recognized multiple ways in which the spaces of Ostiense and the gasometer are patterned in representations of them over many decades of history, we can begin to sort out how the gasometer came to be a multivalent emblem. An accumulation of representations over time contributes to growing numbers of assertions that Ostiense is inherently an ambivalent place.[28] In this section, I provide examples of the plenitude of outlooks in texts less well-known than Pasolini's, but ones that should be factored into the viewpoint that the gas-ometer carries multiplicitous cultural significations.

A text close in date to Vespignani's painting is Alfonso Gatto's dark-toned 'L'eco della sera' (Echo of the Evening). Gatto's gas-factory area, like Pasolini's and Moravia's, appears as wet, forlorn, nocturnal, in around 1950. The terrain is called, interestingly, 'countryside', because of a perspective over the unbuilt land along the riverbank with its scraggly bushes. The landscape appears as bereft of people. A play of light and vapours in the poem brings into visibility two disconnected 'evenings' in a landscape that stretches from the gasometer close by to the western horizon afar. Light from the setting sun better illuminates what is distant as compared to what is nearby, a darkened gas compound almost untouched by rays of light. One 'evening' on the sunlit western horizon lags behind the closer, darker one:

> Il gasometro nero è quasi azzurro
> del suo squallore o sa che è solo
> o sa che sola bagna la campagna
> una pioggia appassita.
> È già finita
> la sera e come nata dalla luce
> un'altra sera s'allontana dove ...
> ... dove sospesa la pioggia vapora
> sfumando nei colori.[29]

> (The black gasometer is nearly blue
> from its squalor and may know its loneliness
> or only know that withering rain
> bathes the countryside.
> The evening is spent
> and as though born of light
> another evening moves farther away where ...
> ... suspended rain evaporates
> blending into colourings.)

The structure here stands unbelonging, already as though posthuman, as a sentient, knowing ('sa') metallic soul in an insubstantial, vaporous world that seems beyond the industrial because of the immaterial qualities the poem invokes. The edifice appears as something tonal and dual because it is both black and blue in parts, according to the distribution of changing natural lighting. The author resists a semantic stabilization of the gasometer as something firm, stable, active, mechanical or industrial. It is as though the edifice has returned to a timelessness made only of vapours, light and darkness rather than matter. The gasometer is a fragment in a world of displaced lights and its dimensions seem to be outside urban space and time; it is beyond industry's causes and effects.

A prose poem in *I segni della corda* (The Signs of the Cord, 1952) by Toti Scialoja, a painter with early links to the 'Scuola Romana', also focuses on striking natural elements around the gasworks compound, again portraying a filthy river bank. It mixes these with 'squalor', to use Gatto's wording, in the form of a couple that embrace on the ground. Though post-industrial, in the sense that the gasometer appears bereft of its mechanical function, the poem gives us a distinctly unethereal, and even an anti-lyrical portrait. The short narrative follows characters promenading or embracing one another near the old river port under the gasworks compound with its overshadowing tower. We find a familiar dirty river zone, but this Ostiense locale is also distinctly chemical, and dangerous:

> L'enorme anfiteatro del gasometro arriva con la sua ombra fino a noi, fin quaggiù. E finalmente la tua saliva che sa di carbone, le tue gengive velate di un acido che disinfetta l'anima. Le coscie bianche scoperte sui tritumi, così abbaglianti sotto la luce chimica delle nuvole accese; il crepuscolo non discende più giù della gola, di lì fino al gorgoglio del fiume non si estrae che la luce, fin dove la tua pelle comprime, bagna la carta spiegazzata, s'intride d'animo, di rimorsi.
>
> Il cielo divenne vuoto sulle nostre teste mentre ci ferivamo il palato con la punta dell'erba serrata tra i denti, aizzata con la lingua a favore di un freddo disgusto.[30]

> (The enormous amphitheatre of the gasometer extends shadows toward us, right down here. Last, your saliva tasting of coal and your gums veiled with acid that disinfects the soul. White thighs uncovered, resting on detritus, dazzling beneath the chemical, switched-on clouds. Dusk can descend no further than down the throat; from that point on to the gurgling river nothing can be extracted but light, from there to where your skin compresses, bathes, crumpled paper soaked with animus, remorse.
>
> The sky emptied over our heads while we wounded our palates with the pointed ends of grass our teeth were clenching, urged on by a tongue favouring cold disgust.)

The structure is a gigantic shadow-maker that can obscure the pair. The piece depicts the gasometro not only as a place of cruel action, akin to a Roman 'amphitheatre', but also as a threatening force because it releases industrial waste, carbon and acid that permeate human bodies. Its darkness reaches over a couple who lie with faces pressed hard into grass, pollution and trash. The human body, 'white thighs', is exposed and hurt ('ci feriva'). The human limbs and body parts and the metallic edifice appear in one frame so that Scialoja's poem stabilizes the linkage of industrialization's dangers and human suffering. The gashouse is no monument. While different from Pasolini's cast of characters, Scialoja's lovers at the empty grounds of the defunct gasworks do occupy the city spaces in ways that mirror Pasolini's attention to the death of industrial commerce and the birth of cold sexual commerce in its place. Pleasure and a deathly danger of extinction are inextricable in the poem's Ostiense scene.

A short chapter in Edoardo Sanguineti's experimental poetic volume *Il giuoco dell'oca* also narrates sexual embraces in Ostiense, and the author increases sexual danger by depicting a rape. The author tells the story of fishermen with nets 'nella zona del gasometro' (in the gasometer zone). The group travels along the riverbanks and over the two bridges nearby, the railway overpass and 'Ponte dell'Industria'. They spot a girl swimming and floating in the Tiber current. She appears to be, in a surreal surprise, a mermaid: 'Sembra una mezza donna e un mezzo pesce, davvero' (She resembles a half-woman half-fish, truly).[31] They catch her between the two bridges with their nets, use a winch to bring her up, she dangles grotesquely for some time, and then they lay her on the bridge and cruelly 'take her': 'Ce la tiriamo fuori dalla rete, tutta agitata, la nostra sirena. Ce la posiamo lì, sopra al ponte. Ce la prendiamo per la coda, per prenderla.' (We pull her all-agitated to us out of the net, our siren. We place her there, on the bridge top for us. We take her tail for us, to take her.) This river section of Ostiense is a metaphorical hunting ground, a place of violation and the setting for an act of male domination. Sanguineti carefully patterns large-scale bridges into his representation, and they dwarf the mythic swimmer, who is outnumbered. In this 'mythic' tale, the lure of the siren of yore has no purchase, and she has no way to stop men from taking her. They land her on the 'Ponte dell'Industria' and rape her.

Sanguineti's landscape eschews the sense of the zone as industrially functional and active: the river scene is folded into a narrative of some length that does not particularly reference Ostiense's post-war urban history. Sanguineti seems not to share an interest in the evolving, historically-detailed Roman setting that Pasolini had portrayed and characterized with a class discourse. His fishermen might promenade along many an Italian river that passes through an urban locale in places of abandoned factories. A prominent interlocutor on the subject of deindustrialization, Sanguineti criticized historical trends to turn dead industrial areas into 'high culture' zones, for example in the port areas of Genova, his home city, making them into grounds where 'si smantellava tutto pur di metter su musei e centri di spettacolo' (where everything was torn down so that museums and centres for spectacles could go up).[32] Sanguineti also wrote an admiring preface to the novel *Fonderia Italghisa*, where Giuseppe Caliceti engages in a critique of the transformation of abandoned industrial structures into massive discotheques. Sanguineti, a proponent of avant-garde aesthetics, observed that a battle was waged throughout the twentieth century over the cultural value of industrial parts of Italian cities, and he did not want to see them either turned into inauthentic places or into wastelands of violence: 'La scoperta dei luoghi industriali è stata una vera battaglia estetica ... Marinetti lo capì subito, considerava più bella un'auto da corsa che la Nike di Samotracia' (The discovery of industrial places was a true aesthetic battle ... Marinetti understood this immediately; he thought a race car was more beautiful than the Nike of Samothrace).[33]

Post-Industrial Poetry: A Non-Classical Palimpsest

For a generation of poets writing in the 1990s or later, the abandonment of the gas factory is well behind them. A prose poem composed by Edoardo Albinati and set at the gas compound carries the title 'Iersera incontrai tre o quattro vestali' (Last night I encountered three or four vestal virgins).[34] As in Sanguineti, surreal mythical women people this zone. They are the 'vestal virgins' of Roman religious practice whose sacred fires are still burning in the present in the text, only as smoke rings rising to a ceiling. The poetry plays with light, once again, and the gasometer sits at the edge of the river and of the known, illuminated world where an observer goes roving:

> Il vagare tra fabbriche dismesse, barconi, rovine che alla lunga influiscono sul modo di vedere rendendolo pericolosamente orizzontale come se la terra fosse davvero piatta e oltre le luci australi del Gasometro si cascasse di sotto.[35]
>
> (Wandering among derelict factories, river boats and ruins that in the long run influence one's mode of vision, rendering it dangerously horizontal as though the earth really were flat and beyond the austral lights of the Gasometer one would fall below.)

Wandering near the abandoned factories affects the gaze ('modo di vedere') so that the world appears as flattened, 'horizontal', without depth. The old gasworks is both a place without historical layers and hyper-updated. Urban renewal is well underway, and identities in the area are undoubtedly shaken when improvements increase the area's wealth and real estate value. The poem features, in a cutting irony, a homeless person untouched by economic progress. He is washing his feet in an unlikely setting: he is eager for an impossible privacy within what we can suppose is the Ostiense quarter's nocturnal 'movida'. The vagrant berates companions who have surrounded him with parked motorcycles, and he utters in Roman dialect: 'E lascaime 'n pace, nun lo vedi che me sto a lava' i piedi?!' ('Leave me in peace. Don't you see I'm washing my feet?')[36] The incongruous directive and the reference to the social fact of homelessness clash with the classical image of vestal virgins of antiquity who have persisted in time to reach the postmodern epoch. The admixture makes Albinati's poem uniquely postmodern – if we define the term according to our volume's focus on a non-classical palimpsest.

An innovative long poem by Sara Ventroni, *Nel gasometro*, fully transforms the landmark almost as though she were following the instructions of theoreticians of postmodern urban spaces. In her *Nel gasometro*, the edifice is a unique, tough, rusty, imposing, long-lived net. It appears variously as a cranium, armour, a burial ground and an ecological disaster. It is also a stage set for the movements of ill-defined, post-human beings:

> Ma guarda quelli vestiti da astronauti, tre uomini e due donne.
> O forse tutte donne, forse non lo so.
> Hanno i muscoli artificiali e stanno sospesi ma non sembrano appesi:
> guarda se non sembrano ragni e che movimenti lenti,
> ci saranno dei fili di acciaio trasparenti o dipinti di smalto:
> si muovono come burattini.[37]

(Oh look at the people dressed like astronauts: three men and two women.
Or could they all be women; or maybe I know not what.
They have artificial muscles and are suspended but don't seem to hang:
look and see if they don't look like slow-moving spiders,
there must be transparent wires of steel or painted with enamel:
they move like puppets.)

The action of the spider-like creatures is untimely, slow. Their astronaut suits eclipse both gender and sexedness. The figures moving inside or on the wiry stage cannot be identified through their belonging to a neighbourhood or a job category or a gender. Ventroni draws on specific cultural genealogies, especially the Italian Metaphysical painters, Giorgio de Chirico, Alberto Savinio and Carlo Carrà, and on Marcel Duchamp. Alchemical themes (including androgyny) abound in Ventroni and can be seen in how she constantly foregrounds a union of upper and lower worlds. Throughout the poem, the upper gasometer structure is not depicted as distinctly separate from an underlying soil that suggests the 'putrefaction' of matter in a process of alchemical transformation. Timeless transformation alternates with distinctly historicizing tableaus in the poem, for instance of heavy work in the gas factory and the toil of transporting coal in barges along the Tiber. Ventroni also brings to the fore the deadly side of gas, its suffocating poison and its historical use in the Shoah. The juxtapositions in Ventroni's poem make the point that, to quote Edward Soja, in postmodern city spaces 'older polarities have not disappeared . . .(but) a much more polymorphous and fractured social geometry has taken shape'.[38]

An 'inhuman' aspect of this industrial, machine-driven zone of Rome takes on new, comic meanings in the poems of Valentino Zeichen. Writing in 2000, he provided a short, satirical piece on the gentrification of the Ostiense area. To Zeichen, the new Ostiense is trite and fake 'picturesque'. Its established position as the epitome of prestigious and trendy 'archeologia industriale' (industrial archaeology) is lampooned. Zeichen plays with the notion of the all-too-familiar industrial ruin in his 'Origine del gasometro' (Origin of the gasometer). In this minimalist tale, something drops out of the sky onto the horizon and lands perpendicular to the earth's surface. The object has come from a star ship. Artistic treasures around the landing zone are sucked up into the vessel through an elevator, and then the giants aboard take time for a nocturnal picnic. They leave detritus behind in the form of the Roman gashouse:

divenne soggetto pittoresco
per scadenti dipinti,
e daccapo riciclato
in un nuovo menù culturale:
l'archeologia industriale.[39]

(it became picturesque scenery
for cheap paintings,
and recycled again
through a new cultural menu:
industrial archaeology.)

The gasometer has turned into a joke. If aliens left the metal on the landscape, would this make it worthy of a 'nuovo menù culturale' bent on novelty? Zeichen begs the question: which old and rusted places obtain the status of postmodern icon? How much of that value is profit-driven?

A counter-example to Zeichen's ironic critique comes in the cinema of Ferzan Ozpetek, who invokes the gasometer prominently in his *Le fate ignoranti* (2001). There it is a landmark in a cityscape viewed from the terrace of a convivial group of friends – gay, straight, lesbian and transgender. It is the backdrop of dance parties, and it references the nightlife that characterizes the Ostiense area. There is nothing dangerous, deathly, forlorn or mythic about it. The gasometer simply puts Ozpetek in a better mood when he is downhearted: 'Mi basta fare due passi dalle parti del Gasometro per smaltire un'arrabbiatura.' ('All I need is a stroll in the direction of the Gasometer to rid myself of a fit of anger.')[40] The gasometer, detached from its industrial function, can now appear as an aesthetic object in a corner of Rome that has become hospitable because the people living there have created a zone of tolerance. Tilde Corsi, who produced Ozpetek's films, declared that the vitality of Ostiense has made it a 'new downtown'.[41]

The contrast between Zeichen's outlook and Ozpetek's outlook indicates a dilemma for the future of the gasworks compound and its four gashouses. Which buildings and spaces will be demolished or transformed, and which will remain as they now are, and for what reason? Some buildings have already taken on administrative uses, and some contaminants, tar and ammonia, have already been removed in small areas within the walls. Questions that have dogged the urban renewal of the Ostiense persist for the Italgas area. Alberto M. Racheli brings up an important question in part of an essay that asks how architects and urban planners could gather the past in their projects. Racheli warns that innovative approaches need not cancel history. He contrasts urban works that engage 'sedimentation' with works that practice 'erasure'. Drawing on Avishai Margalit, Racheli hopes that art will move culture forward 'attraverso una costante e appropriata sedimentazione della memoria che si traduca nel nuovo' (through a constant, appropriate sedimentation of memories that translates into something new).[42] One may wonder that if the compound is turned into a park, according to a current plan, how much more museumification the urban texture could absorb. What if the bulk of the gasworks infrastructure in disuse was to be demolished?[43] To accomplish that, Italgas, its owner, would need the proper permits to modify a landscape that has earned the status of a cultural good, and controversy would certainly hamper decisions. If not demolished, how does the current existing industrial wreckage, along with its contaminants, remain as part of a living city such as Rome? The Roman gasometer's story has yet to play itself out. And its multi-medial depictions are part of the texture of that tale.

7 ECCLESIASTICAL ICONS: DEFINING ROME THROUGH ARCHITECTURAL EXCHANGE

James Robertson

Introduction

This chapter will discuss the way in which many of the churches of the twentieth-century Roman suburbs can aid us in our reading of Rome today. This premise supports the notion of a pluralistic rather than a singular narrative; it is the suggestion of a narrative that has developed outside the Aurelian Walls and therefore peripherally to the gravitas of the traditionally held perspective of the Eternal City. It is hoped that such a reading will be reinforced in considering the sense of architectural dialogue or exchange present in the transition from one iconic architectural epoch to another, namely modernism to postmodernism. Crucially, the role of the Second Vatican Council (1962–5),[1] occurring at the interface of these two philosophies, will be taken into consideration. Specifically I will consider the importance and bearing of Vatican II on the future design philosophy and aesthetic of the Catholic Church in Rome and internationally, and consequently its ability to influence the way in which we read the evolution of this most enigmatic of cities will be foregrounded as an alternative trajectory to de facto postmodernism. Support of this thesis, with the aim of shedding light on ecclesiastical development, will be suggested throughout in several ways. First, I will allude to the depiction of Rome in key texts of the modernist cinema of early 1960s Italy.[2] The coincidence of these films with the eve of Vatican II can perhaps be seen as an ironic reflection of the need to address the way in which an increasingly disaffected post-war society was involved in the liturgy. Second, I will compare the city of Glasgow to Rome, where parallels can be drawn both in terms of its geographical expansion in the twentieth century, and in the building of new churches to serve the resultant new parishes and suburbs. This is largely through a connection with one of its most notable ecclesiastical architectural practices of the twentieth century, that of Gillespie, Kidd & Coia.[3]

The Paradox of Rome

It is not surprising that, like other European cities, during the twentieth century Rome began to overshoot its ancient boundaries as the population increased exponentially: at the reunification and creation of the Italian State in 1870 Rome had some 240,000 inhabitants; in 1900 this had reached 462,000 and by 1920 it was 690,000; in 1944 it had risen to over 1.5 million inhabitants; and by the 1970s it numbered almost 3 million, with a constant increase of around 60,000 people per year.[4] An influx to Rome, as to each of Italy's cities, accords with the country's modernization and a subsequent re-invigoration of a sense of national identity. The great post-war Italian film-makers captured and commented on this phenomenon, shown most poignantly in the new *borgate* (poor and often badly designed suburbs) around the periphery of Rome. The new quarters that were developed during the fascist regime and the post-war period, following the burgeoning population, were, by their nature, not subject to the same urban intensity as the ancient city, and so laid the foundations for an alternative architectural trajectory. Whilst areas planned out under Mussolini's fascist regime did not always have any direct dialogue with the ancient city, some, such as the new city planned for the 1941 (subsequently 1942)[5] World's Fair exhibition – the EUR[6] – still reflected a sense of urban formality and stateliness. Areas that later developed on the far periphery seemed to echo the postmodernist pluralistic tendency in cultural, social and urbanistic terms, as was very much mirrored in architecture and in the pedagogy of architecture in Rome in the post-war period. And in the wake of Vatican II, no longer did the regime exert its influence on architectural matters through such conduits as Marcello Piacentini; what evolved was much more fragmentary. However, the concept of architectural exchange could be said to be nascent in the link between the modern, the post-Vatican and the postmodern.

Internationally, other cities, including Glasgow, were subject to substantial population increases; in the west of Scotland this was largely brought about as a result of mass Irish immigration from the second half of the nineteenth century. A re-structuring of the original inner city parishes of Glasgow, increased numbers of Roman Catholics, and an outward-moving trend of sections of the populace, resulted in large new housing estates being planned and created on the peripheries of the city, particularly to the south and east. These vast new areas of housing of course needed to be sated spiritually. The church-building drive that had begun at the start of the 1930s, with the engagement of architect Jack Coia, continued until well after the changes instigated by Vatican II. The architectural interest, and in fact one of the major differences between Rome and Glasgow in this regard, lies in the fact that the new churches built for the Catholic Church in Glasgow constitute a substantial contribution by one firm both before *and* after Vatican II. In Rome during the rule of the regime, there was a smaller number of church architects – a number that then increased in the post-Vatican II period – and those that were employed were carefully chosen. After the fall of the fascist government in Italy and the end of the Second World War, a new kind of liberated architectural design began to take hold ecclesiastically, with a design tempo that was both referential and forward-looking.

The study of the churches of Rome, then, remains one of the best methods of charting not only the city's religious development, but also its architectural and cultural evolution over the course of the twentieth century. However, the transition from modernism to postmodernism as architectural styles, was by no means straightforward. First and foremost, the concept of modernism in its strictest sense sits uncomfortably with the sacred tradition of the Catholic Church,[7] and postmodernism then, in architectural terms, can be thought of less as a distinct movement than as a mood or approach which consciously aimed to contradict poorly conceived, modernist anti-historicist rhetoric. In other words, while the Catholic Church had always prided itself historically on being a patron of the arts, it had also been aware of the advantages provided by the benevolent modification of history in ecclesiastical architecture. Staunch modernist principles in the context of the twentieth century had sought to dispense with historical references and emphasize the importance of man, society and the community. What one does see, in both Rome and Glasgow, are attempts at church building which, although they often alluded to historical characteristics, were quite radical at the time that they were conceived (for example through the use of contemporary materials or modification of structural form). In both Rome and Glasgow, the mid-twentieth century witnessed a sort of purification of form, structure and adornment: a simplification of essence, where historical references were used. A useful example here is the reductivist classicism of the architecture of the fascist period. Postmodernism, ecclesiastically, is harder to define in this context.

The Vatican II sits on the threshold of a transition from one stylistic grouping to another, yet it would be inaccurate to say that this marked a definitive architectonic turning point in all cases. It did, however, modernize many of the traditional features of the Catholic Church in a succession of constitutions, some of which would impact on the physical design of new churches. In fact, it allowed pre-Vatican II, specifically modernist gestures to develop and come to fruition in the ensuing decades. Indeed, in some instances these churches would be better described as modern churches in a postmodern age. Liturgical revisions included a new emphasis on the total participation of the people in the act of worship, their active inclusion in the Eucharistic rite, and the delivery of the message in the vernacular tongue, with the priest *facing* the people. The constitutions also necessitated the moving forward of the altar toward the congregation. Not all of these changes necessarily coincided stylistically with postmodernism, though some certainly did, in particular the rearranging of seating to afford the congregation improved 'interaction' with the liturgy (in fact this had already begun to occur during the pre-Vatican II period). There was therefore a lack of clearly articulated transition from one to the other, with much stylistic 'to-ing and fro-ing', and, relatedly, a certain exchange of design philosophies. During this period then we can trace a pre-Vatican II anticipation of some of the resultant physical changes, as well as subsequently a maturation of modern architectural design, post-Vatican II, that extended into the postmodern era.

What sense can be made of the paradox of Rome, then? Through the suburbs around the centre of the historic city – strewn with the detritus of Rome's rich past – within this 'Pasolinian', heterogeneous periphery we can begin to map an overlay onto the notion of Rome as a clearly defined and singular city.[8] But the idea of architectural exchange is particularly rich and exciting, and indeed takes on an additional strand of significance given the ideological and quintessential image portrayed of the city, and especially the suburbs, cinematically. The study of this exchange moreover illustrates the way in which architectural internationalism appeared not to change Rome per se, instead influencing its development from the outside in; as well as the city's surprising receptiveness to external influence, in contrast to centuries of Rome as *the* master architectural narrative.

Pre-Vatican II

The seeds of modernism had, by the early twentieth century, germinated in the opportunity presented by Raimondo d'Aronco's contribution to the International Exhibition of Decorative Arts in Turin (1902). Though much criticized and not directly connected to the future trajectory of Italian modernism, it did crystallize the possibility of reacting to the vast burden and responsibility of Italian culture. A reconciling of innovative, international modern with a quintessentially national spirit was subsequently promulgated, and the idea of 'national' architecture was reinforced by Camillo Boito's call for an 'architecture of national expression'.[9]

In 1925, Italy once again had the opportunity to represent herself internationally, this time at the Exposition Internationale des Arts Décoratifs et Industriels Modernes, in Paris. This time, the architect Armando Brasini was chosen to design Italy's pavilion in a political move that sought to challenge the apparent simplicity of European modernism. He was chosen for his ability to re-interpret Italian architectural traditions in a liberal and modern way; and indeed he very much felt that the classical tradition in Italy was, at that point, still evolving.[10]

Two years previously in Rome, Brasini had begun his fantastically and unconventionally composed church of the Sacro Cuore Immacolato di Maria in Rome. This minor basilica was designed by Brasini in 1923, and completed by Marcello Piacentini before 1936. It is a breathtaking montage of semi-deconstructed, simplified classical motifs. It can be loosely arranged within a Neo-Classical canon, although this is undoubtedly tempered by the eclecticism and experimentalism of Brasini. The fervour, courage and sense of experimentation at the Cuore Immacolato di Maria leads to an impassioned, audacious and above all modern form of Baroque.[11]

The church commands a lynchpin position within the locale of the Piazza Euclide; its restless and distorted layout seemingly responds to its dense urban situation with roads radiating out to the south. However, it is surely Brasini's effusive and playful manipulation of classical motifs, his unconventional articulation of structure, void, volume and massing which demonstrate his belief that classical architecture could maintain its integrity without resorting to full-blown international modern.

This demonstrates a spectacular and legitimate stand against mainstream modernism, and Brasini's relative silence during the ensuing years of the fascist regime perhaps attests to this. This church is suggestive of a potential future approach to classicism,[12] given weight by his belief in its continual evolution. Indeed this very notion calls into question the very idea of a straightforward chronology from modernism to postmodernism; the latter seemingly being anticipated by Brasini. However, what came to characterize the subsequent period controlled by the fascist regime was one of compromise: of the modernist avant-garde tempered with a true acknowledgement of the Italian spirit.[13]

Throughout the 1930s and early 1940s, Roman churches were characterized by a seemingly un-Catholic rigidity and rationalism, an interesting display of fascist glory despite the recent Lateran Treaty. Yet some architects active during this period interpreted this with varying degrees of creativity. The church of San Felice da Cantalice (1934) is an interesting example. A staid and haunted exterior becomes increasingly rich on progression to the interior. Mario Paniconi and Giulio Pediconi's church, which is located in the Centocelle area of Rome, presents visitors with one of the first images of the modern expansion of the city, en route from the (then more frequently used) Centocelle Airport. Its presence in Pasolini's *Accattone* (1961)[14] is as an early monument within the urban periphery, though perhaps Accattone's directing of Stella away from the church is suggestive of a questioning of its relevance within a more ephemeral urban setting. The exterior of San Felice is characterized by its temple-like, porticoed ante-space. Here, its vaulted ceiling is painted the colour of sky, with Rodolfo Villani's painted figure of Saint Felice situated on the façade above the main entrance, levitating, as though midway between earth and heaven. Four years later, at Glasgow's 1938 Empire Exhibition, Jack Coia's embellishment of the white stuccoed walls of the Catholic Pavilion with frescoes by Hugh Adam Crawford, elicited a similar aesthetic. The melancholic emptiness of San Felice, externally, is a surprising backdrop for a gathering of the faithful.

Internally, the liturgical space is organized around a large nave with the smaller ancillary spaces of confessionals and chapels, and the traditional form of the transept here subverted by way of short lateral projections. This is architecture with a serious function, but it is fun aesthetically; almost pure art deco in places. It is grotto-like, a temple to the imagination which belies the austerity of its exterior. It is lit by stained glass clerestory fenestration, invoking a kind of multi-hued twilight. Side-aisles permit admiration of the circular columns, which are clad in tiny coloured mosaic tiles, and individual architectural elements are expressed in a wonderful, simplified geometry. Cruise-liner characteristics penetrate even this religious building, with horizontal metal balustrading accompanying semi-circular half-landings, reflecting the circular form of the columns. The altar is lit indirectly and from above by a ziggurat-section aperture, in place of a dome, and behind the altar a fantastical fresco forms the curved apse wall, and it is framed, in the manner of a stage set, by two circular columns. Indeed this very much resonates with Paniconi and Pediconi's audacity and continuing sense of experimentation in the post-Vatican II era. It is the start of an oeuvre which reconciled the limitations of the fascist period with increasing concern for the liturgy, the Vatican II itself, and finally the crisis of modernity.

In 1961 the church was still dressed in a light-coloured render with a base of peperino,[15] whilst today brickwork is the principal architectural skin. If the render was part of the original design, this represents one of the only modern Roman churches to have embraced the international smooth white aesthetic in a similar way to Coia's Roman Catholic Pavilion. Conversely, its current brick-work cladding represents more than mere change: it is in some ways a connection to the vernacular; a very postmodern concern.

Other seminal (and cinematic) churches exist, such as that of Santi Pietro e Paolo, featuring in such films as Michelangelo Antonioni's *L'Eclisse* (1962).[16] The somewhat sinister arrangement of platonic forms holds a significant elevated position within the EUR complex and was designed by a consortium of architects and engineers, headed by Arnaldo Foschini and a team of architects consisting of Alfredo Energici, Tullio Rossi and Costantino Vetriani, between 1938 and 1943. This, more so than Immacolato Cuore di Maria, is a pared down, idealized kind of fascist Baroque. Like so much of Rome's fascist architecture, it seems to be a paradoxically modern reduction of an essentially Italian and above all Catholic style, though the emotive drama normally associated with Baroque architecture has here been tamed, subverted and almost maniacally controlled – an odd reconciling of Italian cultural tradition and fascist aspirations of modernity – down to the rigidly limited degree of light, admitted only from high level within the central cylindrical form. Cinematic use of churches, such as in Antonioni's film invite social criticism, specifically a questioning of the role of Catholicism in the twentieth century. In churches such as Santi Pietro e Paolo, even religion appears to be abstracted and interpreted as fashion, or at least as something that we are able to control and change. In many ways, this iconic church, though highly original, represents a stylistic impasse, due to its level of stylistic reduction, compared to Brasini's earlier church.

The modern period leading up to the Vatican II resonates with that moment of intense national reflection, exposition and moral inquiry in the Italian films of the 1950s and 1960s. The filmic representation of iconic churches such as Bruno Maria Appolonj-Ghetti's church of the Martiri Canadesi (1952–5), which features as the hauntingly iconic setting for the rendezvous between Marcello and Steiner in Fellini's *La dolce vita*;[17] the eerie fascist-era church of Ss Paolo e Pietro; the metaphysical qualities of the church of San Felice da Cantalice; and the monumental church of San Giovanni Bosco, featured in Pasolini's *Mamma Roma* (1962)[18] display a peculiar preoccupation with the world's perception of the Eternal City as a modern city, a desire only reinforced by their inclusion in these internationally disseminated films. The underlying sense of dialogue between these churches and those of architects such as Jack Coia, the Glaswegian–Italian principal of Gillespie, Kidd & Coia, is also particularly striking, and their re-presentation through postmodern eyes only reinforces this.

Rome's post-fascist exportation of herself as a modern metropolis in many of the films to come out of Rome, predominantly Cinecittà, in the 1960s, and her largely home-grown architectural talent, did much to reinforce her standing as the Hollywood of Europe, although it simultaneously drew attention to an emerging crisis of urban narrative and cultural identity. In the opening scenes of *La dolce vita*, Fellini very efficiently uncovers Rome's palimpsest through the reality of viewing it from the air – the figure of Jesus the Labourer being dangled from a helicopter, hovering over both ancient architectural fragments and modern urban development. Perhaps this is a comment not only on the themes that have played a major part in the definition and re-definition of the Eternal City – religion, imperial architecture, modern, fascist-era architecture and beyond – but also on the way in which Mussolini may have viewed himself: as creator of modern Italian society, to be engineered and shaped by diligent toil and endeavour.

The churches of modern Rome are therefore, in some ways, a marker of the tension felt in the twentieth century between religion and modern society – heavily commented on in the films I have alluded to here. *La dolce vita* is suggestive of the moral decline of modern society – especially poignant near the very seat of the Catholic Church itself; Pasolini's *Mamma Roma* debases the idea of the great cultural, religious and historical icon of Rome through the protagonists' continued prostitution, in a clear comment on the spiritual poverty that was contemporary to those years of relative economic prosperity.[19] The replacement of the familiar view of Rome characterizes *Mamma Roma*, and Anna Magnani's character, whose attempted suicide after learning of the death of her son, Ettore, engages in symbolically charged glances towards the dome of San Giovanni Bosco, as if questioning whether she could or should be saved from the eternal damnation of suicide and from a life of immorality. Poignancy swells in response to Pasolini's preoccupation with the migration of an impoverished populace from the countryside around Rome, for example from the new fascist towns such as Guidonia Montecelio – itself the home of the striking fascist-era church of Santa Maria di Loreto – to the new *borgate*; and its churches, like San Giovanni Bosco,[20] as well as being diluted, unflattering references to St Peter's in the Vatican, the churches portrayed as weak or failing signifiers of social improvement.

In their subversive use of architectural imagery, film-makers like Pasolini and Fellini somehow validate, through unsympathetic critique, fascist and modern era architecture and urban spaces. A similar concept of reflective 'validation' exists within the ecclesiastical work of Gillespie, Kidd & Coia whereby the current focus on the distinguished post-1956 work of Isi Metzstein and Andy McMillan (belatedly) only serves to draw attention to and retrospectively establish the international significance of Jack Coia.[21]

In the new neighbourhoods constructed in the fascist era, new churches were built to support the new communities. The 1929 gesture of reconciliation between state and church, the Lateran Pact between the government and the Vatican, provided the means for Catholicism to become recognized by the regime as Italy's official religion. This said, it is very telling how the fascists perceived the church in society: in the new towns in the reclaimed Pontine marshes, for example in Sabaudia, the main public space was reserved for a civic function, with the church confined to a secondary square nearby. Nevertheless, in Rome itself, the number of parishes increased, and with the regime's acceptance of Catholicism, those parishes needed churches. In some instances, a special honour was conferred on those churches whose architectural character was praiseworthy. One example in particular is Marcello Piacentini's Cristo Re, on Viale Mazzini, in 1934 – its design 'continues the tradition of monumentality proper to Rome',[22] and so it was granted the status of minor basilica.

The notion of iconic contrast and juxtaposition, which so characterizes Rome, is further emphasized by the fantastical Nostra Signora Ss Sacramento e Santi Martiri Canadesi (the national church of Canada in Rome), designed by the architectural historian Bruno Maria Appolonj-Ghetti and built between 1952 and 1955 (see Figure 7.1 on p. 145); and by Ildo Avetta's beautifully crafted and somewhat futuristic Sacro Cuore di Gesù Agonizzante, built between 1953 and 1955 in the in Zona Mezzocamino commune on the outskirts of Rome (see Figure 7.2 on p. 146). Both are modern in terms of their use of materials, both use structure to define the quality of the interior space (see comparisons with Coia churches in Figures 7.3 and 7.4 on p. 147 and p. 148), and there is a pointed similarity in the articulation of elements, such as the blocky front façade of Martiri Canadesi and Coia's churches in Glasgow.

Figure 7.1: Apse of the Church of Nostra Signora Ss Sacramento e Santi Martiri
Canadesi in Rome, which was designed by Bruno Maria Apollonj-Ghetti
(1952–5). Photograph: author's own.

Figure 7.2: Apse of the Church of Sacro Cuore di Gesù Agonizzante near Rome, designed by Bruno Maria Apollonj-Ghetti (1953–5). Photograph reproduced with the kind permission of Dr Catherine Keay.

Figure 7.3: Apse of the Church of St Columba in Glasgow, designed by Gillespie, Kidd & Coia (1937). Photograph: author's own.

Figure 7.4: Apse of the Church of St Laurence in Greenock, designed by Gillespie, Kidd & Coia (1952). Photograph: author's own.

That the Italians were aware of international architectural developments is not surprising: they would certainly have known of developments in ecclesiastical architecture elsewhere in Europe, thanks to access to journals such as *Architettura*, which notably included an article on a RIBA conference in London in 1935, given by its then new president Edward Maufe. The article reviews the latest ecclesiastical projects in England and abroad, and evokes the sensation of a new type of architecture in its ascendancy.[23] However, it is the relative obscurity of Coia's early work in an international context that in a sense makes him such an interesting architect to discuss.

The great, blocky bulk of Martiri Canadesi seems to burst out of a roughly hewn travertine plinth. Its articulated entrance elevation is intensified by a group of pilaster strips on either side of a central painted fresco (originally intended to be enhanced with sculpture). Clues to the internal structure are hinted at by the tall, protruding brickwork elements of the side elevation. A narthex, with access to ancillary accommodation below, precedes the principal church. Otherwise, the interior, consisting of nave and side-aisles, galleries and quadrangular apse, is sublime – a still, yet dynamic space, mysteriously lit by high, stained glass clerestory fenestration. A strangely Gothic structure, with a marked vertical inflection defines the interior, and its groin-vaulted ceiling unifies sets of double parabolic arches.[24] As in the case of San Felice, here we find striking parallels with other Coia churches – St Columba's, Glasgow (1937, in Figure 7.3 on p. 147) and St Laurence's, Greenock (1951–4, in Figure 7.4, p. 148). At St Columba's, there is a similar monolithic, rectangular entrance elevation and simplified Gothic structure internally, and at St Laurence's there is, again, a strong structural echo. That Appolonj-Ghetti's church was conceived between St Columba's and St Laurence's is evidently suggestive of an international exchange of ideas and motifs beyond only a common reference source. In *La dolce vita*, Steiner's rather incongruous playing of a jazz piece, followed by Bach's 'Toccata and Fugue' on a jazz organ setting, further attests both to the interesting sense of cultural juxtaposition that is intrinsic to the Roman church, and also to the themes of international exchange and modernism. In the lead up to Vatican II, Rome appeared quite conversant with international popular culture, even in an ecclesiastical setting.

Post-Vatican II

It is at this point that we can begin to recognize the full significance that the Vatican II had on the ecclesiastical scene, going forward into those decades of pluralism. In Rome, the Pontificia Opera Nuove Chiese,[25] which had been criticized for something of a laissez-faire attitude in relation to really valuing architectural innovation prior to the proclamation of the council's directives, suddenly began to promote a more overtly architectonic approach which was seen as more relevant to a modern world.[26] There was a continuation of basilican layouts, as we have seen with all of the churches thus far mentioned, except Cuore Immacolato di Maria and Santi Pietro e Paolo. But these began to be overtaken by a wealth of experimentation, with more centralized plan-types becoming common from the 1970s onwards, a phenomenon that may owe something to the emphasis on the post-Vatican II participation of the congregation in the liturgy. Interestingly though, this overwhelmingly heterogeneous period is rather difficult to pin down, despite a massively successful building programme during the three decades between the Vatican II and the period leading up to the Jubilee in 2000. In Rome, some of the Italian postmodernist 'greats' such as Aldo Rossi, Paolo Portoghesi and Carlo Scarpa remain notably absent on the ecclesiastical scene.[27] Whilst there was some continuation, development and consolidation of pre-Vatican II firms, and several firms that emerged for several decades towards the end of the last century, there is nothing comparable to the consistency or pedigree of design work that we see around Glasgow with Gillespie, Kidd & Coia. What we do see, however, is a multiplicity of approaches by Italian architects, an echo of that (at least, historically) postmodern pluralistic experimentalism which, though sometimes hidden within much contemporary mediocrity, always rewards careful analysis.

Between 1966 and 1970, Mario Paniconi and Giulio Pediconi designed the church of San Giuseppe Cafasso in Tuscolano. It is a modernistic, reductionist block of a building which successfully articulates the sum of its parts, and its modulated reinforced concrete structure is clad in tuff and peperino. It has a centralized plan arrangement, in contrast to the metaphysical and basilican San Felice Da Cantalice, built by the same firm some thirty years previously. The great mass of the roof – a deep slab form with inward-chamfering sides, seemingly levitates over the square bulk of the building below, thanks to the recessed clerestory strip windows, with four columns carrying the load of the roof downwards. The church is undoubtedly reminiscent of the post-Vatican II developments in the work of Gillespie, Kidd & Coia; particularly St Patrick's, Kilsyth (1964), with its blocky base, recessed clerestory and incongruously heavy yet 'floating' roof. And it is unquestionably modern in feel, save perhaps for the vernacular use of tuff and peperino stone, although even this is framed with concrete, its use subverted to mere infill.[28]

Paniconi and Pediconi completed their ecclesiastical oeuvre in the early 1980s with the bizarre circular concrete church of the Sacra Famiglia in Via Portuense (1978–81), in Rome. Its smooth, monolithic walls are all but blank at lower level, the edifice rising as a kind of truncated cone, with angled reinforced concrete columns (an exaggeration of their earlier use at San Giuseppe Cafasso) anchoring enclosing bands of wall, sequentially decreasing in diameter. Half of the structure rises higher, to form a semicircular shaped section over the sanctuary area; this being obliquely lit by a line of porthole windows. The inclined elements supporting a curved structure are suggestive of the supports on the Colosseum, whereas the combination of horizontal ribbon windows and small, rose window-like portholes are architectural anachronisms in such close proximity. The ziggurat recessing of the main entrance has a quasi art deco flavour; a subtle echo of San Felice da Cantalice, perhaps. On the other hand, the light scoop atop the attached weekday chapel, a type of quarter-sphere, speaks of those of St Peter's Seminary at Cardross (designed by Gillespie, Kidd & Coia, completed in 1966). The arrangement of truncated massings and axial elements seems to anticipate Tadao Ando's Museum of Wood (1993–4). Many references can be made, but most seem to be in the spirit of imaginative experimentation rather than overt postmodern wit, irony or significant stylistic re-working.[29]

Other notable architects include Aldo Aloysi and Ernesto Vichi, sometimes working in collaboration. Between them, their work spans from the late 1950s into the 1990s, and represents something of a continuum of architectural inquiry and expression; however, interestingly, their work seems to approach a formal resolution of modernist themes rather than an obvious move to a postmodernist aesthetic.

After the formal experimentation of the 1960s, 1970s and 1980s, the 1990s crept towards some of the more obvious architectural characteristics associated with postmodernism and with certain architects. Historical references began then to be executed with contemporary construction methods and materials, with architectural irony or wit, and the associated philosophies of high-tech and deconstructivist design.

Between 1994 and 1996, Santiago Hernandez designed the church of San Josemaria Escrivá de Balaguer in Ardeatino, just east of the EUR; Hernandez presents a restrained and sober brick-clad basilican church with muted classical aesthetic. A tripartite portico with roundheaded arches and simple bilateral colonnade, a simply fenestrated gable end with carved travertine panel in relief and elegantly detailed attached campanile, provide visual balance to what is otherwise an uncompromisingly plain building. Internally, the large galleried nave eschews kitsch and unmitigated pastiche; instead it appears as a controlled blend of historical references (the carved, coffered ceiling and the seating gallery around three sides) with contemporary liturgical concerns, such as the way in which the nave walls step inwards so that focus is directed at the narrower altar end. The reinforced concrete structure and simplicity of the fenestration also contribute here.[30]

In the late 1990s, another notable church appeared in the form of Ennio Canino's San Liborio in the Monte Sacro Alto district north of Rome. Less overtly 'historical' than Hernandez's church, Canino's work makes symbolic reference to historical plan form, the entire church being contained within a stylized Greek Cross; the reinforced concrete and steel structure is, again, clad in brickwork. The most striking aspect of the building is the incongruous and somewhat awkward reconciling of the entrance arm of the Greek Cross with a pseudo high-tech and seemingly over-engineered entrance canopy. In this arrangement, a substantial steel column, surmounted by a tall cross, is placed either side of a deep entrance canopy, cantilevered out beyond the columns, and angled down toward the entrance to the church. Clad in travertine internally, this chimeric church appears to make bold references to both distant and near history in an unlikely manner, whilst at the same time alluding to the vernacular.[31]

In a sense, the church-building programme that had occurred as a result of the outward expansion of Glasgow, before and after Vatican II, had also occurred in Rome in the lead-up to the Jubilee year of 2000. Gillespie, Kidd & Coia were the continued leaders of this mass church-building drive in Glasgow, whereas many architects were involved in the Roman expansion, Richard Meier being one of the most infamous outsiders. This is particularly significant in the consideration of Rome's periphery; the appropriation of the historic Ager Romanus into the urban demise of the city presented a problem. The socio-architectural wilderness of these peripheral areas – particularly of the 'Tors', the romantic names of the towers of the Ager Romanus – was finally addressed. The 2000 master plan effectively reconnected the periphery and devolved a form of self-governance and identity to these 'microcities'.[32] The Jubilee church-building drive from the Vatican would give these outposts a moral and spiritual heart: Richard Meier's Tor Tre Teste church being a particularly successful example. Meier was the winner of an invited competition which received entries from a host of renowned architects including Frank Gehry, Santiago Calatrava, Peter Eisenmann, Tadao Ando and Paolo Portoghesi. The international competition set for the design of this new beacon of City and Church seems to have engendered a kind of reverse-internationalism, in opposition to the cinematically exported versions of the city in the preceding decades. His design for one of these, yielding possibly the strangest vision of the city's development yet, sits somewhat marooned in its site in the midst of Tor Tre Teste, the grey, 1970s-built estate of apartment blocks, several miles east of Rome's city centre, consisting of a church and integral community centre. After a somewhat unpromising amble through a charming if crumbling neighbourhood of low-rise housing and small-scale retail, the proximity, scale and amount of seemingly anonymous fragments of Roman ruins is startling. Walls with arches that become apertures rather poignantly and iconically frame the remainder of the journey across a vast playing field, looking onto the housing estate and the deconstructed, glittering, dissolving fragments of the church in the distance.

In his church, Meier demonstrates both an internal and external mastery of light with his typically pure and pared down white aesthetic and dramatic play of light and shade. Consisting of a deconstructed composition of three curved, concrete-clad shells – a subtle reference to the Holy Trinity – addressing a 'spine' wall, the west and east ends are back-lit and superbly sculptural in their framing of crucifix and organ.[33]

Meier's choice of materials for the church has been widely documented – particularly for its simplicity and fundamental sensuality. He opted for a mixture of stone, white Roman concrete and light coloured timber internally for the pews and for the partial internal cladding of the nave.[34] The resonance with Alvar Aalto's Finnish Pavilion at New York's World Fair of 1938–9 is striking here. Nevertheless, Meier's bridging of the traditional, contemporary and vernacular seems to reach out metaphysically beyond mere choice of materials.

Conclusion

Historically, the Church and the city of Rome have in many ways remained inseparable. As an examination of even a mere handful of these buildings shows, the (physical) church corroborates its wider importance in tracking cultural and architectural perceptions of the city. The Vatican II, though its intentions were noble, did not necessarily provide a distinct or universal turning point in the design of Catholic churches; indeed, based on the examples highlighted here, one could argue that what ensued was in some ways rather confusing, perhaps due more than anything else to a lack of true liturgical understanding on the part of some architects. However, firms such as Paniconi and Pediconi, Aloysi and Vichi in Rome and Gillespie, Kidd & Coia in Glasgow, demonstrate the maturing of a process already begun pre-Vatican II. Contemporary Italian films portray a sense of people losing their way socially and spiritually after a post-war building boom and a consequent disorientation of the psychogeography of the city; yet the churches featured are iconic markers, even if their use in such films is sometimes derogatory. In the name of clarity and perhaps accuracy, the period would be better referred to as post-Vatican rather than postmodern – certainly as far as churches are concerned. Postmodernism per se appeared relatively late in the church architecture of Rome, though architects such as Armando Brasini leave one wondering whether there was an opportunity that somehow postmodern architects missed: the possibility of further developing a classicism which could have extended into the peripheries and surpassed other forms of ecclesiastical modern.

What is apparent is that there was no obvious, straightforward chronological transition from one architectural 'period' to another. Rather, there has been a prolonged oscillation of stylistic tendencies, which have coexisted in a fluctuating, architectural polemic. The sense of stylistic, cultural and ecclesiastical exchange between them, from a long heritage of modernistic architecture in its various forms that stretch as far as the post-Vatican and even postmodern, has been allowed to exist by the lynchpin of the Vatican II. It surely must contribute to the argument that through the iconic permanence of the Church, despite a changing society, and an experimentation wrought through architectural exchange, Rome's narrative is evolving rather than ephemeral, affectable rather than eternal.

8 'ROMA INTERROTTA': POSTMODERN ROME AS THE SOURCE OF FRAGMENTED NARRATIVES

Léa-Catherine Szacka

It is comprised, not of proposals for urban planning, naturally, but of a series of gymnastic exercises for the Imagination whose course runs parallel to that of Memory.

G. C. Argan[1]

During the late 1970s a group of twelve architects – Piero Sartogo, Colin Rowe, Robert Venturi with Denise Scott Brown, Michael Graves, Costantino Dardi, Antoine Grumbach, James Stirling, Paolo Portoghesi, Romaldo Giurgola, Robert Krier, Aldo Rossi and Léon Krier – were brought together for an exhibition that redrew Giambattista Nolli's 1748 map of Rome and sought to use this reinterpreted map in the production of visionary drawings of architecture and urbanism.

Nolli's map was the first attempt to produce a complete outline of Rome, his adoptive city. Created under the commission of Pope Benedict XIV, the map, entitled the 'Nuova Topografia di Roma' (New Topography of Rome), has since become an important and highly influential representation. The city itself was represented in twelve connected segments, and the map's frame was an architectonic–allegorical capriccio that represented the two Romes: on the left, the antique (and pagan) Rome, on the right, the modern (and sacred) one. It was commissioned to be a precise technical work, intended by the pope as a rational outline of the city's social and legal administration. As Michal Graves notes,

> The vast housing and commercial stock of the city was rendered as urban *poché*, while the religious and state structures were described in a level of detail which encourages the understanding of the city as a spatial sequence of successive rooms.[2]

The 'Topografia' also provided an immediate and intuitive understanding of the city's urban form through the simple yet effective graphic method of rendering solids as dark grey (with hatch marks), and rendering voids as white or light shades of grey to represent terrain such as vegetation or paving patterns. By adopting this iconographic approach – one of the first maps of the city designed in this way –

Nolli (who was not an architect, but a surveyor) sought to offer a street map that was legible in what was, quite interestingly, posited as an *objective* manner, offering a new awareness of the city by emphasizing its internal and external voids.

The new map of Rome represented a synchronic–historical section of the pre-industrial, Baroque city at the peak of its splendour.[3] What remains striking today about Nolli's blueprint is the intrinsic similarity that it illustrated between the ancient cityscape and that of pre-modern Rome, which had changed relatively little (and certainly remained within the Aurelian Walls).[4] It moreover caught that historical moment that signalled the potential for significant change: soon after the map was produced, the city was to face the major urban upheavals ordered in the nineteenth century by King Victor Emmanuel II and King Umberto I, and in the twentieth century by the fascist regime. For both its innovation and its synchronic snapshot of this historical moment, the map's significance endured, and in fact from the late 1950s to the late 1980s, the re-appropriated Nolli map had become the paradigm of modern urban planning – especially in American circles.[5]

During that same latter period, the significance of Nolli's map surged when a Roman non-profit art organization invited a panel of internationally renowned architects, those named above, to develop one of the twelve segments of the map into a personal critique of the city's development in the nineteenth and twentieth century. The result, twelve disjointed narratives that signalled the fragmentariness of the 'Eternal City', was exhibited in Rome's Trajan Markets in 1978 under the title 'Roma Interrotta' (Rome Interrupted).

In spite of its playful nature and form, as I will argue in the following paragraphs, the exhibition embodied and reflected the tensions of the postmodern condition under which it was forged: from the interruption of the city's singular grand narrative and the impossibility of objective–realistic representation, through to the fragmentation of the urbanscape and the shattering of objectivity.

Despite some recent scholarly and museological attention,[6] 'Roma Interrotta' remains notably understudied. By combining close readings of the original drawings produced for the exhibition and analysis of archival material related to the organization of the event with an oral history campaign conducted in the fall of 2010,[7] I aim to shed new light on the history of this unique and significant event. As I will show, by proposing a non-chronological and non-linear image of Rome, 'Roma Interrotta' produced twelve contextualized yet highly individualistic endeavours that correspond to that shift towards a narrative of fragmented and plural subjectivities that is typical of postmodernity. I do so by scrutinizing the genesis, organization and realization of the exhibition in relation to questions of pastiche and history in the first section; and, in the second, by honing in on three specific contributions that very fruitfully illustrate a shift in architectural and artistic thinking, from a unitarian and objective truth to a subjective multiplicity.

The Exhibition Space and Reappropriated History

Embedded in the artistic, political and social context of late 1970s Italy, 'Roma Interrotta' encapsulates the atmosphere of a very specific epoch. It was an unconventional type of architectural exhibition, organized by the Incontri Internazionali d'Arte (IIA, International Art Meetings), a non-profit organization and an underground critical workshop of the avant-garde that had, since the start of the 1970s, been very active on the contemporary Roman art scene. One of the main tenets of this organization was to engage with all forms of art and thus to break down the barriers between disciplines. The founder and general secretary of the IIA, Graziella Lonardi Buontempo, was described as a 'passionate cultural force in Rome since the early 1970s' and a 'tireless promoter of advanced artistic research, organizing great public exhibitions and promoting a new approach to culture'.[8] During the 1970s, Lonardi Buontempo interacted directly with many Italian and international artists such as Andy Warhol, Joseph Beuys, Alighiero Boetti, Mario Merz and Jannis Kounnellis. With the help of the curator and critic Achille Bonito Oliva, she promoted new forms of artistic creativity and performances by creating a 'place of experimentation, where artists and critics interacted with the public in performances and discussions'.[9] Lonardi Buontempo and Bonito Oliva's exhibitions – their most celebrated and revolutionary artistic events being 'Vitalità del negativo nell'arte italiana 1960/70' and 'Contemporanea' – were famous for their choice of venues, often unusual and unconventional public spaces.[10] Following on from these experiments, the IIA decided to hold the 'Roma Interrotta' exhibition in the archaeological space of Trajan's Market. At the time, the space of the disused market was practically unknown to the public (both tourists and Romans). Thus the choice of this particular exhibition space adhered to the contemporary desire to retrieve historical and collective memory, thus guaranteeing the exhibition a permanent and 'real' impact on the destiny of Rome's city centre.

In the particular case of 'Roma Interrotta', not only were the discourses and content of the show innovative, but also the container and the exhibition design – projected by Franco Raggi – made a highly postmodern repertoire of forms and ideas. Raggi, a young designer, director and managing editor of the magazine *Modo*, and previously editor at *Casabella*, had already organized or co-organized important exhibitions at the Milan Triennale ('Architettura-Città' with Aldo Rossi, 1973) and at the Venice Biennale ('Europa-America' with Vittorio Gregotti, 1976), where he was asked to work on 'Roma Interrotta'. For Raggi, the exhibition had a strong 'surreal' component, something that he chose to emphasize in his design, using references from popular culture ('the pop') and allusions to ecclesiastical and ceremonial traditions.[11] It was a matter of surpassing the classical architecture exhibition by playing on languages. The exhibition venue,

Trajan's Market, was ancient Rome's centre for commerce and communication. It was thus a highly 'functional' space. The street's entrance on Via IV Novembre was marked by a very dry and heavy arch that almost predated rationalist architecture. Inside was a central space with six shops on each side. Emphasizing what used to be the commercial function of the building, Raggi gave each architect a shop in which to exhibit his work, creating an historical overlap between the market's original typology and its new function as an exhibition space.

In addition to their 65 by 46 cm section of a revisited Nolli map, each architect produced a variable number of images to be exhibited in their own small space. Yet because of technical constraints, their material had to be hung without ever touching the structural walls of the market. Raggi thus imagined an innovative support system: a series of pale blue grid structures made of lightweight wood and hung from elements that had been left behind after previous exhibitions. In the central space were the *old* 1748 Nolli map and the *new* 1978 'interrupted' one. Set one against the other (over the palimpsest of earlier exhibitions), the two maps generated a physical space, a cube, raised on a fake marble base and preceded by a red carpet, in which visitors could stand. Inside the cube were the maps, while outside were inscriptions in golden letters: on the one side the names of the twelve exhibitors, and on the other 'Giambattista Nolli, Pianta di Roma 1748'. And as a majestic gesture recalling the metaphysical paintings of de Chirico, Raggi planned an extravagant announcement of the title 'Roma Interrotta' by creating an urban sign, a 300 square metre electric blue satin cloth – similar to one employed in religious ceremonies – that would float in the artificial breeze produced by a two-metre wide fan from *Cinecittà*. Raggi's design used several tropes of postmodernism: it recalled the history of the building; it played with a mix and match of rich and poor material (mixing gold letters, red carpet, fake marble and shiny blue fabric with the ruins of the old market and some lightweight wood structures); it mingled the sacred (the fabric and the golden letters were reminiscent of the material traditionally used in the church) and the profane (the market), the banal and the extraordinary; it based itself on a series of signs (such as the blue canvas) and in so doing it became both a critical statement and an urban event.

The Interrupted City

Though originally intended as the first event in a series, 'Roma Interrotta' was ultimately the only IIA exhibition ever dedicated specifically to urbanism and architecture.[12] But in its unconventional (at least for the time) collaboration between an art organization and a group of architects reflecting on urban problems, 'Roma Interrotta' triggered a curious relationship between the architects and their forms of representation (here, principally drawing). The maps and architectural representations of all forms and materials were, of course, produced only for the sake of being exhibited.[13] And yet, by being solely created by architects, the exhibition fostered the idea of the architect's autonomy as put forward by Aldo Rossi and some of the other rationalist architects. Though space prevents an extensive comparison, this tense interplay between the practical and the representational undoubtedly invokes a reading of the exhibition as comment on Rome as 'Thirdspace'. This follows Edward Soja's notion of 'Firstspace' and 'Secondspace': 'Thirdspace ... can be described as a creative recombination and extension, one that builds on a Firstspace perspective that is focused on the "real" material world and a Secondspace perspective that interprets this reality through "imagined" representations of spatiality'.[14] Introducing this intrinsic multi-stability of the city in 'Roma Interrotta' is an important step in understanding the importance of this conception of postmodern Rome.

What was the role and place of 'Roma Interrotta' within the larger history of postmodernism? The Anglo-American architectural historian and critic Charles Jencks has famously argued that modernism died in 1972, with the destruction of Pruitt-Igoe housing estate in St Louis, Missouri. Following that, in 1977, postmodernism was almost immediately codified and disseminated with the publication of Jencks's first edition of *The Language of Post-Modern Architecture*. Yet it was soon after, in 1980, that the Venice Architecture Biennale marked a watershed moment between 'the end of the beginning' and 'the beginning of the end' of postmodernism. Steven Connor distinguishes four different stages in the development of postmodernist architecture: accumulation, through the 1970s and the early part of the 1980s; synthesis, from the middle of the 1980s onwards; autonomy, from the beginning of the 1990s and dissipation later in the 1990s.[15] If we follow Connor's temporality, chronologically at least, 1977–8 would correspond to that early stage of postmodernism during which the hypothesis was under development by people like Jencks, but also Daniel Bell, Jean Baudrillard, Jean-Francois Lyotard and Ihab Hassan.

The changing perspective on the city, a perspective associated with postmodernism, in reality started to occur around 1966, with the publication of two seminal books: *Complexity and Contradiction in Architecture* by Robert Venturi and *L'architettura della città* by Aldo Rossi.[16] While the former served as a virulent critique of modern architecture and urbanism, the latter advocated the return to the traditional city, insisting on the importance of the notion of place and monuments, and arguing that the city was the *locus* of collective memory. Rossi was also innovative in his suggestion of a new relation between urban analysis and architectural projects. Following that, the aftermath of the revolts of 1968 led to important changes in decision-making policies and a renewed interest in the question of urbanity in many countries (mainly France, Italy and the USA).[17] In Rome, for instance, the election in 1976 of the art historian

Giulio Carlo Argan as the first leftist mayor gave rise to a series of artistic experiments funding historical monuments in public places in an attempt to alter the sombre atmosphere in the wake of the *anni di piombo* (years of lead). Argan endorsed Renato Nicolini's *Estate Romana* (Roman Summer), a famous cultural manifestation consisting of a series of ephemeral cultural manifestations – big cinematographic, theatrical or musical events – that took place in various monumental loci of the capital from 1977 onward.

The architects of 'Roma Interrotta' adopted a new attitude towards urban design that was part of a broader historical shift. They perceived the city as a field where they were allowed to 'play', either using a strong analytical methodology, borrowing from sociological studies and learning from observing what was there, or interweaving historical chronicle with fictionalized narratives and fables.[18] 'Roma Interrotta' can be seen as part of that larger cultural phenomenon which from the late 1960s had proliferated in architectural circles, each one contaminating the other, and leading to a definition of the city that was no longer merely a functional organism with transportation network or a series of functional zones (as described and promoted in the CIAM 1933 Athen's Chart), but rather as the product of human culture.

On the occasion of the exhibition, Argan wrote that 'Rome was an interrupted city because there came a time when it was no longer imagined, and it began to be planned (badly)'.[19] It was in reaction to this particular state of affairs described by Argan that the Italian architect Piero Sartago together with the cultural institution *Incontri Internazionali d'Arte*, proposed to step back 230 years and to draw inspiration from the Nolli map. For the purpose of the exercise, architects 'added to, subtracted from, altered, or destroyed the Rome of 1748 to show the city as it might have been'. And since the Nolli map had originally been divided into twelve tables of engravings, due to printing limitations, nothing was easier than to distribute the twelve sections between the participants. As suggested by Thomas Weaver, the result, presented in 'Roma Interrotta', was an assemblage of heterogeneous projects, a map of adjacency, which initiated an altogether new and radical way of approaching Rome's urban design.

The *modus operandi* of 'Roma Interrotta' included a very strong historically speculative and imaginative component: the aim was to imagine 'una nuova Roma' (a new Rome), as though the city had not changed in more than 200 years.[20] In other words, it was a matter of going back to the pre-modern city by fictively erasing all the problematic urban transformation that had been implemented in order to create a more modern and more functional city.

The 'Roma Interrotta' project sprang from a particular theoretical and methodological premise: what the Anglo-Saxon architectural historian Colin Rowe has called 'design speculations and fantasies on historic city plans'.[21] The technique of 'what might have happened' was directly related to Rowe's way of thinking.[22] One of the main figures of the critical revisionism of the Modern movement in architecture and urban design, Rowe's early work at Cornell University led to the Contextualist school of thought. This body of thought was critical of modern urbanist and architectural theory of design wherein modern building types are harmonized with urban forms common to a traditional city.[23] As J. Stevens Curl explains, over the course of a brilliant and very influential academic career Rowe focused on developing an alternative method of urban design that derived in part from the earlier work of Camillo Sitte, and was based on the creation of cities through a process of collage and superimposed pieces.[24] From the early 1970s onwards, Rowe started to make public his contextualist thinking on the city, publishing articles that would eventually become *Collage City*, a book published in 1978. In *Collage City*, Rowe proposed *bricolage* as an alternative to the scientific methods of planning put forward by rationalist modernist planners and architects. For Rowe, collage acts as an antidote to the mental structures responsible for the totalitarian excess.[25] Also very prominent in the book was Rowe's condemnation of the disappearance, in the modern city, of the collective space of the street or the public place.

The interesting question that remains is: how did the contextualist ideas travel from Ithaca to Rome, and eventually influence the *modus operandi* of 'Roma Interrotta'? In the late 1960s Sartogo was invited to Cornell University, where he visited Rowe's contextualist urban design studio on several occasions.[26] The Roman architect moreover had frequent contact with the New York's Institute of Architecture and Urban Studies (IAUS)[27] and in particular with Peter Eiseman, with whom, in 1971, he had put together a special bilingual issue of the magazine *Casabella* – the first ever published – with the title 'The City as an Artifact'.[28] In the introduction to the issue, Alessandro Mendini, then editor of *Casabella*, wrote: 'we resolved that Europe should hear of these ideas – ideas which, in the US, had already brought about approaches to planning radically different from orthodoxy practice and had grafted on as yet unexplored criteria of expressivity'.[29] Thus, when Graziella Lonardi Buontempo and the IIA sought the collaboration of Sartogo to organize an exhibition on the city of Rome, Sartogo drew on the work done for the *Casabella*'s bilingual issue and developed the idea of the 'artefact'. As Sartogo himself has explained,[30] the 'Roma Interrotta' project allow architects to imagine what the city of Rome would look like if the Tiber's embankments had not been built, thus destroying this direct connection between the river and the urban fabric.[31] In the same way, this synchronic approach permits architects to speculate on what Rome could have become if the fascist regime had not destroyed the historical urban fabric of vast portions of the historical city centre.[32]

Fragments and Subjectivities

The primary aim of the 'Roma Interrotta' project was to find ways of revisiting Rome by means of a critical assessment that took the form of a giant collage – that is, a conjunctive operation using 'both/and' rather than a disjunctive one using 'either/or'. This approach was inspired by Colin Rowe's own, which in turn was influenced by Claude Lévi-Strauss's notion of the collage as a mental structure, and one that could serve as an antidote to the totalitarian drift.[33] It may also have owed something to the *cadavres exquis*, a famous surrealist game played by André Breton and his colleagues: a method by which a collection of words or images is cooperatively assembled by a group of collaborators. Yet there was one major difference between the two endeavours: if the technique of *cadavres exquis* implied that each participant should add to a composition in sequence, either by following a rule or by being allowed to see the end of what the previous person contributed, in 'Roma Interrotta' no place was left for collaboration as each architect was responsible for a single piece of the puzzle, without any preparatory group effort or consultation.

Unlike the surrealist image, 'Roma Interrotta' was not only concerned with the pictorial design. It was, contributor Antoine Grumbach notes, concerned with the question of the 'future of the city's past'.[34] And while all participants agreed that the form of future cities should be deduced from history, the responses were of an extremely diverse nature. Offering a multifaceted interpretation of the Nolli map and giving to the city as many 'fictional' meanings as possible, 'Roma Interrotta' fostered the typical postmodern spirit of pluralism and tolerance – as strongly defended by Charles Jencks in his *Language of Post-Modern Architecture*, as well as by Venturi and Scott Brown.

In 'Roma Interrotta', rather than producing an overall and unified result, what really mattered was to show many approaches to the problem of the historical city centre: the aim was to push the architects to produce a set of drawings that would exemplify their own view of the city or what the city meant to them, while liberating designer creativity, freeing them of any sort of constraints. In the following paragraphs, I focus on the output of three of the twelve 'Roma Interrotta' proposals: those of Antoine Grumbach, Léon Krier and James Stirling. Though quite evidently each project brings its own artistic merit and value to the discussion, these three projects have been selected for their relevance to the idea of a shift towards pluralism and subjectivity, whereby each project proposes a personal language, at times megalomaniac, at times deeply introspective and poetic. Rather than being pseudo-objective, the projects elaborate a series of individual rules or logics based on historical, archeological or almost anthropological research.[35]

Antoine Grumbach

Antoine Grumbach's project is a very revealing response to postmodern questions of 'master narratives' and the use of fiction. Entitled 'A Challenge to Architecture', Grumbach's project was an 'inverse archaeology',[36] using the term that he himself coined, based on a critique of the Modern movement and on the employment of collage, so as to generate a fictitious city made of a series of sediments or traces. Thus, in the case of Grumbach's project, the 'new Rome' was no longer linked only to the history of collective memory, but depended on the reader's (or the architect's) personal and subjective interpretation of the urban environment, the sediments and traces coming from fictitious stories or internal myths. In the 'Roma Interrotta' catalogue, Grumbach explains that his project invokes 'the poetic potential of the fragments or of the totality of the object'.[37] Grumbach, like most of the 'Roma Intorrotta' participants, had built little at the time of the exhibition. His approach to urban design was, rather than practical, highly theoretical and linguistic.

Grumbach worked on one of the peripheral parts of the Nolli map: the upper right-hand corner, a sector that included Via Nomentana and Via Salaria but, which in the eighteenth century, was almost completely covered by green areas. Thus Grumbach set out to make the persistence of nature emerge by inventing and putting together a herbarium.

Fiction was used by many of the 'Roma Interrotta' participants. According to the architectural historian Henrich Klotz, the use of fiction in architecture, or specifically in the *fictionalization* of architecture, is the primary characteristic of postmodern projects. It is fiction, in his view, that distinguishes modern from postmodern architecture. Yet, as Klotz explains, it is not so simple to obtain the fictionalization of architecture:

> Fiction is not achieved by merely combining successfully some geometric forms. Only after a building is no longer bound up solely with itself, only when the stereometric autonomy of perfect volumetric wholes is destroyed and allusions and associations are permitted that go beyond the building itself, is there a possibility for creating an architectural fiction.[38]

In Grumbach's case, many allusions to past architects or architecture (from Bruno Taut's glass pavilion to Pierre Chareau's glass house, and historical references to Ledoux, Le Corbusier, Oud, Alphand, etc.) combine in various strange associations and juxtapositions. In constructing three 'fictional profiles', Grumbach refers to the palimpsestical aspect of Rome, perhaps more directly than any other architect taking part in 'Roma Interrotta'. Grumbach almost naively unravels part of his architectural subconscious, revealing, through his fictions, elements that have marked his education as an architect.

Entirely made in situ, Grumbach's project followed the *genius loci* of the city,[39] building on Roman promenades to trace a vegetal route which threads its way between the private houses and their gardens. Sharing some of Christian Norberg-

Schulz's ideas, Grumbach sought to consider not only the practical aspects of architecture but also its psychological implications. The young architect had the will and the possibility of spending a summer (1977) in Rome, working on his project: 'I am obsessed with context and territory, and I wanted to be able to scour the territory I had been assigned, day and night, as well as in its history and its successive sedimentary layers'.[40] Using the medium of photography, Grumbach's approach also involved the meticulous documenting of the territory through the lens of his camera, an activity that automatically entails the subjectivity of the author.

'Roma Interrotta' ultimately proved to be a fundamental and influential step within Grumbach's career. The architect used the exhibition as a way to refine his theoretical and practical approach to urban and architectural design, producing a series of drawings, which, as he has stated, clearly illustrated a conceptual approach used in many subsequent projects:

> In a sense, the 'Roma Interrotta' drawings were an exaggeration, but for the first project I ever realized – some public spaces in the ville nouvelle of Marne-la-Vallée, I used a similar approach. I started by imagining what would have been past's ruins of the ville nouvelle, because I could not conceive a new town without working through its sedimentary traces.[41]

Léon Krier

Léon Krier's 'Roma Interrotta' project was clearly a megalomaniac gesture: instead of restraining himself to his part of the Nolli map, Krier developed a system of urban–social centres to be placed all over the city, in an attempt to revive the physical and cultural centres of the traditional *rioni*.[42] Krier writes: 'The growing popular disbelief in central power, its frustration with the churches, the central committees of the political and economic machinery, will have to result in the administrative decentralization within our cities'.[43] Thus, Krier challenged the notion of a unitary centre, or, in other words, he insisted on one of Ihab Hassan's eleven 'definiens' of the term postmodern, that is 'fragmentation'. In his essay, first published in 1987, Hassan writes that fragmentation's 'ultimate opprobrium is "totalization" – any synthesis whatever, social, epistemic, even poetic'.[44]

Krier was given the bottom right-hand corner of the Nolli map, the one representing an image of the Capitoline Hill within the allegorical–pictorial frame. His intervention required the invention of a new building typology that resulted from a new social need. The *Centri rionali*, or physical and cultural centres, were rational monumental structures made of huge brick pillars carrying a triangular roof that protected part of a piazza from the rain and the sun. The architect chose to place his *Centri* in three Roman loci: Saint Peter's square, Piazza Navona and the intersection of Via Condotti and Via del Corso. For each *Centro*, Krier produced a plan and perspectives constituted of the insertion of the project represented by 'very simple graphical intervention' into some of Piranesi's drawings.[45] Jutting out all of the surrounding palazzi by at least three floors, the *Centro* on Piazza Navona offered a paradoxical vision: that of an extremely open building and simultaneously that of a totalitarian-looking and certainly intimidating construction. Clearly out of scale,[46] Krier's intervention aimed not only at a formal solution: it contained a social critique of the modern city in which no sense of community was pursued. In his words, his project developed 'an alternative model to stop the bureaucratic transformation of the city into purified and controlled functional zones'.[47]

Similarly to most of his colleagues, Krier had realized a series of drawings especially for the exhibition. Yet for Krier, these drawings had real value, and were the property of each architect rather than part of an ensemble that necessarily needed to be preserved as a whole. This particular stance on the exhibition is attested to by a series of letters between Krier and Lonardi Buontempo, located in the IIA archive. This correspondence reveals a sinewy argument between the two parties over the ownership of drawings produced for the exhibition. In October 1980, Krier wrote:

> You know that the drawings, which I did for the 'Roma Interrotta' show, are extremely important to me. They are works of art in their own right and I have only very few of them, because normally the drawings I do are to do with explaining more than with doing works of art in their own right. I have had now several exhibitions and those 20 drawings have been terribly missing there. The most important exhibition however for me now is coming up in New York in January 1981 at the Max Protetch gallery. For me it would be extremely humiliating not to have the 'Roma Interrotta' drawings there, I think that you can understand the reason very well. It would be like presenting myself to a bel-canto contest with a sore throat, (or a piano competition with a broken arm, etc.)[48]

To this request, Lonardi Buontempo replied that: 'It [was] absolutely necessary to continue the travelling tour of "Roma Interrotta", and to maintain the original arrangement of the show during this travel'. She continues, '[m]aybe someday we shall donate the whole to some cultural institution or to some museums however, "Roma Interrotta" must preserve its integrity, i.e. remain such as it has been intended originally'. In the same letter, the art patron also wrote that her wish was 'to let the Incontri Internazionali d'Arte continue to be the depository of the original version of the projects', stating that 'this viewpoint is now largely universally accepted on an international level when dealing with works of visual art, and, obviously, "Roma Interrotta" is one of these'.[49] This exchange illustrates the crucial importance of the drawings both for their author (Krier) and for the exhibition's organizer (Lonardi Buontempo). Though we might dismiss this discussion as being merely personal and thus irrelevant, this incident in fact reveals much about the role of architectural representation in the postmodern era, and on the subjectivity of Krier's approach and resulting production.

James Stirling

While James Stirling's 'Roma Interrotta' project was also to some extent meg-alomaniacal, it distinguished itself from Krier's by using another major trope of postmodernism: irony. Highly self-referential, Stirling's project was ironic in that it 'plays with the ambitious state of meaning between presence and absence' and 'suggests the vitality and depth of endless dialectics.'[50] Testing the validity of displaying some of his project in the territory of 1748 Rome, Stirling was put-ting a lot of seriousness into something he obviously recognized and presented as being the least serious of all gestures. As Stirling specified in the subtitle of his project, he was after the 'demise of the post-war planning profession' and per-haps sought a method of urban composition that would be completely detached from rational and objective planning.

The MFA solution (standing, anecdotally, for Megalomaniac Frustrated Architect, referring to an architect's resentment towards projects that remain unbuilt) consisted in incorporating built and unbuilt projects by James Stirling (as well as projects realized in collaboration with James Gowan or Michael Wil-ford) into places in Rome that were considered essential to preserve/integrate/ intensify. Stirling had been allocated sector 4 of the Nolli plan: the north-west section, constituting mainly the Janiculum Hill and a small section of the Tiber. An extensive amount of research and investigation (conducted by Barbara Weiss, then Stirling's assistant) was necessary to locate Stirling's projects and relate his particular building to the location. Weiss remembers 'spending a huge amount of time looking at every single monument on the Janiculum site and doing some research on the history of particular palaces.'[51] As revealed by a series of sketches found at the Canadian Centre for Architecture,[52] Stirling carefully studied the emplacement of each of his 'interventions', testing his hypothesis by means of plans, perspectives and circulation schemes.

In the exhibition's catalogue Stirling explained his working method, which he qualified as 'contextual–associational': it is a way of planning that is 'somewhat akin to the historic process (albeit timeless) by which the creation of built form is directly influenced by the visual setting and is a confirmation and a comple-ment to that which exists.'[53] Playing with sixty-four images of all sorts (photos of Roman monuments, drawings and models of past projects, photos of James Stir-ling's built projects and even representations of objects such as a vacuum cleaner) and a series of written recommendations, Stirling's team carefully described each of the operations of the megalomaniac architects. For example:

> Along the Tiber (Doha gulf) are aligned the buildings of eleven new ministries (Gov-ernment Centre Doha 1976). The programme required each ministry to have its own personality yet office floor areas were similar. The Minister's suite at the top of each tower overlooks the waterfront. Entry into arcaded courtyards is from Via della Lungara.[54]

Stirling refers to the teaching of Rowe and Ungers that 'stands in comparison to the irrationality of most post-war planning'.[55] Deploring the city's loss of identity while condemning the disband of the planning profession in the UK, Stirling with this project took the opportunity to carefully study not only Baroque Rome but also the hypothetical connection between his projects and potential sites as a way to foster the importance of the context in postmodern architecture and city planning.

Conclusion: The Future of the City's Past

The Roman exhibition closed down on 27 June 1978 after attracting around 20,000 visitors. Despite some bitter criticism, the 'Roma Interrotta' drawings came to be in demand across the globe and went on an impressive international tour that lasted thirty years.[56]

In July 1979, Ada Louise Huxtable published a review of the exhibition at the Cooper Hewitt Museum. Although criticizing the show for being 'an elite and erudite game' as well as an 'obscure, technical, parochial, and private' endeavour, she wrote that the results of the undertaking were 'as interesting for the professional as they are baffling to the layman'. Huxtable declared: 'this is one of these studies that has already became legend, the kind of theoretical exercise that takes a permanent place in the more esoteric annals of art and architecture history'.[57] Defending a similar position, Giorgio Muratore, in a text entitled 'Dodici architetti ai Mercati Traianei giocano con Roma' (Twelve Architects Play with Rome Trajan's Market), published in the daily newspaper *La Repubblica*, strongly deplored the fact that the exhibition had been used as

> pretesto ... per un confronto diretto tra architetture antiche e architetture moderne nell'ipotesi decisamente snob e tipicamente radicale di un corto circuito culturale che, annulati più di duecento anni di storia, desse vita ad una conflagrazione di linguaggi, di materiale e di tecniche capace di simulare una virtuale alternativa ai drammatici fatti reali della vicenda edilizia contemporanea romana in particolare.[58]

> (the pretext for a direct confrontation between antique and modern architecture in a definitely elitist and typically radical hypothesis of cultural short circuit. It deleted more than 200 years of history in favour of a conflagration of language, material and technique, capable of imitating a virtual alternative to the dramatic real facts of the situation of contemporary construction, particularly in Rome.)

The critic went on to suggest that the show looked like a sort of *bal masqué* where every architect read its own part with a tragic determination.[59] According to Muratore, only a few of the contributing architects remained lucid and appreciated that 'Roma Interrotta' was nothing more than a complex and gigantic architectural game. And according to the architectural historian Francesco Dal Co, the exercise was very academic and the project had obviously been imagined only to be exhibited.[60] All these critics refer to the artistic aspect of the endeavour, questioning its true contribution to the architectural field.

However, the impressive tour of the 'Roma Interrotta' project raised questions about the international impact that the individual contributions may have had on the imaginaries of architects and urban planners. The 'Roma Interrotta' drawings were undoubtedly seen by a massive number of people. Confronting visitors with a rich repertoire of languages and representation techniques, the set of drawings of 'Roma Interrotta' somehow symbolize a double paradigm shift: on the one hand, the newly acquired freedom of the architect, and, on the other, the entry of architecture into cultural institutions. Yet 'Roma Interrotta' was also, by touring all over the world, an excuse to circulate a new image of the city of Rome. No longer seen as simply as the one dimensional historical city, Rome was now viewed as a repertoire of postmodern urban and architectural forms with which architects could play and which gave weight and value to their work.

'Roma Interrotta', then, offers a postmodern *image* of Rome, presenting the 'Eternal city' as a diffuse and disorientating place that challenges the notion of a unitarian territory produced by a single overarching plan. The event was the occasion to materialize and make more 'public' an ongoing shift with regard to urban planning: a shift towards a more subjective approach to the city. For the endeavour, architects took as their departure point a past that was no longer there, intermingling that state of affairs with a future that was purely fictional or, at least, not yet present. As such, 'Roma Interrotta's *modus operandi* corresponds perfectly with Steven Connor's definition of postmodernism as

> that condition in which for the first time, and as a result of technologies that allow large scale storage, access, and reproduction of records of the past, the past appears to be included in the present, or at the present's disposal, and in which the ration between present and past has therefore changed.[61]

That new sort of temporality transformed the city by concretizing the rehabilitation of old industrial or commercial structures (such as Trajan's Market) in containers for cultural activities.

'Roma Interrotta' was, first and foremost, an excuse to stage practices and generate a unique set of drawings which travelled the world, triggering debate and discussion. Rather than the overall result, what really mattered in 'Roma Interrotta' was to show one's approach to the problem of historical city centre. While the group with its associate ideology was very important, the figure of the architect as a 'super hero' artist and intellectual was also starting to emerge at precisely that time. By taking part in 'Roma Interrotta', architects produced a series of drawings which, through a sort of narcissistic process, contributed to their own personal language and techniques while blowing up their ego (as exemplified by the exhibition's engorged blue cube containing, on the inside, the Nolli map and the new map of Rome, and on the outside, the names of the twelve architects written in big golden letters). 'Roma Interrotta' is exemplary of the postmodern period: it shows an architecture based on the notions of 'event' and 'mediatization', which suddenly took over the cultural industry; it generated more than a hundred original drawings or *images* that depicted the urban condition as much as it did the personality of each architect. Like many postmodern enterprises, it was the *images* generated by 'Roma Interrotta' rather than the projects themselves, which really influenced the architectural world.

On 20 December 2010 Graziella Lonardi Buontempo died at the age of eighty-two. The (almost) complete set of drawings produced on the occasion of the legendary exhibition were in possession of Lonardi Buontempo, who left no clear directions as to what should be done with them, provoking a frantic competition between different cultural institutions that sought after the drawings. Though this raises many further questions about the precise financial and cultural value of the exhibition, the drawings are testament to the specific crossover of historical instances and fragmented subjectivities and continue to provide an extraordinarily valuable key to understanding the Italian capital's postmodern foundations.

9 LAS VEGAS BY WAY OF ROME: THE ETERNAL CITY AND AMERICAN POSTMODERNISM

Richard W. Hayes

The postmodern movement questioned master narratives that purported to convey eternal truths.[1] Identified by Jean-François Lyotard for its scepticism towards metanarratives, or comprehensive explanations of history, postmodernism would seem to have little to do with the idea of Rome as locus of universal value: the eternal city. In architectural culture, this idea originated in the grand tour of the seventeenth and eighteenth centuries and persisted through the nineteenth and twentieth centuries in the *Grand Prix de Rome* of France's architectural academy and in schools modelled on the French system.[2] With the establishment in 1720 of the annual *Grand Prix de Rome* by the Académie Royale d'Architecture, the predecessor to the École des Beaux-Arts, a pilgrimage to Rome to experience the city's glories at first hand became the culmination of architectural education.[3] Prevailing for two hundred and fifty years, this continuum came to an end in 1968, following the student revolts that transformed architectural education in France.[4] The permanent termination of *Grand Prix* competitions reflected modernism's radical break with history and seemed to signal the *dénouement* of Rome as wellspring of architectural influence.

Yet Rome was inconvertibly a touchstone for two of America's most important postmodern architects: Charles W. Moore and Robert Venturi. In this essay, I discuss the significance Rome held for each of these architects and the differences that mark the lessons they learned from the Italian capital. Their work serves as an entry point for analysing why Rome was so important to postmodernism, particularly in its American manifestation. For both architects, Rome acted as a locus of paradoxical lessons: it served as paradigm of civic space and urbanity, showing how a renewed focus on the city could provide an alternative to what was felt to be the anti-urban ethos and formal impoverishment of late modern architecture. At the same time, it led them, surprisingly enough, to an appreciation of American mass culture. Their recourse to Rome was at once part of a rejection of the inherited verities of architectural modernism and a springboard to an experimental meshing of European high culture with American pop culture, derived from their own personal, subjective experiences of the city. The end results are what have come to be considered the characteristic features of postmodernism in architecture: an opening up of the modernist canon; a syncretic simultaneity of the historical and the contemporary; and a recuperation of historical precedent made vivid by a corresponding enlargement of architecture's purvey to include mass culture, the quotidian, and the symbolic.[5]

Rome's historical centre served as an incubator for Moore and Venturi as they formulated what cultural critic Andreas Huyssen later described as the 'strategic move' of postmodernism: destabilizing high/low cultural divisions from within.[6] For Huyssen, postmodernism can best be understood by its rejection of modernism's 'anxiety of contamination' from popular culture; its 'categorical separation of high art and mass culture'.[7] In their interpolation of European high art and American mass culture, Moore and Venturi exemplify what Huyssen sees as the main feature of postmodernism: 'It operates in a field of tension between tradition and innovation, conservation and renewal, mass culture and high art, in which the second terms are no longer automatically privileged over the first'.[8]

This is what distinguishes their work from another American architect, Michael Graves, a prominent visitor to Rome, who is often labelled a postmodernist. Like Venturi, Graves was a fellow of the American Academy of Rome, the institution founded in 1894. The importance of a Roman sojourn in the careers of Moore, Venturi and Graves points to the city's renewed disciplinary relevance in the second half of the twentieth century.[9] Graves's historicist designs, however, do not evince an attenuation of master narratives, nor does he explore tensions between the high and the low. Moore and Venturi, by contrast, developed out of their separate experiences of Rome as the urban palimpsest *par excellence* a postmodernism which resonates with the key principles identified by Lyotard and Huyssen. They will thus be the focus of my essay.

Charles W. Moore: From Tivoli to New Orleans

First, Charles W. Moore. Born in 1925 in Michigan, Moore was one of the leading architects and educators of the second half of the twentieth century in America. After receiving a modernist education at the University of Michigan, Moore earned a doctoral degree from Princeton University, where he completed a dissertation entitled 'Water and Architecture' in 1957, becoming one of the few practising architects of his era to hold a doctorate.[10] Moore described his reasons for selecting water as a dissertation topic when he stated retrospectively,

> Water, at least in its architectural manifestations, seemed to me an exciting subject when I was looking for a topic for a doctoral dissertation in architecture at Princeton. It seemed then ... that our ways of thinking about the stuff of which architecture is made were too confining: that the symbolic and expressive were viewed with suspi-

cion ... Water, with its extraordinary range of qualities, represented one of the magic substances that could lead us back to a rich and expressive way of building.[11]

As part of his search for 'a rich and expressive way of building', Moore looked to the fountains and public spaces in Europe, particularly those in and around Rome, which he toured in 1950 on a fellowship after his graduation from Michigan. He returned to the city in 1975 and 1981 as a two-time resident of the American Academy, part of life-long enthusiasm for the city that caused him to state, 'Some prefer Rome, some prefer Paris, and some prefer London. I prefer Rome'.[12] While his dissertation is wide-ranging in its historical references, Moore gave extensive focus to Rome's waterworks, such as Gianlorenzo Bernini's Four Rivers Fountain in the Piazza Navona, Nicola Salvi's Trevi Fountain, the Fountain of the Tartarughe in the Piazza Mattei, and the cascades at Villa d'Este in nearby Tivoli. He described how 'Roman fountains probably offer the richest available catalogue of sculptured surfaces made in response to water' and called the Trevi Fountain 'the most magnificent exhibition of water on our planet'.[13] In 1960, he published an analysis of Hadrian's Villa in Tivoli, emphasizing the role of water in the architecture of the second-century villa, particularly in the so-called Maritime Theatre, a round, paved 'island' surrounded by a moat and freestanding colonnade, all of which are encircled by enclosing walls (see Figure 9.1 on p. 174). 'To animate the spaces beyond what we can see today', Moore wrote, 'would have been the rush and the splash of flowing water, which was everywhere'.[14] Set against the backdrop of classical architecture, these waterworks affected the mind and senses of the beholder in a physically direct way, while simultaneously furnishing a locus of historical memory through an eclectic assemblage of references to buildings throughout the classical world. Moore underscored the eclecticism of the Spanish-born emperor, noting how Hadrian created 'representations of celebrated buildings and localities which had impressed him on his extensive travels' across the empire.[15] For Moore, the Maritime Theatre was 'the quintessential magic island, the most compelling place in Tivoli', designed to foster an intensified sense of self-presence.[16] Hadrian's villa was of vital importance to Moore as he evolved his principles of place-making in architecture, which involves both bodily experience and the fostering of memory through cultural allusions.

Moore was not alone in his appreciation of Hadrian's villa; indeed, as architectural critic Charles Jencks observed, 'during the sixties, Hadrian's Villa became *the* exemplar, a model and point of reference' for architects and historians like Louis I. Kahn, Oswald Mathias Ungers, Colin Rowe and Vincent Scully.[17] The previous decade, writers Marguerite Yourcenar and Eleanor Clark took Hadrian and his villa as subject of books that would have a wide influence.[18] By the mid-1970s, architectural historian Colin Rowe placed Hadrian's Villa at the centre of his influential book, *Collage City*, describing it as a miniature Rome and a

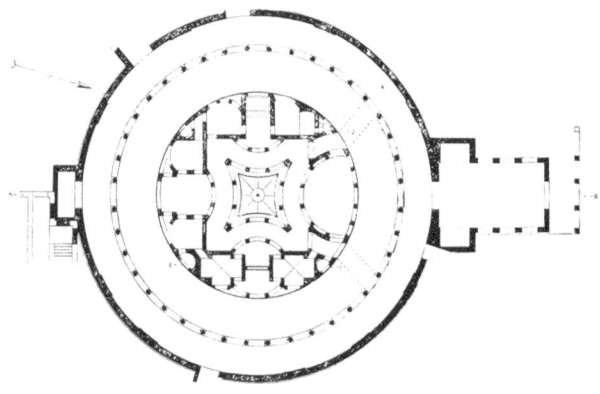

"Maritime Theater"

Figure 9.1: Blueprint and photograph of the Maritime Theatre inside Hadrian's Villa in Tivoli. From C. W. Moore, 'Hadrian's Villa', *PERSPECTA: Yale Architectural Journal*, 6 (1960), pp. 17–27, on p. 22. Copyright: Yale University School of Architecture and Avery Architectural and Fine Arts Library, Columbia University in the City of New York. Reproduced with the kind permission of the copyright holder.

dialectical utopia. For Rowe, the villa was as a paradigm that mediated the ideal and 'the needs of ad hoc', serving to exemplify his evolving concept of urbanistic collage. He wrote,

> The Villa Adriana is a miniature Rome. It plausibly reproduces all the collisions of set pieces and all the random empirical happenings which the city so lavishly exhibited ... It is almost certain that the uninhibited aesthetic preference of today is for the structural discontinuities and the multiple syncopated excitements which the Villa Adriana presents.[19]

Rowe's abstract, formalist interpretation differs from Moore's experiential engagement with the villa and its waterworks, which influenced his designs for the Lovejoy Fountain of 1965 in Portland, Oregon and the Piazza d'Italia of 1975–8 in New Orleans, Louisiana, a project that is often considered to be the single most emblematic work of postmodern design (see Figure 9.2 on p. 176).

The project was commissioned for the city's Italian-Americans, who felt their contributions to New Orleans had not received the recognition accorded the French, Spanish and African-American communities.[20] Located between the business district and the Mississippi River, St Joseph's Fountain was intended to be a symbolic focus for the Italian-American neighbourhood, both memorial and gathering place.[21] Working in association with the New Orleans architects August Perez & Associates, Moore designed a scheme infused with references to Italian architecture and civic space, filtered through a pop sensibility, and used water as a device to engage residents and visitors in a physical experience of the memorial. The plan radiates from a three-dimensional map of Italy criss-crossed by fragmented colonnades painted in intense, saturated colours. Water flows from a Serlian motif at the rear as well as between the colonnades and from jets along the distinctive topography of Italy. A Latin inscription on the entablature of one of the colonnades ('HUNC FONTEM CIVES NOVI AURELIANI TOTO POPULO DONO DEDERUNT', This fountain is a gift to all the citizens of New Orleans) contrasts with the day-glow colours Moore used to create a vivid, scenographic monument, exemplifying the mixture of visual codes that would become a hallmark of postmodern design.

Response to the Piazza d'Italia has ranged from celebration to reproach. Architectural critic Martin Filler, for example, praised Moore's design as 'an ensemble of unqualified pleasure and delight, the perfect expression of the *gioia di vita* that is as characteristically Italian as the vocabulary of forms and colours that makes this such a deeply evocative place'.[22] Patricia A. Morton, by contrast, recently labelled the fountain 'an icon of postmodern kitsch'.[23] One aspect I would like to add to the discussion is the element of active engagement. 'My chief interest', Moore once stated, 'is in doing things that get the participation of the people who are going to live in them or use them or get involved with them'.[24]

Figure 9.2: Design of Charles Moore's Piazza d'Italia in New Orleans. Charles W. Moore and the Urban Innovations Group with Perez Associates. Perspective drawing by Bill Hersey and John Kryk, c. 1977. Reproduced courtesy of the Charles Moore Foundation.

Moore often discussed architecture in terms of choreography, a point made in his 1977 book, *Body, Memory, and Architecture*, in which he and fellow author Kent Bloomer criticized the prevailing ocularcentric, or purely visual, apprehension of the built environment. They argued instead for the restorative value of haptic experience, in which buildings would serve as stimuli for movement, using the Spanish Steps in Rome to illustrate their point.[25] Moore noted how *la Barcaccia*, the fountain of 'the worthless boat' at the Piazza di Spagna evoked 'the mystery and quiet of the sea' while encouraging a physical, bodily response from the public.[26] Located below grade level, the fountain encourages passers-by to step down towards the basin, thus fostering a sense of being immersed in water, even in the midst of city traffic. Fresh from his 1975 residency at the American Academy, Moore animated his design for New Orleans with memories of Rome's public spaces and the intensely haptic responses they provoked. 'Roman fountains', Moore wrote, 'invite contact; people seem irresistibly drawn toward them, to dangle their fingers in the water, then to plunge in their arms'.[27] In addition to the Piazza di Spagna, Moore studied how, in the seventeenth century, Piazza Navona was flooded during Sundays in August, allowing inhabitants the festal experience of walking or driving their carriages through standing water in the midst of the urban realm.[28] In his dissertation, Moore noted how often Italian fountains function as civic focal points.[29]

Consequently, Moore sought to create in the Piazza d'Italia a civic space at the scale of pedestrians, who were encouraged to climb the topographic map of Italy and walk though the fountain's flowing and standing waters, in between the layered colonnades. Using low basins filled to the brim with water was clearly derived from Roman prototypes like *la Barcaccia*. Furthermore, a freestanding rostrum atop a contour map of Sicily allows for impromptu public events. The design thus privileges bodily engagement over visual decoding and it was part of Moore's effort to vivify the diminished public realm in America, the subject of his provocative 1965 essay, 'You Have to Pay for the Public Life'. In the essay, Moore described how hard it is to locate a meaningful public realm in what he called 'the featureless, floating world' of contemporary America, defined largely by car culture. Surveying the unmemorable buildings in this rootless world of incessant mobility, he wrote,

> houses are not tied down to any *place* much more than the trailer homes are or the automobiles. They are adrift in the suburban sea, not so mobile as the cars, but just as unattached. This is, after all, a floating world in which a floating population can island-hop with impunity; one need never go ashore. There are the drive-in banks, the drive-in movies, the drive-in shoe repair.[30]

By contrast, the creation of place became Moore's life work, and he explored how variations of the European *passeggiata* (stroll) could be made relevant to the

North American context. The design of the Piazza d'Italia embodied Moore's attempt to turn observers into participants by inducing bodily engagement and by creating an eclectic assemblage of historical motifs that would encourage people to make connections across space and time. These were among the lessons Moore had learned at Hadrian's Villa in Tivoli and the public fountains in Rome.

Robert Venturi and the Relevance of Michelangelo

Rome offered different lessons for Moore's fellow Princeton graduate Robert Venturi, who once described his first trip to Rome as the formative architectural experience of his life. Born in 1925 in Philadelphia, Venturi is a descendant of Italian immigrants. His maternal grandparents came from Puglia and his father was born in the town of Atessa in the Abruzzi, later immigrating to Philadelphia where he established himself as a produce merchant.[31] From these immigrant origins, Venturi's life has been an American success story: the son of doting parents, his mother a forward-thinking political progressive, he was a brilliant student, graduating with highest honours from Princeton, where he studied with some of the finest architectural educators of mid-century, including Louis I. Kahn, Enrico Peressutti, Jean Labatut and Donald Drew Egbert, the last two of whom would go on to be Moore's dissertation advisors.[32]

In the summer of 1948, after his first year of graduate study, Venturi embarked on a two-month-long tour of Europe, half of which was spent in Italy.[33] In a letter to his parents on his first day in Rome, Venturi wrote,

> My first impression is favourable; I love it. It is really very different from what I expected – there is so much colour in the buildings against a deep blue sky and deep green foliage – something we who have lived in America cannot imagine. Many of the buildings are a deep rouge – a combination of rose and yellow.[34]

The student's experiences were so powerful, he voted to return, and six years later, he won a two-year fellowship to the American Academy in Rome, a period that would prove enormously consequential for American architecture.[35] For it was in the course of these two years in Rome that Venturi laid the groundwork for his 'gentle manifesto', *Complexity and Contradiction in Architecture*. Published in 1966 under the auspices of the Museum of Modern Art, the short book became the foundational text of postmodern architecture, described by Yale professor Vincent Scully as 'the most important writing on the making of architecture since Le Corbusier's *Vers une Architecture* of 1923'.[36] While every page of the book includes examples culled from all periods of architecture, Rome was essential to Venturi's path-breaking indictment of modern architecture and his opening up new critical terms of debate. Of almost two hundred and fifty illustrations in the book, over fifty are of Rome. Italy's Mannerist architecture was Venturi's most important discovery, a fact signalled by the use of a photograph of Michelangelo's Porta Pia on the cover of the book's second edition, where it formed a liminal correlative to the author's conceptual breakthrough (see Figure 9.3 on p. 180). Derived from the Italian word *maniera*, or style, Mannerism refers to works of art, architecture and literature dating from the sixteenth century in Italy which were characterized by self-conscious artifice, complexity and sophistication.[37] For Venturi, Mannerism seemed to echo the tensions, ambiguities and anxieties that characterized much of contemporary life, the condition alluded to by the phrase 'complexity and contradiction'. These were the principles that best described what Venturi called 'the richness and ambiguity of modern experience'.[38]

Interestingly enough, Venturi did not set out to study Mannerist architecture and it was only in the last weeks of his two-year stay that Mannerism became the focus of his analysis. Venturi later wrote,

> I went [to Rome] looking for SPACE – among forms and in piazzas – but I fell in love with Borromini, became enamored of Michelangelo and discovered Mannerism, and later symbolism ... It was in my last few weeks at the Academy that I realized Mannerism was what turned me on – and made Michelangelo relevant – relevant for an American architect of my time. And out of that intuition several years later evolved *Complexity and Contradiction in Architecture*.[39]

It is clear that Rome offered the young architect three separate lessons: first, the city's streets and public spaces taught him that architecture is fundamentally urban and should respond to a context larger than individual buildings, which could now be understood as fragments of larger wholes. This insight offered a way out of the dead end into which modern architecture seemed to have found itself. By the 1950s, many establishment modern architects designed sculptural objects that ignored their surroundings, resulting in what writer Norman Mailer derided as 'empty landscapes of psychosis'.[40] Once in Rome, Venturi looked at urban components like the Piazza Sant'Ignazio, where the building's facade seems to inflect to define exterior space, and, in so doing, acknowledges a larger, societal role for buildings. This was a revelation compared to the modernist object-building standing aloof in an anti-urban way. Other examples Venturi illustrated include the Palazzo Massimo alle Colonne on Corso Vittorio Emanuele, whose gently curving facade follows the bend of its street, and the Piazza del Popolo, where twin churches create an urban ensemble greater than themselves.[41]

The second lesson Rome offered was its Mannerist architecture, in which a dissonant use of classical language stood in strong contrast to the simplistic vocabulary that modernism had dwindled into. By mid-century, the heroic simplification of forms in 1920s high modernism had become boring and vapid in the hands of lesser followers.[42] Italian architecture of the sixteenth and sev-

Figure 9.3: Photograph of Michelangelo's Porta Pia. Reproduced with the permission of Venturi, Scott Brown and Associates, Inc.

enteenth centuries, by contrast, seemed to fuse unlikely elements in complex compositions that Venturi appreciated aesthetically and intellectually. Michelangelo's Porta Pia was prominent in this regard. Constructed between 1561 and 1565 as a gate in the Aurelian Walls, the Porta Pia was one of Pope Pius IV's civic improvements. Art historian James Ackerman (whom Venturi references in *Complexity and Contradiction*) has described the Porta Pia as 'an innovation in city-gate design which had neither forerunners nor imitators'.[43] For Ackerman, the design is notable for its eccentric assemblage of decorative elements that break with prevailing architectural conventions. According to Ackerman,

> The Porta Pia, erected on the inner face of an ancient fortified gate enclosure just north of the original Porta Nomentana, differed in function and form from any city gate of the Renaissance or earlier times. Though set in defensive system, it was an indefensible, thin brick screen barely strong enough to sustain its own weight – a record of the moment when the Romans abandoned hope of using their ancient walls as an effective defense against modern artillery. Furthermore, it faced inwards, towards Rome, evading for the first time a tradition which from prehistoric times had turned gates towards the highway and countryside as an introduction to the city behind. Michelangelo's gate belongs more to the street than to the walls; it was pure urban scenography – a masonry memento of the temporary arches erected in the Renaissance to celebrate the arrival of princes, though without their triumphal connotations. The street, too, was more theatrical than utilitarian, since it crossed one of the least populated and congested quarters of Rome, where no important buildings were raised before the end of the century.[44]

It was precisely the heterodox aspect of the design that attracted Venturi. In *Complexity and Contradiction*, he offered a sustained visual analysis of the city-facing facade, describing how 'in their complex relationships, disparate elements are in varying degrees structural and ornamental, frequently redundant, and sometimes vestigial'.[45] While postmodernists have often been interpreted as harking back nostalgically to a lost humanism,[46] it is important to note that Venturi was attracted to Michelanglo's design precisely for the ways in which it problematized the classical inheritance. Indeed, Ackerman identified the Porta Pia as an expression of 'the twilight of humanism' in which 'a fantastic miscegenation' of forms repudiated many of the conventions established by humanist architects in the High Renaissance.[47]

Michelangelo's masterpiece thus appealed to both the intellectual and nonconformist sides of Venturi. More importantly, it set the criteria with which to interpret architects as diverse as Louis Sullivan, Sir Edwin Lutyens and Alvar Aalto, who were not part of the Mannerist era but whose designs featured ambiguities, visual wit or tense and unresolved interrelationships. Venturi located these qualities in selected examples of contemporary Roman architecture, such as the 1950 Casa del Girasole in the viale Bruno Buozzi, designed by Luigi Moretti with a façade seemingly cleft in two.[48] Venturi later adopted the phrase 'implicit mannerism' to describe examples of mannerism in architecture occurring after the sixteenth century.[49]

The final element of the Roman milieu that would prove influential was the palimpsestic quality of the city, where fragments of the past created startling juxtapositions in scale and time. Venturi's understanding of the city as palimpsest is succinctly conveyed in his photograph, taken in the courtyard of the Capitoline Museums, of the 'accidental collage' of a colossal head of Constantine and everyday, louvered shutters (see Figure 9.4 on p. 183).[50] The theme surfaces as well in an extensive passage he quotes from Nathaniel Hawthorne's 1860 novel *The Marble Faun*, a story of American expatriate artists in Rome. At the opening of the eighth chapter of *Complexity and Contradiction*, Venturi includes Hawthorne's description of a group of artists – 'an aesthetic company' – taking a moonlight ramble through Rome's streets and piazzas, progressing from the Trevi Fountain to the Forum of Trajan:

> The party moved on, but deviated a little from the straight way, in order to glance at the ponderous remains of the temple of Mars Ultor, within which a convent of nuns is now established – a dove-cote, in the war god's mansion. At only a little distance, they passed the portico of the Temple of Minerva ... Within this edifice of an antique sanctity, a baker's shop was now established, with an entrance on one side; for everywhere, the remnants of old grandeur and divinity have been made available for the meanest necessities of our day.[51]

The passage portrays the cityscape as a succession of contrasts between contemporary, quotidian life and ancient grandeur, a nineteenth-century precursor to Venturi's admixture of high and low. Hawthorne's hybrid novel was at once a Gothic romance and a favoured guidebook for nineteenth-century visitors to Rome.[52] By alluding to Hawthorne's text, Venturi aligns himself with a long-standing tradition of cultured American travellers to Rome. As Paul Baker has noted, by the end of the nineteenth century Rome had a permanent colony of 200 American residents in addition to 30,000 annual American visitors.[53] Travel and residence abroad – especially in Italy – became a significant part of the American experience. Hawthorne's novel explores the ambivalence of this experience, as the two American artists become embroiled in a murder, losing the innocence of their initial attempts at self-culture, emerging with a chastened sense of human fragility. In Hawthorne's tale of innocence and experience, the city functions as both beacon of artistic aspiration and harbinger of deviance.

Venturi's invocation of the novel thus reinforces his argument that Rome is the locus of a mature, complex understanding of the human condition, one that embraces ambivalence and ambiguity.[54] The point I would like to underline is that these artistic lessons also offered insights on how one could practice as an architect in the evolving pluralist context of the twentieth century. While

Figure 9.4: Photograph of Constantine's colossal head, which is located in the courtyard of the Palazzo dei Conservatori, Capitoline Museums, Rome. Copyright Alinari/Art Resource, New York.

Venturi's argument is fundamentally formalist, the formalist strategy served to undergird a progressive social position – a position that saw the role of architecture as mediating the varying and sometimes irreconcilable cultures of a pluralist society.[55] In Rome, Venturi studied buildings that accommodated their contexts, compositions that held opposing forces in balance, and fragments of past eras that vivified the present: these features fused in Venturi's imagination, finding an affirmatory position in the principles of complexity and contradiction.

In light of this, it may not seem surprising that the next focus of Venturi's analysis would be a contemporary city. *Complexity and Contradiction* concluded with an image of an American main street, and the author later described how he came to appreciate the American built environment during his Roman sojourn.

> As a temporary expatriate, reveling in the baroque splendors of the city beyond my studio windows and seeping myself in the ambience of all Italy beyond the horizon, I was at the same time peculiarly sensible to a vision of my own land – visualizing old things in new ways and from different angles. The American in Europe, especially the young artist, finding an American identity through absorbing a European heritage can be a most pompous cliché, but here I think it fits. As I immersed myself in baroque city planning, I perceived via perspective and comparison, the genius of the American gridiron plan. It became no longer ordinary but special – as the democratic or egalitarian configuration of streets was explicitly devoid of hierarchy – the mayor's house could sit across from a deli. There was no ducal palace terminating an axial boulevard – rather there was space at the end of streets, infinite space leading toward the frontier, eternally open to opportunity, as Vincent Scully put it.[56]

While the turn towards the American context is thus understandable, the specific choice of Las Vegas as subject for his next book seems disjunctive if not contrarian. 'Sin city', the postmodern simulacrum, a quickly constructed entertainment zone with little history: the Nevada resort is the polar opposite of the urban palimpsest. 'Las Vegas *was* built in a day', Venturi and his co-authors Denise Scott Brown and Steven Izenour joked.[57] It was in fact Scott Brown who first took Venturi to Las Vegas.[58] Born Denise Lakofski in 1931 in what was then Rhodesia – Scott Brown grew up in South Africa – she studied first at the Architectural Association in London and later with architect Louis I. Kahn at the University of Pennsylvania, where she met faculty member Venturi.[59] Scott Brown's parents had vacationed in Las Vegas in the 1950s and in 1966 she took Venturi to the gambling capital, where they toured the infamous 'Strip' in a rented car. Scott Brown later described the unresolved mixture of topophilia and topophobia of their response to the desert oasis: 'we rode around from casino to casino. Dazed by the desert sun and dazzled by the signs, both loving and hating what we saw, we were jolted clear out of our aesthetic skins'.[60] As historian David Brownlee noted, they were also jolted into love for each other and were married in 1967 on the porch of Scott Brown's Santa Monica bungalow.[61]

The couple returned to Las Vegas in the fall of 1968, when, hired by Charles Moore as chairman of Yale's Department of Architecture, they took a class of thirteen graduate students for a ten-day research trip as part of a design studio they called 'Learning from Las Vegas, or Form Analysis as Design Research'.[62] The studio was one of the highlights of an intense era of experimentation and innovation that characterized Moore's tenure at Yale.[63] In 1972, the work of the studio was published in a folio-sized book, a revised version of which, greatly reduced in size and more simply formatted, was published in 1977.

One of the characteristic features of the studio was the use of maps and graphic tools to analyse an urban landscape that seemed to feature so few of the elements traditionally associated with cities. An interest in urban cartography is apparent in Venturi's first publication, based on his Princeton MFA thesis, the 1953 essay entitled 'The Campidoglio: A Case Study', in which he made use of maps, perspective drawings and aerial photographs from the sixteenth century to the present to reveal how the urban context impacts architectural meaning.[64] Venturi's fascination with the Porta Pia could even be seen to anticipate his interest in contemporary urban signs. As Ackerman noted, Michelangelo's portal was an example of festive 'street scenery' notable for its scenographic frontality.[65] The photograph of the gate that Venturi selected for the cover of the second edition of *Complexity and Contradiction* emphasizes its flat, sign-like quality.

Continuing their splicing together of historical Rome and contemporary life, Venturi, Scott Brown and Izenour deployed Giambattista Nolli's 1748 map of Rome as a template for studies of signage, circulation and illumination levels along the Strip (see Figure 9.5 on p. 186). An architect and surveyor, Giambattista Nolli was commissioned in the mid-1730s by Pope Benedict XIV to prepare a map illustrating the boundaries of the city's fourteen administrative districts or *rioni*. Notable for its depiction of important interior spaces as well as outdoor civic spaces, *La Pianta Grande di Roma* (Great Plant of Rome) is one of the most important urban documents in Western culture. Venturi and his co-authors described their attraction to the map's figure/ground clarity, writing,

> Nolli's map of the mid-eighteenth century reveals the sensitive and complex connections between public and private space in Rome ... A 'Nolli' map of the Las Vegas Strip reveals and clarifies what is public and what is private but here the scale is enlarged by the inclusion of the parking lots and the solid to void ratio is reversed by the void of the desert. Mapping the Nolli components from an aerial photograph provides an intriguing crosscut of Strip systems.[66]

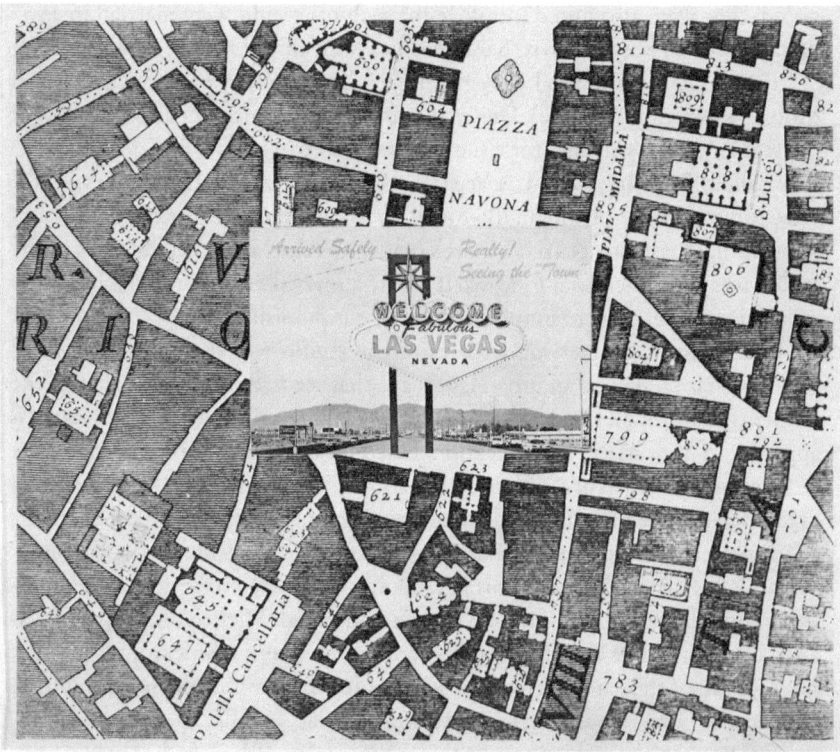

Figure 9.5: Collage of Giambattista Nolli's 1748 map of Rome with a photograph of Las Vegas's Strip used by Robert Venturi, Denise Scott Brown and Steven Izenour in *Learning from Las Vegas* (1972). Reproduced with the permission of Venturi, Scott Brown and Associates, Inc. and Avery Architectural and Fine Arts Library, Columbia University in the City of New York.

Invoking Nolli's map to compare and contrast the two cites, they make several important points:

> Each city is an archetype rather than a prototype, an exaggerated example from which to derive lessons for the typical. Each city vividly superimposes elements of a supranational scale on the local fabric: churches in the religious capital, casinos and their signs in the entertainment capital. These cause violent juxtapositions of use and scale in both cities. Rome's churches, off streets and piazzas, are open to the public; the pilgrim, religious or architectural, can walk from church to church. The gambler or architect in Las Vegas can similarly take in a variety of casinos along the Strip.[67]

On the one hand, the above-detailed invocation of Nolli's map is congruent with Venturi's identification of Rome as fount of urbanism. On the other hand, it is a provocative and irreverent gesture, fitting in with the generally anti-Establishment tone of the late sixties, to use a map originally intended for religious pilgrims in an analysis of the decadent outpost of secular, capitalist society: Las Vegas.[68] In line with this provocation, the architects suspend moral judgment in their commentary. By contrast with other writers on Las Vegas of this era, such as novelists Hunter S. Thompson and Tom Wolfe, Venturi, Scott Brown and Izenour adopted an ethically neutral attitude that sought to defer judgment. They avoided both the dystopian view of Thompson, who saw Las Vegas as a grotesque end to the American Dream, and the florid word paintings of Wolfe, for whom the illuminated signs were wonders of the modern world.[69] In larger terms, Venturi and his co-authors explicitly rejected the expected metanarratives through which Las Vegas has been viewed and critiqued – whether Marxist, Frankfurt School or Humanist – once again suggesting how their work approximates the incredulity that Lyotard identified as key to the postmodern condition. Indeed, in a recent study, Aron Vinegar has highlighted the centrality of scepticism to Venturi, Scott Brown and Izenour's text, picking up Scott Brown's use of the word 'deadpan' to describe the salience of their nonjudgmental approach to the contemporary environment. According to Vinegar, 'Venturi and Scott Brown's interest in the "deadpan" as a technique' disposed them 'to cultivate a responsiveness toward the immanent world that we live in now'.[70] For Vinegar, the recourse to such a dispassionate, deadpan method facilitated the movement between high and low that is at the heart of *Learning from Las Vegas.*[71]

In place of critique, *Learning From Las Vegas* argues for an egalitarian opening up of subjectivity and agency to everyday, ordinary people.[72] Ending on a modest note, Venturi and his co-authors find in the city's illuminated signs 'the vitality that may be achieved by an architecture of inclusion'. They write:

> The Strip shows the value of symbolism and allusion in an architecture of vast space and speed and proves that people, even architects, have fun with architecture that reminds them of something else. Allusion and comment, on the past or present or on our great commonplaces or old clichés, and inclusion of the everyday in the environment, sacred and profane – these are what are lacking in present-day modern architecture. We can learn about them from Las Vegas.[73]

Conclusion: Rome in the Plural

To conclude, a return to Rome. Clearly, it was not populism that Venturi learned in Rome, even if his sojourn gave him an insight into his own identity as an American and a new appreciation – through contrast – of American mass culture. It was the city's unparalleled urbanism and the bracing intellectual features of its Mannerist architecture that allowed his conceptual break with the modernist paradigm. The dissonant yet compelling designs of Michelangelo and Borromini offered lessons in how architecture could once again be complex and in so doing become relevant to a pluralistic society where every day one traverses multiple political and cultural fields, where identity itself is a palimpsest. A renewed appreciation of Rome was something Venturi and Scott Brown learned in Las Vegas. In 1993, he wrote,

> So we went from Rome from Las Vegas, as we said then, and from Las Vegas to Rome ... and could see Rome with new eyes and from a reverse perspective this time ... It is the home of Classicisms in the plural. It is the Rome of evolving juxtapositions – of eternal incompleteness. It is a Rome acknowledging evolutions of many kinds and juxtaposing contexts of many kinds, a Rome that is never complete, a Rome that I love that is ultimately significant for our time.[74]

What remains to be answered is the question I alluded to in my opening paragraph: how does such an unabashedly enthusiastic experience of Rome square with Lyotard's definition of the postmodern condition as one of incredulity towards master narratives? In their responses to Rome, simultaneously heartfelt and irreverent, Charles Moore and Robert Venturi at once instaurated the idea of Rome and destabilized its hegemony – thus distancing themselves from both orthodox modernists and simple revivalists. In particular, Venturi and Scott Brown's unexpected alliance of Las Vegas and Rome coincides with Lyotard's idea of how postmodernism 'reinforces our ability to tolerate the incommensurable'.[75] In identifying Rome as the locus of an eternal *relativity*, Venturi candidly expresses in the above-cited passage the ardour of his passion, a topophilia numerous architects have experienced. But coexistent with this seemingly premodernist zeal was a deadpan impiety through which the city could become relevant to another century, another continent, another condition.

NOTES

Holdaway and Trentin, Introduction

1. J. W. Goethe, *Italian Journey*, trans. W. H. Auden and E. Mayer (Harmondsworth: Penguin, 1970), p. 142.
2. Goethe, *Italian Journey*.
3. S. Freud, *Civilization and its Discontents*, trans. J. Riviere (Mansfield Centre: Martino Publishing, 2011).
4. See V. Vidotto, *Roma contemporanea* [Contemporary Rome] (Rome and Bari: Laterza, 2006), in particular the section 'Crescita demografica e sviluppo urbano' [Demographic Growth and Urban Development], pp. 278–89.
5. P. Bondanella, *The Eternal City: Roman Images in the Modern World* (Chapel Hill, NC, and London: University of North Carolina Press, 1987) and C. Edwards, *Roman Presences: Receptions of Rome in European Culture, 1789–1945* (Cambridge: Cambridge University Press, 1999).
6. M. Herzfeld, *Evicted from Eternity: The Restructuring of Modern Rome* (Chicago, IL: University of Chicago Press, 2009), p. 313.
7. See A. Cederna, *Mirabilia urbis: Cronache romane, 1957–1965* [Wonders of the City: Roman Chronicles 1957–1965] (Turin: Einaudi, 1965), and I. Insolera, *Roma moderna: Da Napoleone I al XXI secolo* [Modern Rome: From Napoleon I to the XXI Century] (Turin: Einaudi, 2011).
8. Vidotto, *Roma contemporanea*, p. 289.
9. For a summary of recent work on Rome see also F. De Pieri, 'Searching for Memories in the Suburbs of Rome', in *Modern Italy*, 15:3 (2010), pp. 372–9.
10. We include in this category: K. Jewell, 'Pasolini: Deconstructing the Roman Palimpsest', *SubStance*, 53 (1987), pp. 55–66; K. Pinkus, *The Montesi Scandal: The Death of Wilma Montesi and the Birth of the Paparazzi in Fellini's Rome* (Chicago, IL: Chicago University Press, 2003); J. D. Rhodes, *Stupendous, Miserable City: Pasolini's Rome* (Minneapolis, MN: Minnesota University Press, 2007); S. Gundle, *Death and the Dolce Vita: The Dark Side of Rome in the 1950s* (Edinburgh and New York: Canongate, 2011); C. Mazzoni (ed.), 'Capital City: Rome 1870–2010', special issue of *Annali d'italianistica*, 28 (2010); and D. Caldwell and L. Caldwell (eds), *Rome, Continuing Encounters between Past and Present* (Farnham: Ashgate, 2011).
11. C. Mazzoni, 'Introduction', in *Annali d'italianistica*, 28 (2010), pp. 13–29, on p. 14.

12. See in particular P. Matteucci and K. Pinkus, 'The Rome of Pasolini's *Petrolio*', *Annali d'Italianistica*, 28 (2010), pp. 295–316; and G. Parati, '*Where Do Migrants Live?* Amara Lakhous's Clash of Civilizations over an Elevator in Piazza Vittorio', *Annali d'Italianistica*, 28 (2010), pp. 431–45.

13. The GaWC (Global and World Cities) network is a research group based at the Geography Department at Loughborough University, which focuses on the external relations of world cities. See online at http://www.lboro.ac.uk/gawc/rb/rb377.html [accessed 2 December 2012].

14. P. Antonello and F. Mussgnug, 'Introduction', in P. Antonello and F. Mussgnug (eds), *Postmodern Impegno: Post-Hegemonic Approaches to Ethics and Socio-Political Commitment in Contemporary Italian Culture* (Bern and New York: Peter Lang, 2009), pp. 1–29, on p. 9.

15. M. Jansen, *Il dibattito sul postmoderno in Italia* [The Debate on the Postmodern in Italy] (Florence: Franco Cesati Editore, 2002), p. 14.

16. *Michelin Green Guide: Rome* (London: Michelin Apa Publications Ltd, 2010), p. 6.

17. For more information about Rome's metropolitan areas see R. Cassetti and G. Spagnesi, *Roma contemporanea: Storia e progetto* [Contemporary Rome: History and Design] (Rome: Gangemi, 2006), and its entry on the website of the province of Rome at http://www.provincia.roma.it/news/capitale-metropolitana-un-nuovo-assetto-istituzionale-garantire-lo-sviluppo [accessed 2 December 2012].

18. M. Dear, *The Postmodern Urban Condition* (Oxford: Blackwell, 2000), p. 1.

19. E. Soja, *Thirdspace: Journeys to Los Angeles and Other Real-and-Imagined Places* (Oxford: Blackwell Publishing, 1996), pp. 21–2.

20. For a comparison between European and American cities in light of postmodernity see E. Mazierska and L. Rascaroli, *From Moscow to Madrid: Postmodern Cities, European Cinema* (London: Tauris, 2003).

21. R. Ceserani, 'Premessa', in Jansen, *Il dibattito*, pp. 9–12, on p. 10. Jansen makes the same point in reference to Luperini, Ceserani and Fredric Jameson on p. 158.

22. These categories no doubt constitute a gross oversimplification of the debates in the name of a succinct approximation. Broadly the first group includes Umberto Eco and the early work of Ihab Hassan; and the second Fredric Jameson, David Harvey and Jürgen Habermas. Linda Hutcheon and Jean-François Lyotard lie in between; they see a historical change in the latter society but they also emphasize the metahistoricity of the postmodern characteristics. See, for example, Lyotard's statement that 'Freud, Duchamp, Bohr, Gertrude Stein, but also Rabelais and Sterne, are postmoderns in that they emphasize paradoxes' in F. Lyotard and B. Massumi, 'Rules and Paradoxes and Svelte Appendix', in *Cultural Critique*, 5 (1986–1987), pp. 209–19, on p. 218. Compare U. Eco, *Postscript to the Name of the Rose*, trans W. Weaver (San Diego, CA: Harcourt Brace Jovanovich, 1984); I. Hassan, *The Postmodern Turn: Essays in Postmodern Theory and Culture* (Columbus, OH: Ohio State University Press, 1987); F. Jameson, *Postmodernism, or, the Cultural Logic of Late Capitalism* (Durham, NC: Duke University Press, 1997), D. Harvey, *The Condition of Postmodernity: An Enquiry into the Origins of Cultural Change* (Oxford: Blackwell, 1990); J. Habermas and S. Ben-Habib, 'Modernity versus Postmodernity', *New German Critique*, 22 (1981), pp. 3–14; L. Hutcheon, *A Poetics of Postmodernism: History, Theory, Fiction* (New York and London: Routledge, 1988); J. F. Lyotard, *The Postmodern Condition: A Report on Knowledge*, trans. G. Bennington and B. Massumi (Manchester: Manchester University Press, 1984).

23. Jameson, *Postmodernism*, pp. 2–3.

24. Althusser quoted in Jameson, *Postmodernism*, p. xx.
25. Vidotto, *Roma contemporanea*, p. 323.
26. A. Friedberg, *Window Shopping: Cinema and the Postmodern* (Berkley, CA, and London: University of California Press, 1992), p. 2.
27. See Jewell, 'Pasolini: Deconstructing the Roman Palimpsest', pp. 55–66, who posits Pasolini's Rome as the latest historical paradigm of the city, and Rhodes, *Stupendous, Miserable City: Pasolini's Rome*, who lucidly indicates the coexistence of the sublime (stupendous) and squalid (miserable) according to this opposition.
28. R. Venturi, 'The Centennial of the American Academy in Rome', in *Iconography and Electronics upon a Generic Architecture* (Cambridge, MA: The MIT Press, 1996), pp. 54–5.
29. A brief bibliography of studies on postcolonial Rome in cinema and literature should include J. Burns, 'Provisional Constructions of the Eternal City: Figurations of Rome in Recent Italophone Writing', in C. Emden, C. Keen and D. Midgley (eds), *Imagining the City*, 2 vols (Oxford, New York: Peter Lang, 2006), vol. 2, pp. 357–73; L. Caldwell, 'Piazza Vittorio: Cinematic Notes on the Evolution of a Piazza', in D. Caldwell and L. Caldwell, *Rome, Continuing Encounters between Past and Present*; and Parati, 'Where Do Migrants Live? Amara Lakhous's Clash of Civilizations over an Elevator in Piazza Vittorio'. See also the documentary *L'orchestra di Piazza Vittorio* [Piazza Vittorio's Orchestra] (Agostino Ferrente, 2006) and the novels A. Lakhous, *Scontro di civiltà per un ascensore a Piazza Vittorio* [Clash of Civilizations in an Elevator in Piazza Vittorio] (Rome: Edizioni e/o, 2006) and I. Scego, *Il mio posto è dove sono* [My Place Is Where I Am] (Milan: Rizzoli, 2010). For a representation of Queer Rome see the documentary *Improvvisamente l'inverno scorso* [Suddenly, Last Winter] (Luca Ragazzi and Gustav Hofer, 2008).

1 Cavietti, 'Between Rome's Walls: Notes on the Role and Reception of the Aurelian Walls'

1. G. C. Argan, 'Roma interrotta', in B. Contardi (ed.), *Storia dell'arte come storia della città* [Rome Interrupted, in History of Art as History of the City] (Rome: Editori Riuniti, 1983), p. 213.
2. R. Cassetti, 'Il ruolo delle "funzioni centrali" nella costruzione di un nuovo ordine urbano della città', in R. Cassetti and G. Spagnesi (eds), *Roma contemporanea: Storia e progetto* [The role of 'centre functions' in the construction of a new, urban order for the city, in Contemporary Rome: History and Plans] (Rome: Gangemi, 2006), pp. 67–107.
3. Cassetti, 'Il ruolo', p. 79.
4. P. Falini and A. Terranova, 'Ecco gli interventi per ri-legare la città' [This is the project that will re-connect the city], *Capitolium*, 1 (2003), pp. 31–7.
5. Falini and Terranova, 'Ecco gli interventi', pp. 31–7.
6. D. Fuina, 'Il parco lineare integrato' [The Integrated Linear Park], *Capitolium*, 1 (2003), p. 30.
7. The project was presented at the fifth national Rassegna Urbanistica [Urban Design Show], held in Venice in 2004. Compare V. Fabietti, C. Giaimo and M. Mininni (eds), *VI Rassegna Urbanistica Nazionale, I Casi in Rassegna* [The Sixth National Urban Design Show: The Houses in the Show] (Rome: INU Edizioni, 2010).

8. R. Mancini, *Le Mura Aureliane di Roma: Atlante di un palinsesto murario* [The Aurelian Walls of Rome: Atlas of a Palimpsest of Building Work] (Rome: Quasar, 2001), and H. Dey, *The Aurelian Wall and the Refashioning of Imperial Rome, AD 271–855* (Cambridge: Cambridge University Press, 2011).

9. Dey, *The Aurelian Wall*, p. 9.

10. Ibid., p. 123.

11. In chapter 2 of this volume Fabio Benincasa develops further the intricate relationship between imagined and concrete Rome, with further emphasis on the *Mirabilia Urbis Romae*.

12. L. Nuti, *Cartografie senza carte: Lo spazio urbano descritto dal Medioevo al Rinascimento* [Cartography Without Maps: The Urban Space Described, from the Middle Ages to the Renaissance] (Milan: Jaca Book, 2008).

13. G. Simoncini, *Topografia e urbanistica da Bonifacio IX ad Alessandro VI* [Topography and Town Planning, from Boniface IX to Alexander VI] (Florence: L. S. Olschki, 2004), p. 141.

14. G. Simoncini, *Roma restaurata: Rinnovamento urbano al tempo di Sisto V* [Rome Restored: Urban Renewal at the Time of Sixtus V] (Florence: L. S. Olschki, 1990).

15. Simoncini, *Roma restaurata*, pp. 64–5.

16. See L. Cassanelli, G. Delfini and D. Fonti, *Le mura di Roma: l'architettura militare nella storia urbana* [The Walls of Rome: Military Architecture in Urban History] (Rome: Bulzoni, 1974), p. 271; S. Debenedetti (ed.), *Valadier: segno e architettura* [Valadier: Signs and Architecture] (Rome: Multigrafica, 1985), pp. 96–7 and p. 209.

17. P. Virgili, 'Mura Aureliane. Usi e abusi: la dimora di Ettore Muti a Porta San Sebastiano', in A. Ceccherelli and P. Virgili (eds), *Museo delle Mura: Guida* [The Aurelian Walls. Uses and Abuses: The House of Ettore Muti at Porta San Sebastiano, in The Museum of the Walls] (Milan: Electa, 2007), pp. 32–5.

18. A. Ricci, *Attorno alla nuda pietra: Archeologia e città tra identità e progetto* [Around the Naked Stone: Archeology and the City, Between Identity and Design] (Roma: Donzelli, 2006).

19. *Il caso Roma: Libro inchiesta su cinque anni di vita della città* [The Rome Affair: A Book Investigation on Five Years of City Life] (Rome: Comune di Roma, 1981); G. C. Argan, *Un'idea di Roma* [An Idea of Rome], intervista di M. Monicelli, (Rome: Editori Riuniti, 1979); A. Latour, *Roma New York Mosca: Tre città, tre mondi* [Rome, New York, Moscow: Three Cities, Three Worlds] (Rome: Edizioni Kappa, 1993).

20. Argan was moreover heavily involved in the 'Roma Interrotta' exhibition in the late 1970s: see Szacka's chapter in this volume for an outline of his important contributions. See also L. Cassanelli, 'Gli studi di Argan sulla città', in *Giulio Carlo Argan: Progetto e destino dell'arte*, special issue of *Storia dell'arte* [Argan's Studies of the City, in Giulio Carlo Argan: The Design and Destiny of Art], 112:37 (2005), pp. 72–8. Argan's students then dedicated many studies to Rome's urban history. See M. Di Macco, *Il Colosseo: funzione simbolica, storica, urbana* [The Colosseum: Symbolic, Historical and Urban Functions] (Rome, Bulzoni, 1971), in which she writes, 'L'obiettivo è la verifica della complessa relazione storica tra arte e città, e il suo primo atto l'individuazione dei grandi temi o delle "strutture primarie" nella determinazione e nella mutazione della forma urbana' (The objective was to verify the complex historical relationship between art and the city, and its first step was the identification of the major themes, or of the 'primary structures' in the determination and mutation of the urban form).

21. Argan, 'Introduzione', in Contardi (ed.), *Storia dell'arte come storia della città*, pp. 230–1.

22. C. Maltese (ed.), *Centri storici di grandi agglomerati urbani* [Historical Centres of Large Urban Agglomerates] (Bologna: CLUEB, 1982), p. 1.

23. Argan, in Contardi (ed.), *Storia dell'arte*, p. 88.

24. L. Ficacci, 'Storia dell'arte e politica dieci anni dopo', [History of Art and Politics, Ten Years Later] in *Giulio Carlo Argan*, p. 151–2: 'É una circostanza rilevante che, più che l'attività parlamentare di Argan, abbastanza documentata e considerata dalla storiografia, sia invece il progetto quale Sindaco di Roma ad essere stato non solo disatteso, ma del tutto archiviato in una zona d'ombra di dimenticanza, nella pratica delle amministrazioni successive e nel dibattito, peraltro irrilevante, sul destino della città. Ma quando le tendenze propagandistiche e l'abuso dei luoghi comuni circa il trattamento del centro storico si saranno fatalmente esauriti, sarà inevitabile che qualche disciplina culturale riprenda la responsabilità almeno dell'elaborazione del progetto. A quel punto sarà di primaria importanza recuperare, almeno al livello di problema, la lucida analisi e il progetto che, da Sindaco, Argan aveva definito nelle sue linee portanti circa l'evoluzione urbana, la distribuzione delle funzioni e la tutela del nucleo storico della città di Roma'. (Argan's parliamentary activity has been reasonably well documented and considered in historiographical work. His projects as Mayor of Rome, on the other hand, and quite relevantly, have been not only neglected, but rather archived within that shadowy zone of the forgotten when it comes to the related activity of subsequent administrations in debates (albeit irrelevant) on the future of the city. But when the propagandistic tendencies and the abuses of communal locations with regard to the historical centre of the city will cease to be, it will be absolutely inevitable that some cultural discipline eventually re-assumes the responsibility for the completion of the project. At that stage, the first and most important step will be to return to Argan's lucid analyses and his blueprints for urban development: the load-bearing routes, the distribution of city functions and preservation of the city of Rome's historical nucleus.)

25. Virgili, 'Mura Aureliane', pp. 32–5.

26. F. Giovanetti, '18 chilometri di monumento minore' [18 Kilometres of a Minor Monument], *Capitolium*, 1 (2003), pp. 19–25.

27. V. Altimari, 'Mura Aureliane: Restauro con droga e lucciole' [Aurelian Walls: Restoration with Drugs and Prostitutes], *Corriere delle Sera*, 30 March 2010, online edition available at http://roma.corriere.it/roma/notizie/cronaca/12_luglio_20/degrado-mura-aureliane-2011107071721.shtml [accessed 10 December 2012].

28. See 'About', on Hural's personal website, available at http://www.mph-work.com/about/index.html [accessed 10 December 2012].

29. C. Dardi, 'Architetture parlanti e Archeologia del silenzio' [Talking Architectures and the Archaeology of Silence], *Metamorfosi*, 1–2, (1986), pp. 31–45.

30. A. Bonito Oliva, *Avanguardia transavanguardia* [Avantgarde Transavantgarde], (Milan: Electa, 1982), p. 9; review of the exhibition: G. Briganti, 'Canta il cigno sotto le mura' [The Swan Sings under the Walls], *La Repubblica*, 13 May 1982, p. 16.

31. N. Miller, *Mapping the City: The Language and Culture of Cartography in the Renaissance* (London: Continuum, 2003), p. 2.

2 Benincasa, 'The Explosion of Rome in the Fragments of a Postmodern Iconography: Federico Fellini and the *Forma Urbis*'

1. A general summary of the influential nature of Roman imagery, especially over the English-speaking world, can be found in P. Bondanella, *The Eternal City: Roman Images in the Modern World* (Chapel Hill, NC, and London: University of North Carolina Press, 1987). See also R. Jenkyns, *The Legacy of Rome: A New Appraisal* (New York: Oxford University Press, 1992).

2. An interesting contemporary overview about it is to be found in *Contro Roma* (Milan: Bompiani, 1975). The volume contains a number of articles that situate themselves 'against Rome' (this is the meaning of the volume's Italian title), written by several eminent Italian intellectuals, including Alberto Moravia, Eugenio Montale and Goffredo Parise.

3. *Intervista* [Interview], film, directed by Federico Fellini (Italy: Rai, 1987).

4. Fellini's interest in Carlo Emilio Gadda's works is well known, see for instance T. Kezich, *Fellini* (Milan: Camunia, 1987), p. 24 and its English translation, *Federico Fellini: His Life and Work* (London: Tauris, 2007).

5. *Lo sceicco bianco* [The White Sheik], film, directed by Federico Fellini (Italy: P.D.C., 1952); 'Toby Dammit', film, directed by Federico Fellini, segment of *Histoires extraordinaires* [Spirits of the Dead], directed by Federico Fellini, Louis Malle and Roger Vadim (France and Italy, Cocinor, 1968); *Roma* [Fellini's Roma], film, directed by Federico Fellini (Italy and France: United Artists, 1972); *Ginger e Fred* [Ginger and Fred], film directed by Federico Fellini (Italy, France and West Germany: PEA, 1986).

6. I refer to M. Marcus, *After Fellini: National Cinema in the Postmodern Age* (Baltimore, MD, and London: Johns Hopkins University Press, 2002).

7. *Caro diario* [Dear Diary], film, directed by Nanni Moretti, (Italy and France: Sacher-Rai, 1993); *L'ora di religione* [My Mother's Smile], film, directed by Marco Bellocchio, (Italy: Rai-Luce, 2002); *L'odore del sangue* [The Scent of Blood], film, directed by Mario Martone, (Italy and France: Mikado, 2004).

8. See Caldwell's chapter in this volume for a broader discussion of Moretti's film in the context of these Roman neighbourhoods, in particular on pp. 65–7.

9. P. Portoghesi, *Roma barocca* [Baroque Rome] (Bari: Laterza, 2002) pp. 11–12.

10. According to Italo Insolera the recurrent planification of the newborn capital 'aveva come sua espressa filosofia di realizzare senza traumi una vasta urbanizzazione, secondo criteri e forme corrispondenti al modello di una media città borghese' (had as its precise philosophy the realization, without trauma, of a wide urbanization, according to the criteria and forms corresponding to the model of an average bourgeois city), in I. Insolera, *Le città nella storia d'Italia: Roma* [Cities in the History of Italy: Rome] (Rome and Bari: Laterza, 2002), p. 428.

11. Compare F. Petrarch, *Familiares*, book 6, letter 2.

12. The so-called *Città ideale* (Ideal City) are fifteenth-century paintings, now dispersed between Urbino, Baltimore and Berlin, variously attributed to Fra Carnevale, Piero della Francesca or Francesco di Giorgio Martini. Inspired by the ideals of organic city theorized by Leon Battista Alberti, these images illustrate how the humanists imagined completing the fragmented ruins visible in Rome with a homogeneous and planned urban centre. In this sense, what they could imagine was more important than what they could *actually see* in the Roman Forum.

13. A. Gnisci, *Noialtri Europei: Saggi di letteratura comparata su identità e luoghi d'Europa* [We Europeans: Essays of Comparative Literature on the Identity and the Places of Europe] (Rome: Bulzoni, 1994), pp. 29–40.

14. Portoghesi, *Roma barocca*, p. 43.

15. See E. Burke, *A Philosophical Enquiry into the Origin of Our Ideas of the Sublime and Beautiful* (Oxford: Oxford University Press, 2009) and J. Winckelmann, *The History of Art in Antiquity*, trans. H. Malgrave (Los Angeles, CA: Getty Research Institute, 2006). On the connection between Baroque sensitivity and Romanticism see E. Raimondi, *Il colore eloquente: Letteratura e arte barocca* [The Eloquent Colour: Baroque Art and Literature] (Bologna: Il Mulino, 1995); and G. Deleuze, *The Fold*, trans. T. Conley (London: Continuum, 2006).

16. See for example G. B. Vico, *The New Science*, trans. D. Marsh (London: Penguin Classics, 2000); Immanuel Kant, *Critique of Judgment*, trans. J. Creed Meredith (Oxford: Oxford University Press, 2007); G. W. F. Hegel, *The Phenomenology of Spirit*, trans. A. V. Miller (Oxford: Oxford University Press, 1977), each of which promote the arrangement of knowledge into a unified, methodologically founded philosophical framework.

17. As Lyotards writes, 'The narrative function is losing its functors, its great hero, its great dangers, its great voyages, its great goal. It is being dispersed in clouds of narrative language elements – narrative, but also denotative, prescriptive descriptive, and so on', in J. F. Lyotard, *The Postmodern Condition: Report on Knowledge*, trans. G. Bennington and B. Massumi (Manchester: Manchester University Press, 1984), p. xxiv.

18. J. L. Borges, *The Aleph and Other Stories, 1933–1969*, trans. N. T. di Giovanni (London: Pan Books, 1973).

19. G. Deleuze, *Cinema 1: L'immagine movimento* [Cinema 1: The Movement Image] (Rome: Ubulibri, 2002), pp. 240–2.

20. G. Simmel, 'The Metropolis and Mental Life', in D. Frisby and M. Featherstone (eds), *Simmel on Culture* (London: SAGE, 2000), pp. 174–86.

21. I. Insolera, *Roma moderna* [Modern Rome] (Turin: Einaudi, 2011), pp. 56–90.

22. The script is included in R. Renzi (ed.), *Il primo Fellini: Lo sceicco bianco, I vitelloni, La strada, il bidone* [The Early Fellini: The White Sheik, the Vitelloni, the Strada and the Bidone] (Bologna: Cappelli, 1969).

23. *La dolce vita* [The Sweet Life], film, directed by Federico Fellini (Italy and France: Cineriz-Pathé, 1960).

24. This has some interesting resonances with Trentin's comments on the 'simulacrization' of monuments and the dislocation of origin in his contribution to this volume.

25. P. Noto, 'Esterno notte: Via Veneto, *La dolce vita* e l'esperienza del luogo', in A. Minuz (ed.), *L'invenzione del luogo: Spazi dell'immaginario cinematografico* [Exterior, Night: Via Veneto, the Dolce Vita and the Experience of the Place, in The Invention of the place: Spaces in Cinema's Imagery] (Pisa: ETS, 2011), pp. 82–4.

26. 'Le tentazioni del Dottor Antonio' [The Temptations of Doctor Antonio], segment of *Boccaccio '70*, film, directed by Vittorio De Sica, Luchino Visconti, Federico Fellini and Mario Monicelli (Italy and France: Cineriz, 1962).

27. P. Nicoloso, *Mussolini architetto: Propaganda e paesaggio urbano nell'Italia fascista* [Mussolini as an Architect: Propaganda and Urban Landscape in Fascist Italy] (Turin: Einaudi, 2011), pp. 196–209.

28. *Satyricon*, directed by Federico Fellini (Italy: PEA, 1969).

29. Federico Fellini, *Fare un film* [Making a Film] (Turin: Einaudi, 1993), p. 104.

30. See Z. Bauman, *Liquid Modernity* (Polity: Cambridge, 2000).

31. F. Jameson, *Postmodernism, or, The Cultural Logic of Late Capitalism* (Durham, NC: Duke University Press, 1991), p. 27. See also D. Harvey, *The Condition of Postmodernity: An Enquiry into the Origins of Cultural Change* (Hoboken, NJ: Blackwell, 1991).

32. B. Zapponi (ed.), *'Roma' di Federico Fellini* [Federico Fellini's Rome] (Bologna: Cappelli, 1972).

33. J. Paul, 'Rome Ruined and Fragmented: The Cinematic City in Fellini's *Satyricon* and *Roma*', in R. Wrigley (ed.), *Cinematic Rome* (Leicester: Troubador, 2008), pp. 109–20, on pp. 114–5.

34. See J. D. Rhodes, *Stupendous, Miserable City: Pasolini's Rome* (Minneapolis, MN: University of Minnesota Press, 2007), pp. 41–74.

3 Caldwell, 'Centre, Hinterland and the Articulation of "Romanness" in Recent Italian Film'

1. *Caro diario* [Dear Diary], film, directed by Nanni Moretti (Italy and France: Sacher-Rai, 1993); *Velocità massima* [Maximum Velocity], film, directed by Daniele Vicari (Italy: Medusa, 2002); *Romanzo criminale* [Crime Story], film, directed by Michele Placido (Italy: Warner Bros. Picture Company, 2005).

2. D. Caldwell, 'Introduction', in D. Caldwell and L. Caldwell (eds), *Rome: Continuing Encounters between Past and Present* (Farnham: Ashgate, 2011), pp. 1–16, on p. 7.

3. J. A. Agnew, *Rome* (Chichester: J. Wiley & Sons, 1995), p. 66.

4. P. Mudu, 'La circonferenza apparente: la periferia romana tra luoghi comuni e non comuni' [The Apparent Circumference: the Roman Periphery between Common and Uncommon Places], *Parolechiave*, 36 (2006), pp. 117–42, on p. 118.

5. Mudu, 'La circonferenza apparente', p. 119. For further detail on domestic migrations to Rome, see Marco Cavietti's contribution to the volume.

6. Agnew, *Rome*, p. 66.

7. M. Salvati, 'Presentazione', *Parolechiave*, 36 (2006), pp. vii–xiii, on p. xi.

8. A. Rossi, *The Architecture of the City*, trans. D. Ghirardo and J. Ockman (Cambridge MA; London: The MIT Press, 1982), p. 120.

9. Ibid., p. 126.

10. P. Avarello, 'L'urbanizzazione', in L. De Rosa (ed.), *Roma nel Duemila* [Urbanization, in Rome in 2000] (Rome and Bari: Laterza, 2000), pp. 159–202, on p. 163.

11. R. Nicolini, quoted in F. Erbani, 'La vita culturale' [Cultural Life], in De Rosa (ed.), *Roma nel Duemila*, pp. 227–39, on p. 233.

12. E. Soja, 'Regional Urbanization and the End of the Metropolis Era', in G. Bridge and S. Watson (eds), *The New Blackwell Companion to the City* (Malden, MA: Wiley and Blackwell, 2011), pp. 679–89, on p. 680.

13. A. Tallis, '"Reconciliation" or "Conquest"? The Opening of the Via della Conciliazione and the Fascist Vision for the "Third Rome"', in Caldwell and Caldwell (eds), *Rome: Continuing Encounters between Past and Present*, pp. 129–52.

14. These areas are Prenestino, Gordiani, Tor Marancia, Peitralata, San Basilio, Tufello, Val Melaina, Tiburtino III, Acilia, Trullo, Primavalle and Quarticciolo. See I. Insolera, *Roma Moderna: Un secolo di storia urbanistca 1870–1970* [Modern Rome: A Century of Urban History 1870–1970] (Turin: Einaudi, 2001), p. 142.

15. L. Ciacci, 'The Rome of Mussolini: An Entrenched Stereotype in Film', in M. Konstantarakos (ed.), *Spaces In European Cinema* (Exeter: Intellect Books), pp. 93–100.

16. Ibid., p. 94.

17. R. Nicolini, 'Introduzione', in C. Aymonino, *Progettare Roma Capitale* [Introduction, in Projecting Rome as Capital] (Rome and Bari: Laterza, 1990), pp. 7–10, on p. 8.

18. Insolera, *Roma Moderna*, pp. 135–6.
19. E. Salzano, 'Le periferie: errori', in F. Indovina, L. Fregolent and M. Savino (eds), *1950–2000 L'Italia è cambiata* [Peripheries: Errors, in 1950–2000 Italy has Changed] (Milan: Franco Angeli, 2000), pp. 355–60, on p. 355.
20. *Mamma Roma*, film, directed by Pier Paolo Pasolini (Italy: Cineriz, 1962). In his contribution, above, James Robertson comments further on the presence of the periphery in Pasolini's film. See pp. 143-4.
21. Mudu, 'La circonferenza apparente', p.121.
22. See Salvati, 'Presentazione', p. xii.
23. E. Nerenberg, 'Re/Constructing Domestic Space: INA-Casa and Public Housing in Postwar Rome or Women's Space in a Man-Made World', in P. Morris (ed.), *Women in Italy 1945–1960: An Interdisciplinary Study* (London: Palgrave), pp. 177–92, on p. 183. On the INA Casa housing project see also P. Biagi (ed.), *La grande ricostruzione* [The Large Reconstruction] (Rome: Donzelli, 2001); M. Guccione, M. Segarra Lagunes and R. Vittorini (eds), *Guida ai quartieri romani INA Casa* [INA Casa Guide to the Roman Neighbourhood] (Rome: Gangemi, 2002).
24. See L. Caldwell, 'What do Mothers Want? An Examination on Three Films', in P. Morris (ed.), *Women in Italy 1945–1960*, pp. 225–38; J. D. Rhodes, *Stupendous, Miserable City* (Minneapolis, MN: University Minnesota Press, 2007), in particular pp. 110–35.
25. Mudu, 'La circonferenza apparente', p. 123.
26. R. Cassetti, *Roma e Lazio: Idee e piani 1870–2000* [Rome and Lazio: Ideas and Plans 1870–2000] (Rome: Gangemi, 2001).
27. G. Cerasa, *La città fuori le mura: Roma come non l'avete mai vista* [The City Outside the Walls: Rome as You Have Never Seen It] (Rome: Gruppo Editoriale L'Espresso, 2005).
28. Law 167 introduced the 'PEEP' or 'Piani di Edilizia Economica Popolare' (Economic-Popular Building Plans), a public body that dealt directly with housing for the poor, at http://www.sicet.it/pages/urbanistica/leggi_urb/legge_167-62.htm [accessed 21 November 2012].
29. Mudu, 'La circonferenza apparente', p. 126.
30. Ibid.
31. Quoted in J. Donald, *Imagining the Modern City* (Minneapolis, MN: University of Minnesota Press), p. 51.
32. S. Paci, 'Through the Looking Glass: Research on the Italian City in Historical Perspective', in R. Lumley and J. Foot, *Italian Cityscapes: Culture and Urban Change in Contemporary Italy* (Exeter: University of Exeter Press, 2004), pp. 15–28, on p. 24.
33. Interview with Vicari in R. De Angelis, *Iperurbs/Roma* (Rome: DeriveApprodi, 2005), p. 99.
34. See L. Furxhi, 'Il mio è un film plebeo. Intervista a Daniele Vicari' [My Film is a Plebeian Film. Interview with Daniele Vicari], in P. Detassis, *Daniele Vicari* (Alessandria: Falsopiano, 2003), pp. 15–31.
35. R. Bartali, 'The Red Brigades and the Moro Kidnapping: Secrets and Lies', in A. Cento Bull and A. Giorgio, *Speaking Out and Silencing: Culture, Society and Politics in Italy in the 1970s* (Oxford: Legenda, 2006), pp. 146–60.
36. J. Benci, 'An Extraordinary Proliferation of Layers: Pasolini's Rome', in Caldwell and Caldwell, *Rome: Continuing Encounters between Past and Present*, pp. 153–88.
37. G. Caudo and A. Coppola, 'Periferie di cosa? Roma e la condizione periferica' [Peripheries of What? Rome and the Peripheral Condition], *Parolechiave*, 36 (2006), pp. 97–116, on p. 98. See also G. Piccinato and G. Caudo, *La citta eventuale* [The Possible City] (Rome: Quodlibet, 2005).

4 Rhodes, 'Topophilia and Other Roman Perversions: On Bertolucci's *La luna*'

1.   *La luna* [The Moon], film, directed by Bernardo Bertolucci (Italy: Fiction Cinematografica, 1979).
2.   S. Kracauer, *Theory of Film: The Redemption of Physical Reality* (Princeton, NJ: Princeton University Press, 1997 [1960]), p. 303.
3.   E. Gorfinkel and J. D. Rhodes, 'Introduction: The Matter of Places', in J. D. Rhodes and E. Gorfinkel (eds), *Taking Place: Location and the Moving Image* (Minneapolis, MN: University of Minnesota Press, 2011), pp. vii–xxix, on p. vii.
4.   This tension is something that Gorfinkel and I explore in 'Introduction', pp. vii–xxix.
5.   J. D. Rhodes, *Stupendous, Miserable City: Pasolini's Rome* (Minneapolis, MN: University of Minnesota Press, 2007).
6.   I have tried to explore the specific nature of this modernity in my essay, 'The Eclipse of Place: Rome's EUR from Rossellini to Antonioni', in Rhodes and Gorfinkel (eds), *Taking Place: Location and the Moving Image*, pp. 31–54.
7.   *London*, film, directed by Patrick Keiller (UK: BFI, 1994).
8.   A film like Fellini's *Roma* (1972) might be said to evoke a specifically postmodern Rome, but it does so largely from inside the confines of a sound stage. The postmodernity of *Roma* does not seem to derive from the postmodernity of Rome, in other words. See Fabio Benincasa's reading of Rome in Fellini's work, in this volume, for some further thought on Fellini's postmodernism (pp. 39–56).
9.   F. Jameson, *Postmodernism, or, The Cultural Logic of Late Capitalism* (Durham, NC: Duke University Press, 1990), p. 44.
10.   K. Lynch, *The Image of the City* (Cambridge, MA: The MIT Press, 1960), p. 32.
11.   Ibid., p. 29.
12.   Ibid., p. 92.
13.   Ibid., p. 93.
14.   B. Brown, 'The Dark Wood of Postmodernity (Space, Faith, Allegory)', *PMLA*, 120:3 (2005), pp. 734–50, on p. 742.
15.   Ibid. Brown cites the work of the architectural historian and theorist Marvin Trachtenberg in making this point.
16.   I will put aside the fact that Ancient Rome – now only visible in palimpsestic traces – was an imageable city par excellence.
17.   E. Bowen, *A Time in Rome* (London: Longmans, 1960), p. 7. Bowen, like the character Caterina Silveri in *La luna*, has come to Rome following the death of her husband.
18.   Bowen, *A Time in Rome*, pp. 10–11.
19.   Brown, 'The Dark Wood', p. 736.
20.   Bowen, *A Time in Rome*, p. 7.
21.   *Beseiged*, film, directed by Bernardo Bertolucci (Italy and USA: Fiction Films, 1998).
22.   B. Bertolucci, in F. S. Gerard, T. J. Kline and B. Sklarew (eds), *Bernardo Bertolucci: Interviews* (Jackson, MS: University of Mississippi Press, 2000), pp. 263–4.
23.   Ibid., p. 119.
24.   *La strategia del ragno* [The Spider's Stratagem], film, directed by Bernardo Bertolucci (Italy: Indipendenti Regionali, 1970).
25.   E. Canniffe, *The Politics of the Piazza: The History and Meaning of the Italian Square* (Aldershot: Ashgate, 2008), p. 131.
26.   Gerard, Kline and Sklarew (eds), *Bernardo Bertolucci: Interviews*, p. 136.

27. T. J. Kline, *Bertolucci's Dream Loom: A Psychoanalytic Study of Cinema* (Amherst, MA: University of Massachusetts Press, 1987), p. 150.

28. Bertolucci quoted in Kline, *Bertolucci's Dream Loom*, p. 152.

29. R. P. Kolker, *Bernardo Bertolucci* (New York: Oxford University Press, 1985), p. 151.

30. Ibid., p. 154.

31. Ibid., p. 153 and p. 157, where Kline says of the film: 'Unlike any of Bertolucci's earlier films, it seems to present itself almost uniquely as an *object for analysis or interpretation*'.

32. Ibid., p. 154.

33. Ibid., p. 155.

34. Ibid.

35. *La commare secca* [The Grim Reaper], film, directed by Bernardo Bertolucci (Italy: Cineteca Nazionale, 1962).

36. Interestingly, perhaps, San Rocco – prayed to for healing from illness – is himself an apocryphal saint, whose legend is a palimpsest of hagiographies.

37. W. S. Hecksher, 'Bernini's Elephant and Obelisk', *Art Bulletin*, 29:3 (1947), pp. 155–82, on p. 155.

38. Ibid., pp. 181–2.

39. Unfortunately, I do not have the space to consider whether the shot of the obelisk is also a self-conscious reference to Freud's allusion to Santa Maria Sopra Minerva at the beginning of *Civilization and its Discontents*. In this passage Freud asks us to imagine a Rome in which all of its monuments, past and present, still exist on the same terrain. The suggested image, Freud tells us, however, is 'unimaginable' because 'the same space cannot have two different contents'. Freud's example is meant to demonstrate 'how far we are from mastering the characteristics of mental life by representing them in pictorial terms'. (S. Freud, *Civilization and its Discontents*, trans. and ed. J. Strachey (New York: Norton & Co., 1989 [1930]), pp. 18–19.) However, as *La luna* makes abundantly clear, the cinematic allusion (perhaps allusion itself) does seem to have the power of making two things appear in the same image.

40. Gerard, Kline and Sklarew (eds), *Bernardo Bertolucci: Interviews*, p. 137.

41. J. M. Merz, *Pietro da Cortona and Roman Baroque Architecture* (New Haven, CT, and London: Yale University Press, 2008), p. 165.

42. R. Krautheimer, *The Rome of Alexander VII, 1655–1667* (Princeton, NJ: Princeton University Press, 1987), p. 49.

43. Ibid., p. 48.

44. Ibid., pp. 50–1; Merz, *Pietro da Cortona and Roman Baroque Architecture*, pp. 168–70.

45. Merz, *Pietro da Cortona*, pp. 169–70.

46. Krautheimer, *The Rome of Alexander VII, 1655–1667*, p. 53.

47. Merz, *Pietro da Cortona*, p. 174.

48. Ibid.

49. This church was initially named Sant' Andrea de Aquarizariis in honour of the water carriers who carried water from the bend in the Tiber into which the abitato is nestled. The abitato became inhabited precisely because of its proximity to water, after the aqueducts were destroyed by the barbarians.

50. *Accattone*, film, directed by Pier Paolo Pasolini (Italy: Cino Del Duca, 1961).

51. For a more extended analysis of the use of these locations in *Accattone*, see my *Stupendous, Miserable City: Pasolini's Rome*, pp. 40–6.

52. S. Freud, 'The Uncanny' [1919], in *The Uncanny*, trans. D. McClintock (London: Penguin, 2003), pp. 121–62, on p. 144.

53. Ibid.

54. Ibid.

55. Ibid.

56. R. J. Stoller, *Perversion: The Erotic Form of Hatred* (London and New York: Karnac, 2003 [1975]), p. 6.

57. Ibid., p. 7.

58. V. Vidotto, *Roma Contemporanea* (Rome and Bari: Laterza, 2001), p. 370.

59. P. Berdini, *La città in vendita: centri storici e mercato senza regole* [The City on Sale: Historical Centres and Markets without Rules] (Rome: Donzelli editore, 2008), p. 30.

60. See P. Ginsborg, *A History of Contemporary Italy: Society and Politics, 1943–1988* (New York: Penguin Books, 1990), pp. 348–405. For a consideration of another, very different film-making practice in some of the same terms and contexts, see M. Siegel, 'The Nonplace of Argento: *The Bird with the Crystal Plumage* and Roman Urban History', in Rhodes and Gorfinkel (eds), *Taking Place: Location and the Moving Image*, pp. 211–31.

61. M. Siegel, 'Identification of a Medium: *Identificazione di una donna* and the Rise of Commerical Television in Italy', in L. Rascaroli and J. D. Rhodes (eds), *Antonioni: Centenary Essays* (London and Houndmills, Basingstoke: BFI/Palgrave Macmillan, 2011), p. 221.

62. Ibid.

63. Bertolucci quoted in Kolker, *Bernardo Bertolucci*, p. 161.

5 Trentin, 'Marcus Aurelius and the Ara Pacis: Notes on the Notion of "Origin" in Contemporary Rome'

1. R. Venturi, D. Scott Brown and S. Izenour, *Learning from Las Vegas* (Cambridge, MA: The MIT Press, 1977), p. 8.

2. F. Jameson, *Postmodernism, or the Cultural Logic of Late Capitalism* (Durham, NC: Duke University Press, 1991), p. 39.

3. E. Soja, 'The Stimulus of a Little Confusion: A Contemporary Comparison of Amsterdam and Los Angeles', in M. P. Smith (ed.), *After Modernism: Global Restructuring and the Changing Boundaries of City Life* (New Brunswick, NJ: Transaction Publishers, 1992), pp. 17–38, on p. 27.

4. 'Disneyland is presented as imaginary in order to make us believe that the rest is real, whereas all of Los Angeles and the America that surrounds it are no longer real, but belong to the hyperreal order and to the order of simulation', in J. Baudrillard, *Simulacra and Simulation*, trans. S. F. Glaser (Ann Arbor, MI: University of Michigan Press, 1994), p. 11.

5. M. Augé, *Non-places: Introduction to an Anthropology of Supermodernity*, trans. J. Howe (London: Verso, 1995).

6. Jameson, *Postmodernism*, p. 24.

7. An example could be the way that tourist guides advertise Rome in global media. See, for example, the description of Rome in the Michelin Green Guide, in the introduction to this volume.

8. M. Foucault, 'Nietzsche, Genealogy, History', in P. Rabinow (ed.), *The Foucault's Reader* (New York: Pantheon Books, 1984), pp. 76–100, on p. 88.

9. See F. Giuliani, 'E sul Campidoglio compare il gemello del Marc'Aurelio' [And on the Capitol Hill appears the Twin of Marcus Aurelius], *La Repubblica*, 20 April 1997, p. 21.

10. According to both the former director of Italy's National Institute for the Restoration, Giovanni Urbani, and Rome's former *sovrintendente ai beni archeologici* (supervisor of Rome's archeological finds), Adriano La Regina, there was no risk in re-arranging the original statue in the Capitol square. See C. Augias, 'Marco Aurelio scende in piazza' [Marcus Aurelius Enters the Scene], *La Repubblica*, 5 January 1993, p. 27 and F. Giuliani, 'Si rischia una città di brutte copie' [There is a Danger of a City of Falsifications], *La Repubblica*, 1 February 1998, p. 1.

11. See G. Casadio, 'Marc'Aurelio torna in copia. Tutti i segreti del restauro' [Marcus Aurelius Comes Back as a Copy. All the Secrets of the Restoration], *La Repubblica*, 23 January 1997, p. 6.

12. Augias, 'Marco Aurelio scende in piazza', p. 27.

13. Giuliani, 'Si rischia una città di brutte copie', p. 1.

14. Foucault, 'Nietzsche, Genealogy, History', p. 78.

15. See F. Giuliani, 'Statue di plastica per abbattere i vandali' [Plastic Statues to Fight Against the Vandals], *La Repubblica*, 3 February 1998, p. 5.

16. See J. Lenaghan, 'Equestrian Statue of Marcus Aurelius', in A. Boestrom (ed.), *The Encyclopedia of Sculpture vol. 1* (New York, Fitztroy Dearborn, 2004), p. 524.

17. Ibid., p. 524.

18. L. Storoni 'No, non era Costantino' [No, it was not Constantine], *La Repubblica*, 22 December 1984, p. 20.

19. 'Il Marco Aurelio ottenne invece una nuova sistemazione in Laterano a patto di non venire ufficialmente riconosciuto sotto il profilo iconografico ed archeologico, e prestarsi quindi più facilmente alla intellettualistica connotazione voluta dal pontefice per i suoi fini politici' (The Marcus Aurelius was moved to the Lateran under the condition that its iconographical and archaeological profile was not revealed, as in this way it could be used according to the intellectualist connotations desired by the Pope, favouring his political aims). In L. De Lachenal, 'Il gruppo equestre di Marco Aurelio e il Laterano. Ricerche per una storia della fortuna del monumento dall'età medievale fino al 1538' [The Marcus Aurelius Equestrian Statue and the Lateran. Historical Research on the Fortune of the Monument from the Middles Ages until 1538], *Bollettino dell'arte*, 62–3 (1990), pp. 1–56, on p. 22.

20. C. L. Frommel, 'Papal Policy: The Planning of Rome during the Renaissance', *Journal of Interdisciplinary History*, 17:1 (1986), pp. 39–65, on p. 41. See also Cavietti's contribution to this volume for further insight on the Papal alterations to the city's form, with particular emphasis on the Aurelian Walls. Cf. in particular pp. 25-31.

21. See De Lachenal, 'Il gruppo equestre di Marco Aurelio e il Laterano', p. 42.

22. Frommel, 'Papal Policy: the Planning of Rome during the Renaissance', p. 64. See also C. D'Onofrio, *Renovatio Romae: Storia urbanistica dal Campidoglio all'Eur* [Roman Renovation: An Urban History, from the Capitoline to the EUR] (Rome: Edizioni Mediterranee, 1973), p. 177.

23. Baudrillard, *Simulacra and Simulation*, p. 18.

24. Ibid.

25. Ibid., pp. 18–19.

26. G. Pullara, 'Sgarbi agli studenti: mettete una bomba sotto l'Ara Pacis' [Sgarbi Tells the Students: Put a Bomb under the Ara Pacis], *Corriere della sera*, 2 June 2004, p. 43.

27. See 'L'Ara Pacis inaugurata tra le polemiche', *Corriere della sera*, 22 April 2006, p. 17 [The Ara Pacis Inagurated With Controversies]. The candidate Gianni Alemanno eventually got elected but decided to keep the museum where it is.

28. See A. Capponi, 'Berlusconi: Ara Pacis mostruosa. E a Roma i politici si ribellano' [Berlusconi: The Ara Pacis is Monstrous: And in Rome Politicians Rebel], *Corriere della sera*, 4 May 2006, p. 29.

29. See P. Conti, '"Via la teca dell'Ara Pacis": si riapre il caso' [Get Rid of the Shell for the Ara Pacis: The Case Re-opens], *Corriere della sera*, 1 May 2008, p. 13.

30. See Pullara, 'Sgarbi agli studenti', p. 43.

31. Quoted in P. Favretto, *Un museo per l'Ara Pacis. La storia, il progetto, i materiali* [A Museum for the Ara Pacis. History, Design, Materials] (Milan, Motta, 2007), p. 13.

32. Favretto, *Un museo per l'Ara Pacis*, p. 19.

33. For an analysis of the altar's symbology see D. Castriota, *The Ara Pacis Augustae* (Princeton, NJ: Princeton University Press, 1995).

34. See A. Cederna, *Mussolini urbanista: lo sventramento di Roma negli anni del consenso* [Mussolini as an Urbanist: Rome's Demolitions during the Fascist Period] (Rome and Bari: Laterza, 1979).

35. Foucault, 'Nietzsche, Genealogy, History', p. 89.

36. See S. Settis, *Futuro del classico* [The Future of the Classical] (Turin: Einaudi, 2004), p. 84.

6 Jewell, 'A Postmodern Gaze on the Gasometer'

1. Ibid.

2. F. Proietti, 'E il gazometro divenne la "rive gauche" dei romani' [The Gasometer become the 'rive gauche' of Romans], *Il Corriere della sera*, 21 March 2010, p. 34, at http://archiviostorico.corriere.it/2010/marzo/21/Gazometro_divenne_rive_gauche_dei_co_9_100321018.shtml [accessed 2 December 2012].

3. KTONB, 'KITONB - "LUXOMETRO" - Official Video - Italiano', on Youtube, at http://www.youtube.com/watch?v=hoqlCU_P6-k [accessed 2 December 2012].

4. Racheli is an adamant critic of renewal in the Ostiense area, who finds that the Walter Veltroni mayoral administration propounded 'una mescolanza di stili diversi, tutti parimenti concorrenti a raggiungere l'esasperazione delle forme e quindi ad esaurire ogni possibilità espressiva delle medesime' (a mixture of different styles, all equally concurring to reach a point of exasperation of forms which evenetully estinguish their expressive potentialities). Racheli wonders if the presence of the University *Roma Tre* has damaged or ameliorated this city zone. A. Racheli, 'La perdita della bellezza dell'architettura del paesaggio', in B. Elia (ed.), *Ostiense dal passato al futuro* [The Loss of Beauty in the Architecture of the Landscape, in Ostiense from Past to Future], (Rome: Gangemi, 2008), p. 13.

5. Ibid.

6. Several planning documents are pertinent, and details are provided in ibid., p. 19, including Comune di Roma, Piano Regolatore di Roma, 2000, point 4.7; Nuovo piano regolatore di Roma enacted in March, 2003; Piano Urbano Ostiense Marconi (approved 22 December 1999 C.C. 240 and updated C.C. n. 10/2003).

7. Uribe González, *Roma città capolavoro*, p. 220.

8. I. Insolera, *Roma: Immagini e realtà dal X al XX secolo* [Rome: Images and Reality from the 10th to the 20th Centuries] (Bari: Editori Laterza, 1985), pp. 427–8.

9. A news 'cinegiornale' film in the archive of the Archivio Storico Luce asserts the Italianicity of the new gasometer and how it will satisfy the energy demands of Italians. See

L. U. C. E. G. Sonoro, 'L'edificazione del più grande gazometro d'Italia fuori Porta San Paolo a Roma' [The Edification of Italy's Biggest Gasometer Outside Porta San Paolo in Rome], Archivio Storico Luce, at http://www.archivioluce.com/archivio/indice. jsp?content_2=http%3A%2F%2Fwww.archivioluce.com%2Farchivio%2Fjsp%2Fsche de%2FschedaCine.jsp%3Fdb%3DcinematograficoCINEGIORNALI%26section%3D %2F%26physDoc%3D13220%26theTerm%3Dgazometro%26qrId%3D3se05618488 102dd%26findCine%3Dtrue%26findFoto%3Dtrue [accessed 2 December 2012].

10. For a propaganda film on the production of gas from coal see G. Ferroni, 'I figli del carbone' [Sons of Coal], Cinecittà Luce, at http://www.archivioluce.com/archivio/jsp/ schede/videoPlayer.jsp?tipologia=&id=&physDoc=3116&db=cinematograficoDO CUMENTARI&findIt=false&section=/ [accessed 2 December 2012]. The wording 'nero e pulsante' is applied to the coke gas machinery.

11. F. R. Archivio storico Italgas 'Il gasometro dell'area ostiense (Roma): Le vicende cos- truttive dai documenti dell'epoca (1934–1936)' [Historical Archive Italgas, The Gasometer in Ostiense (Rome): Its Construction in the Historical Documentation], at http://www.eni.com/portal/search/search.do?keyword=ostiense&x=0&y=0&locale =it_IT&header=search [accessed 2 December 2012]. We read: 'In realtà è facile intuire che l'ambizioso progetto, oltre a richiedere un complesso piano di lavoro, si scontrava inevitabilmente con i principi dell'autarchia' (In reality it is easy to grasp how the ambi- tious project, beyond requiring a complex work plan, would clash inevitably with the principles of autarchy).

12. G. Federico, 'Autarchia', in V. a. S. L. De Grazia (ed.), *Dizionario del fascismo* [Autarchy, in Dictionary of Fascism] (Turin: 2005), p. 667.

13. M. e. a. Furnari, *La fabbrica del Gas all'Ostiense: Luogo e forma di un'area industriale* [The Gas Factory in Ostiense: Place and Shape of an Industrial Area] (Rome: Gangemi Editore, 2005), p. 66.

14. F. Tonkiss, *Space, the City and Social Theory: Social Relations and Urban Forms* (Cam- bridge: Polity Press, 2005), p. 9.

15. The formulation is Henri Lefebvre's, from his *Production de l'espace* (1974), cited in J. D. Rhodes, *Stupendous, Miserable City: Pasolini's Rome* (Minneapolis, MN, and London: University of Minnesota Press, 2007), p. xv.

16. F. R. Archivio storico Italgas 'Il gasometro dell'area ostiense (Roma): Le vicende costrut- tive dai documenti dell'epoca (1934–1936)'.

17. R. Vespignani, *Paragone delle arti* 6, 2005, at http://testoesensoold.uniroma2.it/ assets/download/press/numero6/paragonedellearti/Vespignani/index.htm [accessed 2 December 2012].

18. 'Comunicato stampa: BNL presenta la sua collezione "Cinquanta Pittori per Roma"' [Press Release: BNL Presents its Collection 'Fifty Painters for Rome'], at http://www. exibart.com/profilo/imgpost/doc/061/doc-7244-1061-518-36795.pdf [accessed 2 December 2012].

19. A. Moravia, *Racconti romani* [Roman Tales] (Milan: Bompiani, 2011), p. 34.

20. Ibid.

21. Rhodes, *Stupendous, Miserable City*, p. 77.

22. P. P. Pasolini, *Ali dagli occhi azzurri* [Blue-Eyed Alì] (Milan: Garzanti, 2005; repr., 2007), p. 31.

23. Ibid.

24. Tonkiss, *Space, the City and Social Theory*, p. 144.

25. Ibid., 79.

26. Rhodes, *Stupendous, Miserable City: Pasolini's Rome*, p. 123.

27. Alessandro Giammei, my expert research assistant, located poems by Gatto, Scialoja, Sanguineti and Albinati, and credit is due to him in these cases.

28. F. Marcoaldi, 'Ostiense', in G. Cerasa (ed.), *La città fuori le mura: Roma come non l'avete mai vista* [The City Outside the Walls: Rome as You Have Never Seen It] (Rome: Gruppo Editoriale L'Espresso, 2005), p. 217.

29. A. Gatto, *Nuove poesie* [New Poems] (Milan: Mondadori, 1949), p. 89.

30. T. Scialoja, *I segni della corda* [The Signs of the Cord] (Milan: Edizioni della Meridiana, 1952), p. 73.

31. E. Sanguineti, *Il giuoco dell'oca* [Game of the Goose] (Milan: Feltrinelli, 1991; repr., 1967), p. 32.

32. P. Di Stefano, 'Sanguineti: I proletari smarriti nella Genova senza più industrie' [Sanguineti: The Lost Proletarians in a Genoa without Factories], *Corriere della Sera*, 13 April 2006, p. 56, at http://archiviostorico.corriere.it/2006/aprile/13/Sanguineti_proletari_smarriti_nella_Genova_co_9_060413109.shtml [accessed 11 December 2012].

33. Ibid.

34. E. Albinati, *Orti di guerra* [Gardens of War] (Rome: Fazi, 1997), pp. 35–6.

35. Ibid.

36. Ibid.

37. S. Ventroni, *Nel gasometro* [In the Gasometer] Florence: Casa Editrice Le Lettere, 2006), p. 25.

38. E. W. Sonja, *Postmetropolis: Critical Studies of Cities and Regions* (Oxford: Blackwell, 2000), p. 265.

39. V. Zeichen, *Poesie 1963–2003* [Poems, 1963–2003] (Milan: Mondadori, 2004), p. 347.

40. F. Proietti, 'E il gazometro divenne la "rive gauche" dei romani', p. 34.

41. Ibid.

42. Racheli, 'La perdita della bellezza dell'architettura del paesaggio', p. 11.

43. The gasometer building is a public good even though it sits on the Italgas property, and it would therefore be subject to Ministry regulations governing the 'landscape'. These are found in 'Codice dei beni culturali e del paesaggio, ai sensi dell'articolo 10 della legge 6 luglio 2002, n. 137', ed. M. d. B. Culturali, 28 (Rome: Gazzetta Ufficiale 2004).

7 Robertson, 'Ecclesiastical Icons: Defining Rome through Architectural Exchange'

1. The Second Vatican Council (or Vatican II) represented a key moment of the Catholic Church's scrutiny of itself, as well as the broad promotion of peace and harmony within the world in which it found itself. It emerged as the climax of decades of restlessness in the form of the Liturgical Movement and deep and damaging frustrations in reconciling modernism with Catholicism. Its importance cannot be underestimated because one of its fundamental aims was to focus on the role of the people in the liturgy. In architectural terms, it could be said that it represented official sanctioning of design experimentation which looked at the unified rather than segregated liturgical space. In Rome, this would manifest itself in a plurality of methodologies in the post-Vatican II era, some of which would eventually reject a boldly modernist approach for a broadly postmodernist aesthetic. However, these two philosophies never remained wholly chronological.

2. These, rather than the immediate post-war films of the late 1940s and 1950s, hold particular resonance within the context of this essay, as by the early 1960s, the focus had in some instances begun to shift from concerns of real poverty to a kind of spiritual poverty and ennui (although films such as Pier Paolo Pasolini's 1961 *Accattone* were controversial because of their insistence that previous social and welfare concerns had not gone away).

3. Jack Coia was the principal of the firm from 1927.

4. S. Mavilio, *Guida all'architettura sacra: Roma 1945–2000* [A Guide to Sacred Architecture] (Milan: Mondadori Electa S.p.A., 2006), p. 9.

5. A new date of 1942 was imposed to mark the twenty-year anniversary of the fascist regime.

6. Originally termed E42, the exposition site subsequently became known as the EUR: Esposizione Universale Roma (Universal Exhibition Rome).

7. Symbolically, in 1909 Pope Pius X enforced the 'Oath against Modernism', which aimed to protect the sanctity of the Roman Catholic tradition.

8. Mavilio gives an outline of the urban development of Rome from the late nineteenth and twentieth centuries: *Guida all'architettura sacra*, p. 10.

9. T. Kirk, *The Architecture of Modern Italy,* 2 vols (New York: Princeton Architectural Press, 2005), vol. 2, p. 28.

10. Kirk, *The Architecture of Modern Italy*, vol. 2, p. 63.

11. M. Alderman, 'The Modern Baroque of Armando Brasini', *New Liturgical Movement* (February 2009), at http://newliturgicalmovement.org/2009/02/modern-baroque-of-armando-brasini.html [accessed 7 September 2010].

12. Ibid.

13. Kirk, *The Architecture of Modern Italy*, vol. 2, p. 63.

14. *Accattone*, film, directed by Pier Paolo Pasolini (Italy: Cino Del Duca, 1961).

15. Peperino is a composite stone of lava and tufa that comes from Viterbo.

16. *L'eclisse* [The Eclipse], film, directed by Michelangelo Antonioni (Italy: Cineriz, 1962).

17. *La dolce vita* [The Sweet Life], film, directed by Federico Fellini (Italy: Cineriz, 1960).

18. *Mamma Roma,* film, directed by Pier Paolo Pasolini (Italy: Cineriz, 1962).

19. See M. Viano, *A Certain Realism: Making Use of Pasolini's Film Theory* (Berkeley, CA, and London: University of California Press, 1993).

20. The church of San Giovanni Bosco is also featured in *La dolce vita*.

21. Examples of the architect's retrospective re-appraisal includes, for instance, the exhibition, from 2 November 2007 to 10 February 2008 at The Lighthouse, Glasgow, 'Gillespie, Kidd & Coia: Architecture 1956–1987' and accompanying publication, J. Rodger (ed.), *Gillespie, Kidd & Coia: Architecture 1956–1987* (Glasgow: RIAS in partnership with The Lighthouse, Scotland's Centre for Architecture, Design and the City, 2007).

22. B. W. Painter Jr., *Mussolini's Rome: Rebuilding the Eternal City* (New York and Basingstoke: Palgrave MacMillan, 2007), p. 82.

23. See *Architettura*, 14 (1935).

24. See the description in Mavilio, *Guida all'architettura sacra*, p. 54.

25. Ibid., p. 24.

26. Ibid.

27. Whilst there is an absence of any of their churches in Rome, Portoghesi for one did in fact design religious buildings in Rome, such as the Islamic Cultural Centre and Mosque (1975–95). He also submitted an entry for the design of Dio Padre Misericordioso.

28. See Mavilio, p. 140.

29. Ibid., p. 249.
30. Ibid., p. 186.
31. Ibid., p. 87.
32. Kirk, *The Architecture of Modern Italy*, vol. 2, p. 255.
33. See Richard Meier & Partners, *Jubilee Church*, at http://www.richardmeier.com/www/#/projects/architecture/name/1/132/0/ [accessed 18 December 2012] and S. Glynn, *Church Dio Padre Misericordioso, Rome*, at http://www.galinsky.com/buildings/jubilee/index.htm [accessed 18 December 2012]
34. Richard Meier & Partners, *Jubilee Church*.

8 Szacka, '"Roma Interrotta": Postmodern Rome as the Source of Fragmented Narratives'

1.   J. Franchina (ed.), *Roma Interrotta*, trans. J. Franchina (Rome: Incontri Internazionali d'Arte/Officina edizioni, 1979), 208, p. 12.
2.   M. Graves, 'Roman Interventions', *Architectural Design*, 49:3–4, Profile 20, (1979), p. 4.
3.   M. Bevilacqua (ed.), *Nolli, Vasi, Piranesi: Immagine di Roma Antica e Moderna* [Nolli, Vasi, Piranesi: Images of Ancient and Modern Rome] (Rome: Artemide Edizioni, 2004), p. 12.
4.   See Marco Cavietti's contribution to this volume for a broader discussion of the city's expansion outside these perimeter walls, pp. 19–37.
5.   See A. P. Latini in Bevilacqua (ed.), *Nolli, Vasi, Piranesi: Immagine di Roma Antica e Moderna*, p. 65.
6.   As examples of scholarly attention compare T. Weaver, 'Civitas Interruptus', in *Postmodernism: Style and Subversion, 1970–1990* (London: Victoria and Albert Museum, 2011), pp. 126–131 and M. Delbeke, 'Baroque Rome as a (Post)Modernist Model', in OASE 86, pp. 74–85. As an example of museological attention, see the exhibition 'Roma Interrotta' at the 11th Venice Architecture Biennale, 'Out There: Architecture Beyond Building', curated by Aaron Betsky, 14 September to 23 November 2008. Also, on 7 September 2012 the archive of the Incontri Internazionali d'Arte was assimilated into the collection of the MAXXI thanks to a donation by the late Graziella Lonardi Buontempo of 100,000 documents and 8,000 books, including all the original documents of 'Roma Interrotta'.
7.   I would like to thank the British School at Rome and the Giles Worsley Travel Fellowship, which enabled me to undertake this research.
8.   These descriptions of Lonardi Buontempo are taken from the documentary *A Roma La Nostra Era Avanguardia: Un omaggio alle grandi mostre degli anni '70. Vitalità del negativo e Conteporane* [In Rome, ours was an Avantgarde. A Homage to the Great Exhibitions of the 70s: 'The Vitality of the Negative' and 'Contemporary'], film, directed by L. Massimo Barbero and Francesca Pola (Italy: MACRO (Museo d'Arte Conteporanea di Roma) and Incontri Internazionali d'Arte, 2010).
9.   L. M. Barbaro and F. Pola, *A Roma La Nostra Era Avanguardia*.
10. For example, 'Contemporanea [Contemporary]', an interdisciplinary and international exhibition presented in 1973–4, was held in the new underground car park of the Villa Borghese, designed by Luigi Moretti, and the 1979 exhibition 'Le stanze [The Rooms]', curated by Bonito Oliva, took place in the Castello Colonna, Gennazzano, Rome.
11. Franco Raggi, interview with the author, 23 November 2010.

12. 'This cultural event whose theme is Rome, the "capital" city, is the first in a series of specific initiatives which the Incontri Internazionali d'Arte is dedicating to urban studies'. In Franchina (ed.), *Roma Interrotta*, p. 10.

13. In addition to the twelve tables of engraving, each architect had to produce a series of graphic documents (drawings, collage, etc.) that represented his or her ideas. The archive of the IIA includes more than 130 graphic documents related to the 'Roma Interrotta' exhibition.

14. E. Soja, *Thirdspace: Journeys to Los Angeles and Other Real-and-Imagined Places* (Oxford: Blackwell Publishing, 1996), p. 6.

15. See S. Connor (ed.), *The Cambridge Companion to Postmodernism* (Cambridge: Cambridge University Press, 2004), pp. 1–2.

16. R. Venturi, *Complexity and Contradiction in Architecture* (New York: Museum of Modern Art, 1966); A. Rossi, *L'architettura della città* [The Architecture of the City] (Padua: Marsilio Press, 1966).

17. J.-L. Cohen, *The Future of Architecture Since 1968* (London: Phaidon, 2012), p. 404.

18. There are many other examples of this trend, one of the most famous being Rem Koolhaas's retroactive manifesto for Manhattan, published the same year as 'Roma Interrotta'. See R. Koolhaas, *Delirious New York: A Retroactive Manifesto for Manhattan* (New York: Oxford University Press, 1978) where Koolhaas proposes urbanism as a journalistic text in which urbanism is architecture and architecture is urbanism. See H. White, *Metahistory: The Historical Imagination in Nineteenth-Century Europe* (Baltimore, MD: Johns Hopkins University Press, 1973).

19. Franchina (ed.), *Roma Interrotta*, p. 11.

20. Piero Sartogo, presentazione del progetto, at the 11th Venice Architecture Biennale, 'Out There: Architecture Beyond Building', Roma Interrotta, 14 September to 23 November 2008.

21. See C. Rowe, *As I was Saying: Recollections and Miscellaneous Essays*, 3 vols (Cambridge, London: The MIT Press, 1996), vol. 3, p. 6.

22. In 1945, Rowe had completed an MA thesis for Professor Rudolf Wittkower at the Warburg Institute in London, a work starting from the assumption that Inigo Jones may have intended to publish a theoretical treatise on architecture, analogous to Palladio's Four Books. This first theoretical work established Rowe's way of speculating and imagining what might have happened: an approach to the history of architecture that was largely imaginary and factually questionable, but which he gradually built into a vastly erudite, coherently argued way of thinking and seeing that exasperated conventional historians and became the inspiration for a generation of practising architects to consider history imaginatively, as an active component in their design process.

23. Rowe accepted, in 1962, a professorship at Cornell University. There he would soon develop his own urban design studio, aiming to reconcile modern architecture with the urban context (or what he called the 'theatre of memory' in reference to the work of Frances Yates).

24. The ideal model for this pragmatic, anti-doctrinaire approach was the ruined villa of the Roman Emperor Hadrian at Tivoli, outside Rome. For Rowe this villa (as opposed to the 'perfect' model of Versailles) was the model of a collage, for it was a seemingly disjointed amalgam of discrete enthusiasm in an attempt to conceal any reference to guiding principles. See J. Stevens Curl, *A Dictionary of Architecture and Landscape Architecture* (Oxford: Oxford University Press, 2006), p. 880.

25. S. Malfroy, 'Présentation', in C. Rowe and F. Koetter, *Collage City* (Geneva: In Folio, 2002), p. 16.

26. Piero Sartogo, interview with the author, 5 December 2010.

27. The IAUS was an independent research, design and educational corporation in the inter-related fields of architecture, urban design and planning. It was created in 1967 by the Board of Regents of the State University of New York. The aims of the institute were to propose and develop methods and solutions for problems of the urban environment; to develop a body of theory and criticism with regards to architecture, urban design and planning; to function as a forum for public criticism and debate; to amplify and develop present methods of architectural education and practice.

28. 'The City as an Artifact', *Casabella*, n. 359–60, December 1971. In this issue were assembled a sequence of hitherto unpublished articles especially written by Alesssandro Mendini, Franco Alberti, Denise Scott Brown, Robert Venturi, Peter Eisenman, Joseph Rykwert, William Ellis, Stanford Anderson, Emilio Ambasz and Piero Sartogo.

29. A. Mendini, 'The City as an Artifact', *Casabella* 359–60, (December 1971), p. 9.

30. This was in the film *Roma Interrotta*, presented at the 11th Venice Architecture Biennale, 2008.

31. During the second half of the nineteenth century, the riverbanks and road along the Tiber were radically reconstructed to improve the city's flooding defences and transport connections. As a consequence of that, Rome saw the destruction of many of the city's historical places such as the Porto di Ripetta, a port designed and built in 1707 by the Italian Baroque architect Alessandro Specchi, and famous for its steps descending into the water and producing a sort of scenographic space in the city.

32. Three main circulation axes were introduced by Mussolini during the 1930s.

33. Rowe refers to C. Lévi-Strauss, *La Pensée Sauvage* [The Savage Mind] (Paris: Plan, 1962).

34. See A. Grumbach, 'Roma Interrotta', in J. Dethier and A. Guiheux (eds), *La ville, art et architecture en Europe 1870–1993* [The City, Art and Architecture in Europe, 1870–1993] (Paris: Centre Pompidou, 1994), p. 445.

35. Other 'Roma Interrotta' projects also suggest the change from objectivity to subjectivity. A key example is Paolo Portoghesi's project: based on a planimetry of the physical environment of the Chia Ravine, it analyses the city by means of a series of visual analogies with naturalistic environments. Another interesting approach was put forward by Colin Rowe and his team, and was based on a totally fictitious scenario involving Vincent Mulcahy, a Jesuit scholar based in Rome. This project was described by Rowe and his team as 'an alibi for topographical and contextual concern' and 'a city which represents a coalition of intentions rather than the singular presence of any immediately apparent all-coordinating idea', see Franchina (ed.), *Roma Interrotta*, p. 150.

36. His term probably refers to Michel Foucault's *The Archaeology of Knowledge* (1969).

37. Franchina (ed.), *Roma Interrotta*, p. 66.

38. H. Klotz, 'Postmodern Architecture', in C. Jencks (ed.), *The Postmodern Reader* (London: Academy Editions, 1992), pp. 238–47, on p. 241.

39. See C. Norberg-Schulz, *Intentions in Architecture* (Oslo: Universitetsforlaget, 1963) and C. Norberg-Schulz, *Genius Loci: Towards a Phenomenology of Architecture* (New York: Rizzoli, 1979).

40. Antoine Grumbach, interview with the author, 19 October 2010.

41. Ibid.

42. Rione (pl. rioni) is a term designating the fourteen different districts of Rome according to the administrative division of the Middle Ages.

43. Franchina (ed.), *Roma Interrotta*, p. 195.
44. I. Hassan, 'Pluralism in Postmodern Perspective', in C. Jencks, *The Postmodern Reader* (London: Academy Editino, 1992), pp. 196–207, on p. 196. Essay originally published in I. Hassan, *The Postmodern Turn: Essays in Postmodern Theory and Culture* (Columbus, OH: Ohio State University Press, 1987).
45. Franchina (ed.), *Roma Interrotta*, p. 196.
46. Such a radical solution can be surprising when we know that in the same year that the 'Roma Interrotta' exhibition took place, Krier, together with Pierluigi Nicolin, Angello Villa and Maurice Culot, signed the 'Declaration of Palermo', the first articulation of the Movement for the Reconstruction of European Cities.
47. Franchina (ed.), *Roma Interrotta*, p. 195.
48. Letter from Léon Krier to Graziella Lonardi Buontempo, 10 October 1980, Archive IIA.
49. Letter from Graziella Lonardi Buontempo to Léon Krier, 1 December 1980, Archive IIA.
50. E. Petit, 'Irony and Postmodern Architecture', in G Adamson and J. Pavitt (eds), *Postmodernism: Style and Subversion 1970–1990* (London: Victoria and Albert Museum, 2011), pp. 120–5, on p. 121. For more insight into the concept of irony in postmodern architecture see E. Petit, *Irony; or, The Self-Critical Opacity of Postmodern Architecture* (New Haven, CT: Yale University Press, 2013).
51. From author's telephone interview with Weiss, 9 November 2010.
52. Canadian Centre for Architecture's collection, James Stirling and Partner, Roma Interrotta, Mercati di Traiano, 1977–9, AP140.S2.SS3.D7.
53. Franchina (ed.), *Roma Interrotta* p. 84.
54. Ibid., p.89.
55. Ibid., p. 91.
56. From October 1978 to May 1994 the drawings (or part of the drawings) were exhibited in Mexico City, London, Bilbao, New York, Toronto, Zurich, Tokyo, São Paolo and Paris.
57. A. L. Huxtable, 'Rome and the Artistic Fantasy', *New York Times*, 15 July 1979, p. 35.
58. G. Muratore, 'Dodici Architetti ai mercati Traianei giocano con Roma' [Twelve Architects play with Rome in Trajan's Market], *La Repubblica*, 21–2 May 1978, p. 21.
59. Ibid.
60. F. Dal Co, 'Review Roma Interrotta', *Oppositions*, 12 (Spring 1978), pp. 112–13.
61. S. Condor (ed.), *The Cambridge Companion to Postmodernism* (Cambridge: Cambridge University Press, 2004), p. 10.

9 Hayes, 'Las Vegas by Way of Rome: The Eternal City and American Postmodernism'

1. J.-F. Lyotard, *The Postmodern Condition: A Report on Knowledge*, trans. G. Bennington and B. Massumi (Minneapolis, MN: University of Minnesota Press, 1993), p. xxiv.
2. For a concise summary of the Grand Tour as it relates to Robert Venturi, see M. Stierli, 'In the Academy's Garden: Robert Venturi, the Grand Tour and the Revision of Modern Architecture', *AA Files*, 56 (2007), pp. 41–62, on p. 43.
3. D. D. Egbert, *The Beaux-Arts Tradition in French Architecture* (Princeton, NJ: Princeton University Press, 1980), p. 11.

4. Ibid., p. 85.
5. For an analysis of the formal and thematic trends in postmodern architecture, see M. McLeod, 'Architecture', in S. Trachtenberg (ed.), *The Postmodern Moment: A Handbook of Contemporary Innovation in the Arts* (Westport, CT: Greenwood Press, 1985), pp. 19–52.
6. A. Huysens., *After the Great Divide: Modernism, Mass Culture, Postmodernism* (Bloomington, IN: Indiana University Press, 1986), p. vii.
7. Ibid., p. ix.
8. Ibid., pp. 219–17.
9. D. R. Costanzo, 'The Lessons of Rome: Architects at the American Academy, 1947–1966' (PhD dissertation, Pennsylvania State University, 2009), p. 5.
10. K. Keim, *An Architectural Life: Memoirs and Memories of Charles W. Moore* (Boston, MA: Little, Brown and Company, 1996), p. 56.
11. C. W. Moore, quoted in ibid., p. 200.
12. Ibid., p. 119.
13. Ibid., p. 201.
14. C. W. Moore, 'Hadrian's Villa', *PERSPECTA: Yale Architectural Journal*, 6 (1960), pp. 17–27, on p. 19.
15. Ibid., p. 18.
16. C. W. Moore, 'Water and Architecture' (PhD dissertation, Princeton University, 1957), p. 140.
17. C. Jencks, *The Language of Post-Modern Architecture* (New York: Rizzoli International Publications, 1977), p. 111.
18. M. Yourcenar, *Mémoires d'Hadrien* (Paris: Plon, 1951); E. Clark, *Rome and a Villa* (Garden City, NY: Doubleday, 1952).
19. C. Rowe and F. Koetter, 'Collage City', *Architectural Review*, 158:942 (1975), pp. 66–90, on p. 80.
20. M. Filler, 'The Magic Fountain', *Progressive Architecture*, 59:11 (1978), pp. 81–7, on p. 81.
21. Ibid.
22. Ibid.
23. P. A. Morton, 'Kitsch and Postmodern Architecture: Charles Moore's Piazza d'Italia', in G. Adamson and J. Pavitt (eds), *Postmodernism: Style and Subversion, 1970–1990* (London: V&A Publishing, 2011), pp. 116–19, on p. 117.
24. Untitled Interview, Charles W. Moore Papers, Archives of American Art, Smithsonian Institution (n.p, n.d.).
25. K. C. Bloomer and C. W. Moore, *Body, Memory, and Architecture* (New Haven, CT: Yale University Press, 1977), p. 88.
26. Moore, 'Water and Architecture', p. 78.
27. Quoted in K. Keim (ed.), *You Have to Pay for the Public Life: Selected Essays of Charles W. Moore* (Cambridge, MA: 2001), p. 30.
28. Moore, 'Water and Architecture', p. 41.
29. Ibid., p. 80.
30. C. W. Moore, 'You Have to Pay for the Public Life', *PERSPECTA: Yale Architectural Journal*, 9:10 (1965), pp. 57–65, on p. 59.
31. D. B. Brownlee, D. G. DeLong and K. B. Hiesinger, *Out of the Ordinary: Robert Venturi, Denise Scott Brown and Associates* (Philadelphia, PA: Philadelphia Museum of Art, 2001), p. 7.
32. Ibid., p. 8
33. Ibid., p. 9.
34. Quoted by Stierli, 'In the Academy's Garden', p. 54.

35. Costanzo, 'The Lessons of Rome', pp. 234–6.

36. V. Scully, 'Introduction' to R. Venturi, *Complexity and Contradiction in Architecture* (New York: The Museum of Modern Art, 1966), pp. 9–11, on p. 11.

37. J. Shearman, *Mannerism* (Harmondsworth: Penguin Books Ltd., 1967), pp. 17–22.

38. Venturi, *Complexity and Contradiction*, p. 22.

39. R. Venturi, 'The Centennial of the American Academy in Rome', in *Iconography and Electronics Upon a Generic Architecture* (Cambridge, MA: The MIT Press, 1996), p. 53.

40. N. Mailer, 'Mailer vs Scully', *Architectural Forum*, 120:4 (April 1964), pp. 96–7, on p. 97.

41. As Vincent Scully observed, 'Venturi's primary inspiration would seem have come from ... the urban facades of Italy, with their endless adjustments to the counter requirements of inside and outside and their inflection with all the business of everyday life'. Scully, 'Introduction', p. 12.

42. Venturi decried the 'forced simplicity' in designs of architect Philip Johnson, for example: 'Blatant simplification means bland architecture. Less is a bore'. Venturi, *Complexity and Contradiction*, p. 25.

43. J. Ackerman, *The Architecture of Michelangelo* (Chicago, IL: Chicago University Press, 1986), p. 256.

44. Ibid., pp. 243–6.

45. Venturi, *Complexity and Contradiction*, p. 65.

46. According to Mary McLeod, 'postmodern architects ordinarily accept the canons of pre-modern humanism'. McLeod, 'Architecture', p. 24.

47. Ackerman, *The Architecture of Michelangelo*, pp. 256–7.

48. For a discussion of Venturi's interest in mid-twentieth century Italian architecture, see Stierli, 'In the Academy's Garden', pp. 49–51.

49. R. Venturi and D. Scott Brown, *Architecture as Signs and Systems for a Mannerist Time* (Cambridge, MA: Harvard University Press, 2004), p. 77.

50. Ibid., p. 69.

51. N. Hawthorne, *The Marble Faun*, quoted in Venturi, *Complexity and Contradiction*, p. 60.

52. S. Manning, 'Introduction' to N. Hawthorne, *The Marble Faun* (Oxford: Oxford University Press, 2002), pp. ix–xxxix, on p. xxxiv.

53. P. Baker, *The Fortunate Pilgrims: Americans in Italy, 1800–1860* (Cambridge, MA: Harvard University Press, 1964), p. 3.

54. Venturi quotes August Hecksher's 1962 book, *The Public Happiness,* in which 'a view of life as complex and ironic' is associated with maturity. Venturi, *Complexity and Contradiction,* p. 24.

55. Although Venturi does not use the word 'pluralism' in *Complexity and Contradiction in Architecture*, he does use it in later essays, such as 'Diversity, Relevance and Representation in Historicism, or Plus Ça Change ...', *Architectural Record*, 170:8 (June 1982), pp. 114–9.

56. Venturi, *Iconography and Electronics*, pp. 53–4.

57. R. Venturi, D. Scott Brown, and S. Izenour, *Learning From Las Vegas* (Cambridge, MA: The MIT Press, 1972), p. 14.

58. Brownlee, DeLong and Hiesinger, *Out of the Ordinary*, p. 37.

59. D. Scott Brown, 'Some Ideas and Their History', in R. Venturi and D. Scott Brown, *Architecture as Signs and Systems for a Mannerist Time*, pp. 105–19.

60. Brownlee, DeLong and Hiesinger, *Out of the Ordinary*, p. 37.

61. Ibid.

62. Venturi, Scott Brown and Izenour, *Learning From Las Vegas*, p. ix.

63. E. Blau, *Architecture or Revolution: Charles Moore and Yale in the Late 1960s* (New Haven, CT: Yale School of Architecture, 2001), n.p.

64. R. Venturi, 'The Campidoglio: A Case Study', *Architectural Review*, 113:677 (May 1953), pp. 333–4.

65. Ackerman, *The Architecture of Michelangelo*, p. 251.

66. Venturi, Scott Brown and Izenour, *Learning From Las Vegas*, pp. 14–15.

67. Ibid., p. 14.

68. In a recent interview, Denise Scott Brown emphasized the anti-establishment ethos of the Las Vegas studio. See K. Rattenbury and S. Hardingham (eds), *Supercrit #2 Robert Venturi and Denise Scott Brown: Learning From Las Vegas* (Milton Park: Routledge, 2007), p. 113.

69. H. S. Thompson, *Fear and Loathing in Las Vegas* (New York: Modern Library, 1971); T. Wolfe, *The Kandy-Kolored, Tangerine-Flake, Streamline Baby* (New York: Farrar, Straus and Giroux, 1965).

70. A. Vinegar, *I Am a Monument: On Learning from Las Vegas* (Cambridge, MA: The MIT Press, 2008), p. 73.

71. Ibid., p. 77.

72. M. DeKoven, *Utopia Limited: The Sixties and the Emergence of the Postmodern* (Durham, NC: Duke University Press, 2004), p. 113.

73. Venturi, Scott Brown and Izenour, *Learning From Las Vegas*, p. 58.

74. Venturi, *Iconography and Electronics*, pp. 54–5.

75. Lyotard, *The Postmodern Condition*, p. xxv.

INDEX

1900, 87, 97, 100

Aalto, Alvar, 153, 181
Accattone, 14, 68–9, 71, 95, 99, 141
Accorsi, Stefano, 71
Ackerman, James, 181, 185
Agucchi, Giovan Battista, 49
Ai margini della metropoli (At the Limits of
    the Metropolis), 62
Albinati, Edoardo, 132–3
Alighieri, Dante, 82
Alì dagli occhi azzurri (Blue-Eyed Alì), 127
Allen, Woody, 56
Aloysi, Aldo, 151
Alphand, Jean-Charles, 163
Ando, Tadao, 151–2
Antonello, Pierpaolo, 5
Antonioni, Michelangelo, 55, 71, 95, 98,
    142
Apollonj-Ghetti, Bruno Maria, 143–4
Ara Pacis Augustae, 2, 13–14, 16, 101, 103,
    111, 113, 115–16
Argan, Giulio Carlo, 19, 31, 33, 155, 160
d'Aronco, Raimondo, 140
art galleries in Rome
    Macro, 18, 121
    Maxxi, 9
    Montemartini, 18, 121
Asimov, Isaac, 2
Augé, Marc, 102
Avetta, Ildo, 144
Aymonino, Carlo, 104

Bach, Johann Sebastian, 149
Baker, Charles, 182
Barry, Matthew, 86
Baudelaire, Paul, 45

Baudrillard, Jean, 100, 102, 110, 159
Bava, Mario, 52
Beijing, 4
Bell, Daniel, 159
Bellocchio, Marco, 40
Bellori, Pietro, 49
Bencivenga, Ulderico, 121
Benjamin, Walter, 45
Berlin, 39, 80–1, 126
Bernini, Gianlorenzo, 4, 43, 49, 88, 90, 92,
    173
Bertolucci Bernardo, 11, 14, 79–80, 83–8,
    90, 92, 94–5, 97–100
    1900, 87, 97, 100
    auto-citation, 87
    Besieged, 84
    La commare secca (The Grim Reaper), 87,
        94–5, 98
    La luna (The Moon), 11, 14, 79–80, 83,
        85–7, 90, 95, 97–100
    Il conformista (The Conformist), 87, 88,
        181
    La strategia del ragno (The Spider's
        Stratagem), 85–6, 88, 90
    Partner, 87
    psychoanalysis, 85–6, 97
    Ultimo tango a Parigi (Last Tango in
        Paris), 87–8
Besieged, 84
Beuys, Joseph, 157
Blade Runner, 13
Bloomer, Kent, 177
Blue Velvet, 13
Boccioni, Umberto, 124
Boeti, Alighiero, 157
Boito, Camillo, 140

Bolognini, Mauro, 63
Bondanella, Peter, 2
Bonello, Angelo, 120
Bonito Oliva, Achille, 36, 157
Borges, Jorge-Luis, 44
Borgese, Giuseppe Antonio, 39
Borromini, Francesco, 49, 179
Brasini, Armando, 140–1, 143, 153
Breton, André, 162
Brown, Bill, 82–3
Brownlee, David, 184
Brunelleschi, Filippo, 44
Burke, Edmund, 44

Cabiria, 46
Cairo, 4
Calatrava, Santiago, 152
Caldwell, Dorigen, 8, 57
Caliceti, Giuseppe, 132
Camerini, Mario, 46
Canino, Ennio, 151
Canniffe, Eamon, 85
Capponi, Giuseppe, 115
Caro diario (Dear Diary), 40–1, 57, 65, 67
Carpenter, John, 13
Carrà, Carlo, 134
Carracci, Annibale, 43
Cassetti, Roberto, 19
Cederna, Antonio, 2
de Certeau, Michel, 129
Ceserani, Remo, 7
Chareau, Pierre, 163
de Chirico, Giorgio, 134, 158
Christo (artist), 36
churches in Rome
    Cristo Re (Christ King), 144
    Josemaria Escrivá de Balaguer, 151
    Martiri Canadesi (Canadian Martyrs), 16, 143–4, 149
    Sacro Cuore di Gesù Agonizzante, 144
    Sacro Cuore Immacolato di Maria, 140–2, 150
    San Clemente, 8–9, 57
    San Felice da Cantalice, 141, 143, 150–1
    San Giovanni Bosco, 16, 143–4
    San Giovanni Laterano, 28–9, 57–8, 72, 144, 164
    San Giuseppe Cafasso, 58, 150

San Liborio, 16, 142–3, 150
San Pietro, 26, 40, 57–8, 72, 144, 164
Santa Croce in Gerusalemme, 28–9, 34
Sant'Ignazio, 58
Santi Pietro e Paolo, 16, 142–3, 150
Tor Tre Teste, 9, 16, 152
Clark, Eleanor, 173
Clayburgh, Jill, 86
Coia, Jack, 138, 141–4, 149
Connor, Steven, 159, 168
Coppola, Francis Ford, 13
Corsi, Tilde, 135
da Cortona, Pietro, 43, 49, 94
Crawford, Hugh Adam, 141

Dal Co, Francesco, 167
Dardi Costantino, 36, 155
Dazzi, Arturo, 69
Dear, Michael, 6
De Lachenal, Lucilla, 108
De Palma, Brian, 76
De Sica, Vittorio, 62
Dey, Hendrik, 24–5
Donatello, di Niccolò di Betto Bardi, 44
Duchamp, Marcel, 134
von Duhn, Friedrich, 114

Edwards, Catharine, 2
Egbert, Donald Drew, 178
Eisenmann, Peter, 152
Energici, Alfredo, 142
Escape from New York, 13
Europa '51 (Europe '51/No Greater Love), 62

Falini, Paola, 20
Favino, Pierfrancesco, 71
Favretto, Paola, 114
Fellini, Federico, 10, 12, 40–1, 44–53, 55–6, 62, 143–4
    fragment, 10, 12, 40, 44–5, 48, 50, 56
    La dolce vita (The Dolce vita), 12, 47–52, 56, 143, 149
    Intervista (Interview), 40
    presence–absence, 12, 46
    Roma, 12, 40, 51, 53, 55–6
    Satyricon, Fellini, 12, 50–1, 53, 55

Sceicco bianco (The White Sheik), 12, 40, 46–7, 56
  'Toby Dammit', 12, 40, 51–3, 56
Filler, Martin, 175
Florence, 25, 82
Fontana, Domenico, 41, 43
Foschini, Arnaldo, 142
Foucault, Michel, 15, 103, 107, 113, 116–17
Freud, Sigmund, 1, 84, 97
  'The Uncanny', 97
Friedberg, Anne, 10
Frommel, Christopher, 109

Gadda, Carlo Emilio, 40, 46
Gatto, Alfonso, 129–30
Gehry, Frank, 152
Gillespie, Kidd & Coia, 16, 137, 143–4, 150–3
Giovannoni, Gustavo, 74
Giurgola, Romaldo, 155
Gnisci, Armando, 42
Godard, Jean-Luc, 56
Goethe, Johann Wolfgang, 1, 103
Gorfinkel, Elena, 80
Graves, Michael, 155, 172
Gregotti, Vittorio, 157
Grumbach, Antoine, 17, 155, 162–4
Guazzoni, Enrico, 46

Hadid, Zaha, 9
Harvey David, 52
Hassan, Ihab, 159, 164
Hawthorne, Nathaniel, 182
Hernandez, Santiago, 151
Herzfeld, Michael, 2
Hural Matthew, 34, 36–7
Huxtable, Ada Louise, 167
Huyssens, Andreas, 172

Il conformista (The Conformist), 87, 88
Il ferroviere (The Railroader), 127
Il tetto (The Roof), 127
Insolera, Italo, 2, 62
Intervista (Interview), 40
I soliti ignoti (Big Deal on Madonna Street), 127
Izenour, Steven, 184–5, 187

Jameson, Fredric, 7–8, 52, 82–3, 102
Jansen, Monica, 5
Jencks, Charles, 159, 162, 173
Jung, Carl Gustav, 55

Kahn, Louis I., 173, 178
Keiller, Patrick, 81
Kill, Baby Kill, 52
Kline, T. Jefferson, 87
Klotz, Henrich, 163
Kolker, Robert, 87–8, 97, 100
Kounellis, Jannis, 157
Kracauer, Siegfried, 79–80
Krautheimer, Richard, 94
Krier, Léon, 17, 155, 162, 164–6

La banda degli onesti (The Band of Honest Men), 127
Labatut, Jean, 178
Lacan, Jacques, 86
La commare secca (The Grim Reaper), 87, 94–5, 98
La luna (The Moon), 11, 14, 79–80, 83, 85–7, 90, 95, 97–100
  auto-cinephilia, 100
  fetishization of the centre, 97–9
  haunting past, 95
  perversion, 97–8
  search for father, 86
  topophilia, 95, 100
Lang, Fritz, 10
La commare secca (The Grim Reaper), 87, 94–5, 98
La dolce vita (The *Dolce vita*), 12, 47–52, 56, 143, 149
  kaleidoscope, 48
  reality and fiction, 49–50
Ladri di biciclette (Bicycle Thieves), 62
La giornata balorda (A Crazy Day), 63
La notte brava (The Good Night), 63
La strategia del ragno (The Spider's Stratagem), 85–6, 88, 90
  labyrinth history, 85
  search for father, 86
Las Vegas, 9, 15, 17, 81, 101, 116, 184–8
Le ceneri di Gramsci (Gramsci's Ashes), 128
L'eclisse (The Eclipse), 55, 71, 142
Le Corbusier, 82, 115, 163, 178

Ledoux, Claude Nicolas, 163
Le fate ignoranti (His Secret Life), 135
Lenagham, Julia, 108
Le notti di Cabiria (Nights of Cabiria), 62
Leopardi, Giacomo, 39
Levi, Carlo, 39
Lévi-Strauss, Claude, 162
Libera, Adalberto, 69, 115
Lizzani, Carlo, 62
L'odore del sangue (The Scent of Blood), 40
Lonardi Buontempo, Graziella, 157, 165, 169
London, 4, 6, 39, 45, 81, 149, 173, 184
L'onorevole Angelina (The Honourable
    Angelina), 62
L'ora di religione (My Mother's Smile), 40
Los Angeles, 4, 6, 14–15, 56, 81–2, 101–2,
    116
Lo sceicco bianco (The White Sheik), 12, 40,
    46–7, 56
    non-linearity, 47
Lutyens, Sir Edwin, 181
Lynch, David, 13, 56
Lynch, Kevin, 82, 84
Lyotard, Jean-Francois, 44, 159, 171–2,
    187–8

McMillan, Andy, 144
Magnani, Anna, 143
Mailer, Norman, 179
Maltese Corrado, 32–3
Mamma Roma, 63–4, 143
Mancini, Rossana, 21, 24
Manila, 4
Mann, Michael, 56
Marcus Aurelius, 108
    equestrian statue, 9, 13–14, 101, 103–4,
        107–11, 113, 117
    simulacrum, 110–11, 117
Martone, Mario, 40
Maufe, Edward, 149
Mazzoni, Cristina, 3–4
Meier, Richard, 2, 9, 14–16, 101, 103, 111,
    113, 115–17, 152–3
Melli, Roberto, 123, 124–6, 129
    Il gazometro a San Paolo (The Gasometer
        in San Paolo), 123–5
Mendini, Alessandro, 161
Merz, Jorgin, 94

Merz, Mario, 157
Metzstein, Isi, 144
Michelangelo, di Lodovico Buonarroti
    Simoni, 108–9, 179, 181, 185, 187
Mida, Massimo, 62
Milan, 4, 9, 10, 25, 72, 157
Miller, Naomi, 36–7
Monicelli, Mario, 62
Moore, Charles W., 17, 171–3, 175, 177–8,
    185, 188
Morandi, Giorgio, 49
Moravia, Alberto, 127–8, 130
Moretti, Luigi, 30, 181
Moretti, Nanni, 40–1, 57, 65–7, 74, 77
Moro, Aldo, 71–2, 103
Morpurgo, Vittorio Ballio, 113–16
Morton, Patricia A., 175
Mudu, Paolo, 64, 66
Muratore, Giorgio, 167
museum
    Ara Pacis Augustae, 2, 13–14, 16, 101,
        103, 111, 113, 115–16
    Capitoline, 104, 121
    Cooper Hewitt, 167
    Macro, 18, 121
    Maxxi, 9
    Montemartini, 18, 121
    of Wood, 151
Mussgnug, Florian, 5
Mussolini, Benito, 41, 48–9, 62, 81, 102,
    113–16, 122, 138, 143

Naples, 76, 126
New York, 4, 9, 39, 56, 80–1, 102, 153, 161,
    165
Nicolini, Renato, 36, 60, 62, 160
Nolli, Giambattista, 17, 155–6, 158, 160,
    162–4, 166, 169
Norberg-Schulz, Christian, 163–4

Oud, Jacobus, 163
Ozpetek, Ferzan, 15, 135

palimpsest
    baroque, 45
    classical, 1, 8, 24–5
    non-classical, 132–3, 143
    postmodern, 7, 8, 40, 48–9, 81–3, 92,
        163, 172, 182, 188

Paniconi, Mario, 150, 153

Pannini, Giovanni Paolo, 43–4

Paris, 4, 9, 25, 39, 45, 56, 80, 87, 126, 140, 173

Partner, 87

Pasolini, Pier Paolo, 13–15, 55–6, 63–4, 67, 71, 74, 80, 87–8, 94–5, 98, 126–31, 141, 143–4

    Accattone, 14, 68–9, 71, 95, 99, 141

    Alì dagli occhi azzurri (Blue-Eyed Alì), 127

    Le ceneri di Gramsci (Gramsci's Ashes), 128

    Mamma Roma, 63–4, 143

    modernity, 80–1, 127–9

    periphery, 15, 64, 67, 95, 98, 126–9

    'Squarci di notte romane' (Lights of Roman Nights), 129

Pastrone, Giovanni, 46

Pediconi, Giulio, 141, 150, 153

Peressutti, Enrico, 178

Petrarch, Francesco, 12, 42, 44

Petri, Elio, 76

Piacentini, Marcello, 69, 74, 102, 138, 144

Picciafuoco, Ernesto, 40

Pirandello, Luigi, 39, 46

Piranesi, Giovan Battista, 43, 165

Placido, Michele, 71, 74, 76–7

Polidoro, da Caravaggio, 43

Pope

    Alexander VII, 90

    Benedict XIV, 155, 185

    Julius II, 27, 108

    Martin V, 27

    Nicholas V, 108

    Paul III, 108–9

    Pius II, 108

    Pius IV, 181

    Pius IX, 29

    Sixtus IV, 27–8

    Sixtus V, 28–9, 37, 90

Portoghesi, Paolo, 41, 43, 150, 155

postmodern

    after-image, 100

    auto-citation, 87

    baroque, 40–5, 48–9, 92, 141–2, 167

    Bonaventure Hotel, 82, 102

    churches, 139–40

cityscape, 1–2, 6–8, 101–2, 124–5, 156, 182

deconstruction, 7, 10, 15, 18, 45, 103, 115–17, 140, 151–2

end of grand narratives, 40, 177

fragment, 3, 8, 10–13, 17, 19–20, 32, 34, 40, 42, 44–6, 50–1, 56, 129–30, 138, 143, 156, 162–4, 179, 182, 184

gentrification, 2, 98–9

Herkunft versus *Ursprung* (onset point versus pure origin), 103, 113, 116–17

history, 107

horizontality, 102, 133

labyrinth, 6, 32, 52, 55, 85–6, 90, 94–5

Lascaux caves, 110–11

Las Vegas, 9, 15, 17, 81, 91, 116, 184–8

Los Angeles, 4, 6, 14, 81–2, 101–2

mappability, 36–7, 44–6, 76, 140

    see also unmappability

origin

    see also Herkunft versus *Ursprung*

pastiche, 172

polycentrism, 67, 164, 168

post-humanism, 133

post-Vatican II, 138–40, 142, 149–50, 153, 204

Pruitt-Igoe housing estate, St Louis, Missouri, 159

Rameses II (mummy), 110–11

rejection of totality, 9, 11, 41, 44, 82, 102, 161–2, 168, 188

scientism, 110

simulacrization, 6, 15, 103, 110–11, 117, 184

topophilia, 95, 100, 184, 188

unmappability 14–5, 55, 82–4

    see also mappability

Proietti, Fernando, 120

Quo vadis, 46

Raggi, Franco, 157–8

Raphael, Sanzio, 45

Rhodes, John David, 128–9

Roma, 12, 40, 51, 53, 55–6

'Roma Interrotta' (exhibition), 9, 11, 16–17, 156–66, 168–9

    fragmentariness, 156, 164

Roman Holiday, 98
Romano, Giulio, 43
Romanzo criminale (Criminal Story), 57,
    66–7, 71, 76
Rome
    1883 *piano regolatore* (1883 master plan),
        60
    1931 *piano regolatore* (1931 master plan),
        60, 122
    2003 *piano regolatore* (2003 master plan),
        6, 19, 21, 60–1, 121
    anni di piombo (years of lead), 99, 103,
        160
    Ara Pacis Museum, 2, 13–14, 16, 101,
        103, 111, 113–16
    Aurelian Walls, 6, 9, 11, 14, 16, 20–2,
        24–31, 33–4, 36–7, 58, 65, 92, 119,
        137, 156, 181
    borgate, 13, 48, 56, 61–2, 64, 71, 81, 95,
        127, 138, 144
    Capitoline Hill, 14, 26, 103–4, 121, 164
    Casa del Girasole, 181
    Casalpalocco, 66–7
    Centocelle, 58, 141
    centre–periphery, 1, 3, 6, 13–4, 18, 20,
        31–3, 57, 59, 61, 66–7, 71, 77, 81, 95,
        98–9, 102, 113, 140
    Cinecittà, 9, 40–1, 48–9, 143
    classical, 1–3, 7–9, 27, 39, 42–4, 46, 49,
        51, 55, 72, 76, 82, 101–3, 109, 111,
        113–7, 133, 140–4, 151, 188
    Eternal City, 1–3, 5, 7–8,11, 13, 17–18,
        29, 40, 53, 103, 107, 137, 143, 153,
        156, 168, 171, 188
    EUR, 37, 49, 60, 68–9, 71, 94, 138, 142,
        151
    Garbatella, 41, 66, 74, 76, 122–3, 129
    Gasometer, 13, 15, 119–24, 126–31,
        133–6
    Glasgow, 137–9, 141, 144, 149–50,
        152–3
    Grande Raccordo Anulare (ring road),
        53, 64
    INA Casa (public housing project), 64
    Janiculum, 34, 66, 87, 92, 166
    Lateran, 28, 90, 108–9, 141
    Magliana, 65, 71, 94

Marcus Aurelius equestrian statue, 9,
    13–14, 101, 103–4, 107–11, 113, 117
Mirabilia Urbis Romae, 12, 27, 42
modernity, 2–4, 31, 46, 48–9, 56, 59,
    80–1, 102, 121–2, 124, 127, 142
Monti quarter, 2, 72, 90
New Orleans, 17, 175, 177
nineteenth-century, 24, 29–30, 45–6, 58,
    83, 102, 156, 182
Ostiense, 6, 15, 18, 119, 121–4, 126–9,
    131–5
Palazzo Massimo alle Colonne, 179
Palazzo Senatorio, 104
palimpsest, 7–8, 24–5, 40, 45, 48–9,
    57–8, 81–3, 92, 132–3, 143, 158,
    163, 172, 182, 188
Parco Lineare Integrato (Integrated
    Linear Park), 20
Piazza del Campidoglio, 72, 74, 98, 101,
    104, 107–10, 185
Piazza Cavour, 88, 92
Piazza Euclide, 141
Piazza del Popolo, 26, 90, 98, 179
Piazza Sant'Ignazio, 58, 179
Pigneto, 95
Porta Pia, 29, 58, 179, 181, 185
Renaissance, 4, 28, 42, 44–5, 108–9,
    124, 181
San Michele Institute for Restoration,
    104
sventramenti (urban demolitions), 13, 27,
    61, 74, 81, 83, 94, 98, 102
ruins, 1, 5, 16, 19, 29, 31, 42–3, 45, 55,
    59, 63, 72, 88, 102, 119, 124, 128,
    132–3, 152, 158, 164, 194
Testaccio, 14, 58, 74, 98, 123, 128–9
Torpignattara, 58
Trajan Markets, 72, 88, 156–8, 167–8,
    182
Trastevere, 72, 74, 92, 98
Vatican, 9, 11, 16, 27–8, 108–9, 137–44,
    149–50, 152–3
Via Veneto, 48–9
Rome in cinema
    Accattone, 14, 68–9, 71, 95, 99, 141
    Ai margini della metropoli (At the Limits
        of the Metropolis), 62
    Besieged, 84

Cabiria, 46
Caro diario (Dear Diary), 40–1, 57, 65, 67
Europa '51 (Europe '51/No Greater Love), 62
Fellini Satyricon, 12, 50–1, 53, 55
Il conformista (The Conformist), 87–8
Il ferroviere (The Railroader), 127
Il tetto (The Roof), 127
I soliti ignoti (Big Deal on Madonna Street), 127
La banda degli onesti (The Band of Honest Men), 127
La commare secca (The Grim Reaper), 87, 94–5, 98
La dolce vita (The *Dolce vita*), 12, 47–52, 56, 143, 149
La giornata balorda (A Crazy Day), 63
La luna (The Moon), 11, 14, 79–80, 83, 85–7, 90, 95, 97–100
La notte brava (The Good Night), 63
L'eclisse (The Eclipse), 55, 71, 142
Le fate ignoranti (His Secret Life), 135
Le notti di Cabiria (Nights of Cabiria), 62
L'odore del sangue (The Scent of Blood), 40
L'onorevole Angelina (The Honourable Angelina), 62
L'ora di religione (My Mother's Smile), 40
Lo sceicco bianco (The White Sheik), 12, 40, 46–7, 56
Ladri di biciclette (Bicycle Thieves), 62
La luna (The Moon), 11, 14, 79–80, 83, 85–7, 90, 95, 97–100
Mamma Roma, 63–4, 143
Quo vadis, 46
Roma, 12, 40, 51, 53, 55–6
Roman Holiday, 98
Romanzo criminale (Criminal Story), 57, 66–7, 71, 76
'Toby Dammit', 12, 40, 51–3, 56
Totò cerca casa (Totò Looks for a House), 76
Un giorno in pretura (A Day in Court), 127
Velocità massima (Maximum Speed), 13, 57, 67–9, 71
Rosi, Francesco, 76

Rossellini, Roberto, 62
Rossi, Aldo, 59, 65, 150, 155, 157, 159
Rossi, Tullio, 142
Rossi Stuart, Kim, 71
Rowe, Colin, 155, 160–2, 167, 173, 175
Rumble Fish, 13
Rutelli, Francesco, 60, 104, 171

Sabaudia, 85, 144
Sabbioneta (town), 85, 88, 90
Salvati, Mariuccia, 59
Salvi, Nicola, 173
Sanguineti, Edoardo, 131–3
Santamaria, Claudio, 71
Sartogo, Piero, 155, 161
Saturday Night Fever, 95
Satyricon, Fellini, 12, 50–1, 53, 55
Savinio, Alberto, 134
Scarpa, Carlo, 150
Sceicco bianco (The White Sheik), 12, 40, 46–7, 56
Scialoja, Toti, 130–1
Scorsese, Martin, 56
Scott, Ridley, 13
Scott Brown, Denise, 155, 162, 184–5, 187–8
Scully, Vincent, 173, 178, 184
Shanghai, 4
'Squarci di notte romane' (Lights of Roman Nights), 129
Siegel, Michael, 99
Silverstone, Roger, 66
Simmel, Georg, 46
Simoncini, Giorgio, 27–8
Sironi, Mario, 124
Sitte, Camillo, 161
Soja, Edward, 6, 61, 102, 134, 159
Steno, 62
Stevens Curl, James, 161
Stirling, James, 17, 155, 162, 166–7
Sullivan Louis, 181

Taut, Bruno, 163
Tel Aviv, 4
Terranova, Antonio, 20
Thompson, Hunter S., 187
'Toby Dammit', 12, 40, 51–3, 56
Tokyo, 4
Tonkiss, Fran, 123, 129

Totò cerca casa (Totò Looks for a House), 76
Truffaut, Jean-Francois, 56

Ultimo tango a Parigi (Last Tango in Paris),
 87–8
Ungers, Oswald Mathias, 167, 173
Un giorno in pretura (A Day in Court), 127

Van Wittel, Caspar, 43
Velocità massima (Maximum Speed), 13, 57,
 67–9, 71
Veltroni, Walter, 60, 104, 120–1
Venice, 157, 159
Ventroni, Sara, 15, 133–4
Venturi, Robert, 9, 17, 101, 155, 159, 162,
 171–2, 178–9, 181–2, 184–8
Vespignani, Renzo, 29, 124–6, 129–30
 Periferia con gasometro (Periphery with
 Gasometer), 124–6

Vetriani, Costantino, 142
Vicari, Daniele, 13, 57, 68–9, 77
Vichi, Ernesto, 151, 153
Vidotto, Vittorio, 3, 9–10, 98
Villani, Rodolfo, 141
Vinegar, Aron, 187

Warhol, Andy, 157
Weaver, Thomas, 160
Williams, Raymond, 8
Winckelmann, Johann, 44
Wolfe, Tom, 187

Yourcenar, Marguerite, 173

Zampa, Luigi, 62
Zeichen, Valentino, 134–5